Designing
and
Implementing
Two-Way
Bilingual Programs

Para Conchita Medina por su gran contribución a la educación bilingüe

To Eduardo and Luis Mauricio
Thanks for always being there

To Carolina for her courage and determination

Designing *and* Implementing *Two-Way* Bilingual Programs

A Step-by-Step Guide for Administrators, Teachers, and Parents

Margarita Espino Calderón
Liliana Minaya-Rowe

CORWIN PRESS, INC.
A Sage Publications Company
Thousand Oaks, California

Copyright © 2003 by Corwin Press, Inc.

All rights reserved. When forms and sample documents are included, their use is authorized only by educators, local school sites, and/or noncommercial entities who have purchased the book. Except for that usage, no part of this book may be reproduced or utilized in any form or by any means, electronic or mechanical, including photocopying, recording, or by any information storage and retrieval system, without permission in writing from the publisher.

For information:

Corwin Press, Inc.
Sage Publications Company
2455 Teller Road
Thousand Oaks, California 91320
www.corwinpress.com

Sage Publications Ltd.
6 Bonhill Street
London EC2A 4PU
United Kingdom

Sage Publications India Pvt. Ltd.
B-42 Panchsheel Enclave
Post Box 4109
New Delhi 110 017 India

Printed in the United States of America

Library of Congress Cataloging-in-Publication Data

Calderón, Margarita.
Designing and implementing two-way bilingual programs: A step-by-step guide for administrators, teachers, and parents / by Margarita Espino Calderón and Liliana Minaya-Rowe.
p. cm.
Includes bibliographical references.
ISBN 0-7619-4565-2 (cloth)—ISBN 0-7619-4566-0 (paper)
1. Education, Bilingual-United States. 2. School improvement programs-United States. 3. Second language acquisition-United States. I. Minaya-Rowe, Liliana. II. Title.
LC3731 .C29 2003
370.117'0973—dc21

2002151762

This book is printed on acid-free paper.

03   04   05   06   10   9   8   7   6   5   4   3   2   1

Acquisitions Editor:	Rachel Livsey
Editorial Assistant:	Phyllis Cappello
Production Editor:	Diana E. Axelsen
Copy Editor:	Gillian Dickens
Typesetter:	C&M Digitals (P) Ltd.
Cover Designer:	Tracy E. Miller
Production Artist:	Sandra Ng Sauvajot
Indexer:	Judy Hunt

Contents

Foreword   ix
    Robert E. Slavin
Preface   xi
About the Authors   xvi

PART I: STARTING A TWO-WAY BILINGUAL PROGRAM   1

1. **Moving Toward Two-Way Bilingual Programs**   3
   What Is a Two-Way Bilingual Program?   4
   The Benefits of Two-Way Bilingual Programs   5
   What Two-Way Bilingual Programs Are Not   6
   Reasons to Develop a Two-Way Bilingual Program   7
   Reasons in Support of Two-Way Bilingual Programs   10
   How Can We Use These Concepts in the TWB Program?   20
   Summary   21

2. **Planning and Designing a Two-Way Bilingual Program**   23
   Gathering Information on Program Development
      and Implementation   24
   Sharing Information With All Stakeholders   24
   Involving All Stakeholders in the Critical Decisions
      and Their Roles   25
   Summary   36
   Checklist for Planning   38

3. **Comprehensive Curriculum Models for a Two-Way Program**   39
   Schoolwide Program Models for Two-Way
      Immersion Programs   40
   The Alicia Chacón Model   40
   An Example of the 50-50 Model   41
   A Comprehensive School Reform Model
      Developed for TWB   42
   Summary   48

4. **Case Study: The Alicia R. Chacón International School**   53
    Setting   54
    Site Selection   56
    Fieldwork Procedures/Data Gathering   56
    The Chacón Two-Way Bilingual
        School and Program   57
    What Makes Chacón School a Successful
        TWB Program?   64
    What Do Chacón School Parents Think
        of the TWB Program?   71
    What Do Chacón School Students Think
        of the TWB Program?   78
    Summary   81

PART II: IMPLEMENTING EFFECTIVE INSTRUCTION   83

5. **Instructional Techniques and**
    Activities for Second-Language Learners   85
    What Is Sheltered Instruction?   86
    Strategies for Instructional Delivery   86
    Teaching Techniques for Vocabulary Building   89
    Teaching Techniques for Reading
        Subject Matter Texts   96
    Instructional Tips for Different Stages
        of Language Acquisition   97
    Cooperative Learning Strategies for
        Second-Language Learning   101
    Summary   105

6. **Literacy in Two Languages: The Importance of**
    Research-Based Instructional Models   107
    Types of Instructional Models   108
    Traditional Models for Teaching Reading   108
    Effects of Literacy Instruction in the Primary Language   109
    Emerging Models of Reading for Two-Way Instruction   110
    Sequencing Instruction for Reading   112
    Structuring Components for Integrating
        Listening, Speaking, Reading, and Writing   116
    Summary   131

7. **Using Writing to Promote**
    Reading and Oral Language Development   133
    Teaching Writing From the Start   134
    Explicit Skill Instruction to Meet the Standards   134

Vocabulary and Oral Language for Writing 135
A Community of Writers 135
Culturally Responsive Instruction 136
Setting a Context for TWI Writing 136
Extensive Guided Conversation
and Discussions for Writing 138
Summary 146

8. **Assessing Second-Language Learners** 149
Student Assessment 150
A Definition of Assessment 150
What Are the Purposes of Assessment in TWB Programs? 151
Choosing Assessment Measures in TWB Settings 153
Authentic Assessment of SLLs 153
Assessment and Teaching in TWB Programs 156
What Is a Portfolio Conference? 162
Standards-Based Effective Teaching Connected
to Authentic Assessment 163
Summary 164

PART III: INVOLVING TEACHERS AND PARENTS **167**

9. **Staff Development and Teacher Learning Communities** 169
Topics for Staff Development 170
What Have We Learned From the Study of TLCs? 184
Summary 186

10. **Reaching Out to Parents** 189
Who Are the Parents of SLLs? 190
A Definition of Parent Involvement 191
Conventional Parent Involvement Activities 192
Nonconventional Parent Involvement Activities 193
TWP Program Parents in the Global Scene 195
Considerations for Successful Parent
Involvement in a TWB Program 195
Family Literacy Workshops 197
An Example of a Productive School-Parent Partnership:
The Alicia R. Chacón International School 202
Parent Training Recommendations 203
Summary 204

11. **Evaluation, Research, and Conclusions** 207
TWB Program Evaluation 207
Student Assessment in Evaluation 208
A TWB Program Evaluation Design 209

Five Principles of Effective Evaluation Design   210
Evaluation-Related Questions   212
Evaluation Steps   213
Action Research for TWB Programs   214
Action Research Criteria   215
Action Research and Evaluation   216
Summary   219

Resource A: Resources for Two-Way Bilingual Programs   221
Resource B: List of Acronyms   227
References   229
Index   241

Foreword

When my grandfather arrived in New York from Argentina in the early 20th century, he spoke Spanish, Yiddish, and Russian. My grandmother, a refugee from Poland, spoke Polish, Yiddish, and Russian. Yet they spoke to my father only in English. They used Yiddish among themselves only to exchange insults or otherwise keep my father (or, later, me and my brothers and sister) from understanding them. They were adamant that my father would speak only English and would become a "good American."

America—and Americans new and old—has always been deeply ambivalent about the preservation of languages other than English. In general, immigrants have been expected to keep their language at home, if they wished, but to use English in the broader world, especially in school. Many Latino adults today remember being punished or sent to "Spanish detention" for speaking Spanish among their friends on the school playground, and speakers of other languages have similar memories. As a result, many children of immigrants lost their parents' language. I know adults who can hardly communicate with their own parents. Ironically, America, a nation of immigrants, has extraordinarily low levels of skill in languages other than English compared to other advanced nations.

All of this changed starting in the 1970s with the advent of bilingual education, which usually provides some degree of native-language instruction while children are developing proficiency in English. The goal of bilingual education is not primarily language maintenance, but it is to enable English-language learners to progress in school subjects even though their English skills are not sufficient for academic content. When their English skills are at a high level, the children are transitioned to all-English instruction. While maintenance of a home language is not the main purpose of bilingual education, it is an important by-product, helping to maintain children's cultural and family linkages as well as bilingualism itself, a skill of great value in an increasingly integrated and interdependent world.

In recent years, bilingual education has come under attack, especially (but not exclusively) in California. Yet English-language learners need instruction that is comprehensible to them, and genuine bilingualism among children of all backgrounds needs to be developed.

Dual-language instruction is a rapidly growing response to these needs. In a two-way bilingual (TWB) school, both languages (usually Spanish and English) are equally respected. Spanish-proficient children are seen as a resource to all. Learning a new language is seen as an adventure for all, not a remediation for one group. English-dominant children have an opportunity to gain real facility in Spanish. For some English-dominant students in TWB schools, the Spanish language is a gateway to the rich Latino culture of the Americas and (typically) of their own community. For others, the Spanish language gives them access to their own culture and history, reforging a link that may have been broken between their own grandparents and themselves.

As educators and policymakers turn increasingly toward comprehensive TWB schools, they need to know what such programs look like, what they can accomplish, and how to best take advantage of the opportunities they provide for English- and Spanish-dominant children alike. That is the purpose of this volume. Although TWB programs have existed in some form for a long time, very little is written about them in the education literature. This book fills this gap in an effective and compelling way. It provides a rationale for dual-language instruction, descriptions of TWB programs in action, and a guide to help educators responsible for TWB schools make informed choices about all aspects of their program, from curriculum and instruction to the appropriate roles of the two languages to staff development and evaluation.

This book is certain to be an indispensable guide to planning and practice in dual-language schools. It is practical, down-to-earth, and firmly based in broad experience and research. Every TWB school has its own needs, resources, and constraints, so no one can prescribe exactly how each one should be structured. However, the TWB movement has long needed a wise and well-informed guide. This book fulfills that need, and as such, it is sure to help the movement itself grow, develop, and better serve the growing numbers of children fortunate enough to be learning in two languages.

Robert E. Slavin
Johns Hopkins University

Preface

More and more educators are interested in implementing two-way bilingual programs (also known as two-way immersion (TWI), dual language, and developmental bilingual education) in K–12 schools and in adult workforce development. Practitioners, university professors, charter school entrepreneurs, and reform model developers are anxious to find ways of orchestrating and implementing successful two-way bilingual (TWB) programs. We use *TWB* and *TWI* interchangeably throughout the book since both terms have wide audiences.

The TWB programs aim for full proficiency in two languages, an understanding and appreciation of the cultures associated with those languages, and high levels of achievement in all core academic domains. Furthermore, TWB programs can be considered a "bridge" between bilingual education programs and general education programs because they promote bilingualism, respect, and equity for all students in a school.

Two-way bilingual programs also provide a way to address comprehensive school reform for those schools seeking positive solutions to their ever-growing populations of language minority students. In national reviews of TWB programs, researchers found that when comparison groups are available, evaluations typically show that English-language learners in two-way programs outperform those in English as a Second Language (ESL) or other types of bilingual transitional programs (Lindholm-Leary, 2001).

Despite these preliminary studies and a fairly elaborate theoretical justification for TWB programs, there has been no uniformity in the programs that have been implemented (August & Hakuta, 1997). Programs vary in respect to student selection, assessment, and placement practices; time devoted to instruction in each language; policies for admitting newcomer students; and strategies for involving parents. These practices go hand in hand with the variations of professional development practices and curriculum selection. As educators begin to explore these programs, they are faced with these complex issues as they make critical decisions.

While the published studies focus on the linguistic and academic benefits of the programs for all students, very few studies describe what a TWB program is like. To focus on the characteristics and basic components of successful TWB programs, we set out to study three programs in depth and to build on previous studies of these and other programs.

Our intent is to provide school administrators, teachers, and parents with basic knowledge needed for planning and implementing an effective two-way bilingual program. Therefore, we have structured the chapters to provide a panorama of the basic components of a program. The book is divided in three parts: Starting a Two-Way Bilingual Program (Part I), Implementing Effective Instruction (Part II), and Involving Teachers and Parents (Part III).

PART I: STARTING A TWO-WAY BILINGUAL PROGRAM

Chapter 1 attempts to provide the background information that schools need to initiate their study of TWI by (1) defining the program, (2) summarizing the theoretical and research background, (3) giving exemplars and nonexemplars of its critical features, (4) enumerating the benefits for all students, and (5) contrasting the benefits of TWB/TWI for language minority students with those from other ESL and bilingual programs. Due to the dramatic gap between mainstream and language minority students, we felt it would be important to elaborate on this issue. This chapter also demonstrates that TWB programs have the potential to promote a more equitable school climate in the context of school improvement and systemic reform.

Chapter 2 describes a process for planning and designing a school's program and the types of program models currently in the field. The process of program selection begins with ideas for getting the buy-in from the community and engaging all stakeholders in the school and district.

Chapter 3 examines comprehensive school reform models and offers three approaches to whole-school program implementation. Although there are many exciting and successful TWB/TWI schools, we have selected certain schools because each has taken a different path in developing its curriculum and instructional approach. We also limited our descriptions to English-Spanish programs since we have studied these more intensely, over several years, and know the culture and language firsthand.

We devote Chapter 4 to one of these schools because its TWI has the longest and most stable implementation. The critical features of its success are exemplified through the voices of the principal, teachers, parents, and students. Chacón School has a cohesive TWB program in which its curriculum system and extra-classroom activities play a role in structuring and reinforcing a multilingual and multicultural experience. The model assumes the continuing importance of trilingual competence and the developing needs of the students.

PART II: IMPLEMENTING EFFECTIVE INSTRUCTION

Chapters 5 through 7 are written for teachers as they begin their classroom implementation. After extensive study of the program types and background, as well as the planning or designing phase, teachers need succinct information to guide their daily instructional practice. For this reason, we use a boxed text technique that teachers have requested for these chapters. Teachers find the boxes useful because they can easily convert these into individual teacher cards or posters. The narrative is brief, and the steps to a teaching strategy or technique are succinctly stated.

Chapter 5 begins with the basic premises for English as a Second Language and Spanish as a Second Language instruction. This chapter emphasizes oral language development in the first and second languages because oracy is finally being recognized as a critical precursor to reading comprehension. Effective reading comprehension leads to the learning of content, which in turn leads to success in school. The chapter suggests ways teachers can deliver instruction not just to make it comprehensible to second-language learners but also to ensure vocabulary and discourse development. Ways of organizing learning through quality interaction and cooperative learning strategies end the chapter.

Chapter 6 provides an extensive bank of research-based reading strategies for second-language learners. Since reading has been one of the most problematic aspects of even monolingual children, this chapter provides a framework for developing a comprehensive range of reading skills. The framework also integrates some of the latest research on reading and second-language learning for developing literacy in two languages.

Chapter 7 creates a bridge between reading and writing. The writing process integrates writing skills and ways of assessing the writing progress. It begins with effective teacher-student and student-student interaction strategies, following the notion that interaction is key to the development of oracy-comprehension-writing skills. The boxed narratives in this chapter are intended to be used as student tools as well as classroom posters.

Chapter 8 describes additional ways to assess students across domains. The chapter presents a brief overview of assessment practices and individual student assessment for placement in a program, ongoing classroom assessment, and completion of a school program. It also includes samples of rubrics and practical ways to design assessment and illustrates ways to incorporate them in daily instructional activities for oral, reading, and writing skill development.

PART III: INVOLVING TEACHERS AND PARENTS

Chapter 9 takes the content from the previous chapters and gives suggestions for a comprehensive professional development program and teachers learning communities. It gives the research background on collegiality and teacher support systems through concrete studies that have been conducted in TWI and other bilingual schools. Specific activities that teachers conduct in their learning communities are given, as well as what pitfalls to avoid. An outline for designing a staff development plan ends the chapter.

Chapter 10 offers the positive ways other TWI schools are actively engaging parents in a variety of activities. Programs use two languages for instruction, which facilitates the effective integration of second-language learners (SLLs) and parents with common goals. The chapter contrasts conventional with nonconventional parent involvement activities with the added linguistic and cultural dimension. These activities range from helping their children with homework to participating in school governance and management decisions. Chapter 10 also elaborates on the role of parents in TWB programs and resources schools have used with their successful parent components. Parent involvement functions very well, regardless of parents' background factors such as economic background, ethnicity, language background, status as immigrant or native born, or educational background.

Chapter 11 closes with evaluation components that can be integrated into the program design from the initial stages. The TWB program evaluation includes a planning process with components—such as outcomes of project objectives, standards or criteria to attain when implementing the objectives, and measuring devices (e.g., rubrics, tests, surveys, interviews, observations)—that reveal what was accomplished when implementing the objectives. Evaluation incorporates input of all TWI program participants and guides the improvement of the program. It is our hope that with this sequence, as well as the final recommendations in the chapter, schools will generate rich data and thick descriptions of such important and popular programs. Their contributions to the field will be most invaluable.

ACKNOWLEDGMENTS

We would like to thank all the teachers, administrators, parents, and students who have participated in our study. We are particularly grateful to the educators from three schools in El Paso, Texas, for giving us so much of their time and letting us observe them day in and day out: Alicia Chacón Elementary School in the Ysleta Independent School District, Hueco Elementary School from the Socorro Independent School District, and Rusk and Rivera Elementary Schools in the El Paso Independent School District. Many other talented and dedicated teachers throughout the nation participated in our surveys, as well as trainers and administrators. All their contributions have been most valuable to authenticate theories and procedures.

We are grateful to our colleagues and staffs for assisting with the research and development of manuscripts, graphics, and editing: Eduardo Calderón, María Elena Vasquez, Kay Taggart, Bob Guidry, and Ramón Becks. The research on TWB programs would not have been possible without the support and interest of Dr. Robert Slavin, codirector of the Center for Research on the Education of Students Placed At Risk.

Finally, we are grateful to researchers and practitioners who have devoted their careers to study and promote two-way bilingual education, such as Donna Christian and Liz Howard from the Center for Applied Linguistics; Virginia Collier, Mary Cazabon, Katherine Lindholm-Leary, Elsie Hamayan, Nancy Cloud, Fred Genesee, and Shelley Spiegel-Coleman from the California Association for Bilingual Education; and the many other educators who have been pioneers in these endeavors.

Portions of this study were funded by the Office of Educational Research and Improvement, U.S. Department of Education (Grant No. OERI-R-117-D40005).

The contributions of the following reviewers are gratefully acknowledged:

Tilly Arias
Curriculum Specialist
ELD/Bilingual Department
Santa Ana Unified
    School District
Santa Ana, CA

Rebecca Castro
Resource Teacher
Montebello Unified School
    District
Montebello, CA

Suzanne C. Fonoti
Principal
Cromer Elementary School
    (Flagstaff USD)
Flagstaff, AZ

Marcia Vargas
Curriculum Coordinator for Dual
    Immersion Programs
San Bernardino County
    Superintendent of Schools
San Bernardino, CA

About the Authors

Margarita Espino Calderón, Ph.D., is a Principal Research Scientist for the Center for Research on Education of Students Placed At Risk (CRESPAR), Johns Hopkins University. She is in charge of conducting longitudinal studies and developing curriculum for two-way bilingual and ESL programs, teachers learning communities, and the Success for All/Éxito Para Todos programs. She has taught ESL and bilingual classes in elementary, middle, and high schools and has been a bilingual program director. Her 100+ publications include teachers manuals, journal articles, books, and reading basal series published in the United States and México.

Dr. Calderón is also coprincipal investigator with Diane August and María Carlo on the National Institute of Child Health and Human Development (NICHD) study on the transition from Spanish reading into English reading. She directs the El Paso Adult Bilingual Curriculum Institute, funded by the Department of Labor, whose task is to develop bilingual workplace curriculum and training programs for the Latino labor force. She has recently been appointed to the National Literacy Panel on Language Minority Children and Youth.

A native of Juárez, México, she has a Ph.D. from Claremont Graduate School with an emphasis on multicultural education and organizational development. She has taught graduate courses on educational leadership/administration and on bilingual teacher education.

Liliana Minaya-Rowe, Ph.D., is Bilingual Training Coordinator at the Hartford Public Schools, where she works in a number of projects, including professional development plans and practices for two-way immersion, bilingual, and ESL programs; effective first- and second-language instruction; teachers learning communities; and parent/family involvement practices. She is also Professor Emerita of the Neag School of Education at the University of Connecticut. Her research interests, publications, and teaching include teacher education, literacy, bilingual program development and implementation, and discourse analysis of bilinguals. She holds an M.A. in applied linguistics and a Ph.D. in education from the University of Texas at Austin. Her publications include more than 80 journal articles, books, chapters, teacher manuals, and guidebooks.

Part I

Starting a Two-Way Bilingual Program

1

Moving Toward Two-Way Bilingual Programs

This how-to book is for teachers, school and district administrators, policymakers, program coordinators, evaluators, and community leaders in the United States and other countries who are planning two-way bilingual (TWB) programs, Grades K–12. We call them TWB programs because they are bilingual education programs and meet bilingual education and school objectives. Schools transformed into two-way bilingual programs promote bilingualism, academic achievement, and cross-cultural understanding in all of their students, along with the other important goals of a regular school program. TWB programs provide instruction for native English speakers and native speakers of another language (e.g., Spanish and English, Chinese and English, French and English, Navajo and English, Korean and English). These programs are developed using the same challenging academic and language development standards as basic K–12 education.

Throughout this chapter and this entire how-to book, we have referred to many sources that provide the rich detail of TWB programs. These sources are in the form of textbooks, research reports, summary briefs, conference papers, and speeches and provide an understanding of the topic without which this book would not have been possible. There are several authors who have contributed to what we know in the field of

TWB programs. They include, to name a few, Cazabon (2001), Christian and her coworkers (Christian, Montone, Lindholm, & Carranza, 1997), Genesee and his coworkers (Cloud, Genesee, & Hamayan, 2000; Genesee, 1999), Howard and Sugarman (2001), and Lindholm-Leary (2000, 2001), among others. Information about TWB programs can also be found at the World Wide Web sites for the Center for Applied Linguistics (CAL); the National Clearinghouse for English Language Acquisition and Language Instruction Educational Programs (NCELA), formerly called the National Clearinghouse for Bilingual Education (NCBE); the Center for Research in Education, Diversity, and Excellence (CREDE); and the ERIC Clearing-houses, sponsored by the U.S. Department of Education.

WHAT IS A TWO-WAY BILINGUAL PROGRAM?

A TWB program is a bilingual education program that integrates second-language learners (SLLs)—that is, English learners and English-speaking students—for instruction in and through two languages (Cazabon, 2001; Lindholm-Leary, 2001). For English learners, the first language (L1) is their native language (e.g., Spanish, Chinese, French, Korean, Navajo), and the second language (L2) is English. For English speakers, their L1 is English and their L2 may be Spanish, French, Russian, and so forth. This program provides language, literacy, and content area instruction to all its students in both languages. TWB programs are also known as two-way immersion, bilingual immersion, dual-language immersion, developmental bilingual education, dual-language education programs, and two-way programs (Baker & Prys Jones, 1998; Brisk, 1998).

CAL has documented the growth of TWB programs in the United States. As of 2001, there were 260 programs in 23 states, and the majority of these programs—more than two-thirds—use English and Spanish (CAL, 2002). A TWB program integrates SLLs for instruction in and through two languages. It provides language, literacy, and content area instruction to all its students in both languages.

> A two-way bilingual program integrates Spanish learners, Vietnamese learners, Navajo learners, and so on for instruction in and through two languages.

Academic, language, and affective goals are at the core of TWB programs. Another important goal of these programs is to eliminate the isolation of English learners from English speakers by providing them with a rich English-language environment and by supporting their academic learning with no risk to their native-language development, language maintenance, or academic achievement (Howard & Sugarman, 2001; Thomas & Collier, 1997). On the other hand, English speakers are given the opportunity to learn a second language with native-speaking peer models (Cazabon, 2001; Christian et al., 1997).

A TWB program can also be considered a bridge for all students to have access to and benefit from bilingual education and general education programs. It is bilingual education for all students, for the general population, and for language minority and language majority students. It embodies the latest educational research and practice, whether these are published in general education or bilingual education quarters. It can also be considered an enrichment approach and an asset to bilingualism, and it is thoroughly bilingual. There is a valuing of and respect for the language and culture of the participants. It is a bilingual way for educating all students (Calderón & Carreón, 2000; Cloud et al., 2000).

TWB programs emphasize challenging standards in the core curriculum domains while enriching the students' development in both their first and second languages (Lindholm-Leary, 2000). These programs aim for full proficiency in two languages, understanding and appreciation of the cultures associated with those languages, and high levels of achievement in all core academic domains (Cloud et al., 2000; Montague, 1997).

> A two-way bilingual program is a bilingual way for educating all students—a bridge for all students to have access to and benefit from bilingual education and general education programs.

THE BENEFITS OF TWO-WAY BILINGUAL PROGRAMS

Research on TWB programs points to educational, cognitive, sociocultural, and economic benefits of bilingualism and instruction in two languages (Calderón & Carreón, 2000; Cloud et al., 2000). A summary of these benefits follows.

- *Educational.* TWB programs benefit all students, whether they are minority or majority, rich or poor, young or old. Students can acquire high levels of proficiency in their L1 *and* in their L2.

- *Cognitive.* Bilingual students achieve cognitive and linguistic benefits on academic tasks that call for creativity and problem solving. They also know about the structural properties of the language, including its sounds, words, and grammar. This knowledge is beneficial in reading development because it facilitates decoding academic language.

- *Sociocultural.* Bilingual persons are able to understand and communicate with members of other cultural groups and to expand their world. They are able to respect the values, social customs, and ways of viewing the world of speakers of other languages and their communities.

- *Economic.* There are jobs that call for bilingual or multilingual proficiency. Students who come to school speaking important languages, such as Spanish, Korean, Navajo, and Albanian, are valuable resources who can contribute to the nation's economic relations with other countries because they already know another world language.

- *Global.* Due to the recent terrorist attacks to the United States and the threat of a long-term war, our nation can benefit from bilingualism and biculturalism as strategies and initiatives to bring peace are put in place in different parts of the world with non-English-speaking communities. It follows that our country would benefit if negotiations, protocols, and deliberations were conducted using local languages to defend democracy and protect the general welfare of the citizens of the world.

TWB programs are also potentially beneficial to comprehensive school and/or district reform movements as these reform efforts attempt to address the shortage of educational programs that meet the needs of SLLs, who can be provided with a genuine schooling environment that sees to their language and academic competence and social well-being (Lindholm-Leary, 2001). In a school or district, the goal is to have a balanced bilingual population of native English speakers and speakers of a non-English language who are both able to function effectively in two languages (Amrein & Peña, 2000; Cazabon, Nicoladis, & Lambert, 1998).

WHAT TWO-WAY BILINGUAL PROGRAMS ARE NOT

Research and practice have demonstrated that for TWB programs to be successful, they should do justice to both languages and cultures based on a strong program design and implementation (Calderón, 2001a, 2001b). Consequently, TWB programs are

- NOT subtractive. TWB programs promote native-language literacy skills and balanced bilingualism.
- NOT remedial programs. TWB programs are quality program designs for standards-based education while promoting proficiency in two languages.
- NOT compensatory programs. TWB programs educate first-class students who are able to achieve at the highest levels and who are bilingual. These programs need to be at the core of school and/or district efforts.

- NOT superimposed on traditional school or district structures or on an infrastructure that was set up for an existing bilingual program. The structures need to be reorchestrated, redesigned, and integrated to make time for and do justice to the two languages.
- NOT superimposed on existing mind-sets of an "enrichment" versus a "remedial" model. TWB programs promote enrichment, a position that needs to be clarified and addressed before and during program development and implementation.

REASONS TO DEVELOP A
TWO-WAY BILINGUAL PROGRAM

By the year 2020, the majority of students in our nation's schools will be living in circumstances traditionally regarded as placing them at risk of educational failure (Riley, 2000; Rossi & Stringfield, 1996). Many students will be poorly housed, undernourished, subject to the effect of others' abuse of drugs, provided with few adult role models, and linguistically and culturally diverse (Laturnau, 2001). Researchers, practitioners, and policymakers unanimously agree that urban schooling is in dramatic need of improvement to meet the needs of linguistically and culturally diverse students (August & Hakuta, 1997; Hess, 1999). They point to statistical social indicators that continue to account for the negative public schooling programs, practices, experiences, and circumstances offered to English learners (National Center for Education Statistics [NCES], 1999, 2001; Waggoner, 1999). The graduation rate continues to range between 50 and 60 percent (National Clearinghouse for Bilingual Education [NCBE], 1999; Valenzuela, 1999). By age 25, about 25 percent of these students have completed high school compared to 79 percent for English speakers (Carnevale, 1999; O. Garcia, 1999). Recent research confirms that at-risk students continue to enter school later, leave earlier, and receive proportionately fewer high school diplomas and college degrees than other U.S. students (Fashola & Slavin, 2000).

Since the 1980s, demographers have reported substantial increases in the linguistic-ethnic diversity of student populations at state, regional, and national levels. In the past two decades, they have observed that students of Euro-American heritage grew by 5.5 percent, whereas Latinos grew by 65 percent. As Euro-American students are projected to decrease

> Students at risk of educational failure continue to enter school later, leave earlier, and receive fewer high school diplomas and college degrees than other U.S. students.

by 10 to 11 percent between 2000 and 2020, Latinos are expected to grow by 54 percent (González, 2000; NCES, 1997). In 1996, Latinos represented 11 percent of the nation's population but will increase to 25 percent in 2050

(Osterling, 1998). The U.S. Bureau of the Census predicts that in the near future, one in every four Americans will be of Latino ancestry (August & McArthur, 1996; Rong & Preissle, 1998).

This massive U.S. demographic shift challenges educators in every segment of the country (Riley, 2000; Sizer, 1996). Scholars define their education as elusive and problematic (Donato, 1997; Garcia, 2001). A 1996 White House report described Latinos' overall school experience as "a history of neglect, oppression, and periods of wanton denial of opportunity . . . [by a system that continues to] deny equitable educational opportunities to Hispanic Americans" (President's Advisory Commission on Educational Excellence for Hispanic Americans, 1996, cited in Osterling, 1998, p. 3). Since the 1960s, the dropout rate for Latinos has been regularly cited at between 40 and 50 percent (Cummins, 1986) and as high as 90 percent for Puerto Ricans (Nieto, 1998). Currently, 53 percent of Latinos age 25 or older complete high school, while only 9 percent of this population earn college degrees (Valencia, 1997). August and Hakuta (1997) suggested that the educational status of Latinos is problematic because this group is perceived as a threat to the status quo and scarce symbolic resources. Yet another dynamic contributing to differentiated academic achievement is the structure of schooling as an instrumental means to individualism and social mobility that gives advantages to the dominant middle class (Hoffman, 1998; Macedo & Bartolomé, 1999).

That 3 out of 10 Latino students are reported to have difficulty understanding and speaking English is another critical factor (NCES, 1997; Valdés, 1998). Some of these students are in transitional bilingual education (TBE) programs that are subtractive, resulting in the loss of native-language literacy skills and limited bilingualism (Garcia, 2001; Wong Fillmore, 1991). Evidence strongly suggests that in TBE programs, bilinguals exit at a critical point that does not allow them to develop more fully their native-language literacy and higher cognitive skills that could translate into higher achievement in English-only classes (Slavin & Calderón, 2001; Spener, 1988). Exiting at this critical moment limits their biliteracy skills, jeopardizes their cognitive growth, and lowers their academic achievement (Brisk, 1998; Hakuta, 1986).

> Transitional bilingual education programs often result in limited bilingualism. Students exit these programs at a critical point that limits their biliteracy skills, jeopardizes their cognitive growth, and lowers their academic achievement that could translate into higher achievement in English-only classes.

Along with language, cultural factors are linked to the underachievement of Latino students (Durán, 2000; Goldenberg, 1993). Latino students new to the United States lack knowledge of specific features of the school, known as "culture of the classroom" (Crawford,

1997; Cummins, 1996). They face the challenge of learning not only local and national values but also the hidden cultural patterns of interacting in the classroom such as the following:

- Learning to talk
- The value of participating in sports or other co-curricular activities
- Effective ways of communicating with school authorities
- The value of competing for grades and recognition and so forth (Hoffman, 1998)

Moreover, Brisk (1998) posited that the pressure to assimilate to a new educational system and a new culture is an expensive proposition for Latinos, especially when it means rejecting their language and culture. Forcing newcomers to make personal choices of language and culture often affects their self-esteem, motivation, and ability to learn English and the academic curriculum (Echevarria, Vogt, & Short, 2000).

For more than three decades, bilingual education programs in the United States have had as a goal the social integration of language minority groups who have been at least partially socially disenfranchised (Hernández-Chávez, 1984; Secada, 1990). However, the policies of and practices for these programs have reflected attitudes toward bilingualism versus monolingual-

> The pressure to assimilate to a new educational system and a new culture is an expensive proposition for Latinos, especially when it means rejecting their language and culture.

ism on the part of the socially dominant group (Crawford, 1989, 2000; Cummins, 2000). Consequently, the establishment and operation of bilingual education programs have largely proceeded on the assumption that one can be a "real" member of U.S. society only by assimilating to the new culture and by becoming a monolingual English speaker, thus giving up one's first language and ethnic identity (Crawford, 1992; Minaya-Rowe, 1988).

For the most part, bilingual education programs have been compensatory in nature, much like the Head Start programs of the 1970s; they have also been based on the academic and sociocultural deficit model (Cummins, 2000; E. Garcia, 1999). Programs developed for non-English speakers have provided diluted curriculum instruction and nonchallenging academic content, focusing mostly on second-language development. They have frequently been described as sink-or-swim or submersion programs with the goal to eradicate the first language and to underestimate the first culture (Cummins, 1991; Ovando & McLaren, 2000).

There also have been TBE programs with some instruction in the first language, but they move as quickly as possible into English. For the most part, all federally funded programs have been transitional in nature

> The establishment and operation of bilingual education programs have largely proceeded on the assumption that one can be a "real" member of U.S. society only by assimilating to the new culture and by becoming a monolingual English speaker, thus giving up one's first language and ethnic identity.

and provide early exit bilingual education services to "limited English-proficient students" for the period of time that the students are considered deficient in English communication skills (Tse, 2001). Once they are identified as "ready" to be mainstreamed, the laws do not require any specialized instructional services.

Also, during the past two decades, a number of practitioners and theoreticians have promoted other programs as alternatives to transitional bilingual education, namely, language maintenance programs, dual-language programs, or two-way bilingual programs—in general, programs that fall under the category of enrichment language education (Cloud et al., 2000; Genesee, 1999). They have posed the inclusion of language majority students in bilingual schooling as a way to promote enrichment bilingual education for language minority students. All SLLs are part of a bilingual program—a TWB program—and both languages and cultures are valued and used in instruction (Calderón, 2001a, 2001b; Lindholm-Leary, 2001).

> Language minority and language majority students are part of a bilingual program—a two-way bilingual program—and both languages and cultures are valued and used in instruction.

REASONS IN SUPPORT OF TWO-WAY BILINGUAL PROGRAMS

In this chapter, we examine three reasons important for successful TWB program development. These issues have been conceptual building blocks and generically applied in educational theory and effective practices of education. They also have been linked to the education of linguistically and culturally diverse students and are used to support this book's main focus: how to best meet the educational needs of both SLLs in terms of TWB program development and implementation. The issues are as follows:

- Access to and equity in education, which include sociopolitical issues, attitudes toward bilingualism, and adequate education, among other issues
- Educational innovation, which includes the commitment, time, and perseverance of the entire school to sustain change and professional development, among others

Figure 1.1   Conceptual Issues for Successful Two-Way Bilingual Programs

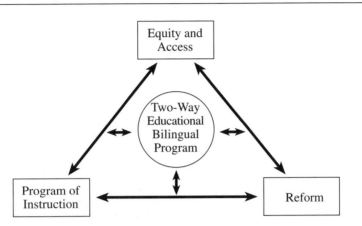

- Program on instruction for all students through language development, academic achievement, and effective instruction, among others

These three issues can roughly define a sequence for TWB program development, as presented in Figure 1.1. They can complement each other, occur simultaneously, and be used again and again as a rationale to develop, implement, and sustain a program. The sequence may be used to explain procedures of initial steps in TWB program development, as well as the rationale of the program, how the program works, how to plan and disseminate a program, and so forth. Furthermore, these three issues can be considered organizational tools as those involved in planning TWB programming—be it teachers, administrators, staff, and so on—design and develop it. The components may vary depending on the school characteristics and varied needs, such as student composition, diverse ethnic backgrounds, linguistic needs, and teachers' levels of expertise. One should bear in mind that the same TWB program design in one school may not exactly serve another school. However, as schools experience change every time they promote a TWB program innovation, at first tentatively, they have the opportunity to ground the procedures to develop an innovative program that meets the particular school's needs. Specifically, this process helps both mainstream and bilingual educators to become aware of common goals and be more sensitive to students' needs. The program components are refined as educators gain a deeper understanding of the interplay of the three issues. Finally, theory and practice are integrated into these issues.

TWB program planners can use the sequence as something practical and immediately useful—something we might even call a directive—to identify the program's potential in the context of the three issues in order

> As schools experience change when the two-way bilingual program is implemented, they have the opportunity to ground the procedures to develop an innovative program that meets the particular school's needs.

to find the most adequate approach to educate all students. The sequence can be used as conceptual support every time an innovation is introduced, whether it is related to standards-based curriculum, staff development, or student assessment. Over time, the process becomes more efficient and is accomplished more quickly as planners and educators develop expertise.

The three issues overlap and are so intertwined that it is difficult to separate them, but they can be used to fit specific school needs. For example, professional development can be related to the program of instruction and to sociocultural aspects of schooling, language and academic achievement can be related to attitudes toward bilingualism and to school commitment, and so forth. What follows is a brief description and rationale of what the spiral represents.

The Two-Way Bilingual Program as an Opportunity for Access and Equity

When properly implemented, TWB programs provide *all* students, including English learners (ELs), a quality education—that is, equal access to academic programs and activities and equal opportunity for academic achievement and bilingualism. A TWB program is an equitable educational program that respects and treats all students as equal members of the school community. It is equitable instruction because it welcomes and challenges all students and staff to do their best regardless of race, national origin, education, language, and culture.

> A TWB program is an equitable educational program that respects and treats all students as equal members of the school community and challenges students and staff to do their best regardless of race, national origin, education, language, and culture.

The literature reveals that creating an equitable TWB school environment is a complex and very demanding process. However, when schools or districts design and implement TWB programs, they can accomplish the following:

- They help ensure equity in education as English-language learners have an equal chance to achieve their full potential.
- They promote equal access to programs and activities.
- They practice equal opportunity for academic achievement.

A TWB program can be at the core of this goal as schools become more racially balanced and can equitably ensure equal opportunity for academic achievement, decrease conflict, and involve parents and community members (Thomas & Collier, 2002). TWB programs also have the potential to promote philosophies and policies of equity and access with respect to all of their students. These programs are grounded in theories concerning education, assessment, teacher growth, parental involvement, organizational structures, and social constructivism. Social constructivism recognizes that all students construct knowledge socially through meaningful interactions with parents, teachers, and peers regardless of ethnicity, class, and language background (Baker & Prys Jones, 1998; Tharp, 1999).

The main benefit TWB program planners can derive from a theory in support of the equity and access to a quality program is the guidance such a theory can provide in judging the soundness of the program designed to meet the needs of both groups of SLLs. For example, we can examine the relationship between the TWB program and community background factors (those social factors that go beyond the school and the program) in terms of the contextual interaction model proposed by Cummins (1979) and Cortes (1986). Figure 1.2 on page 14 illustrates this relationship.

For the contextual interaction model, the TWB program can work as follows.

- The *community background factors,* such as language use patterns in the home and community attitudes toward the student's first language and second language, contribute to *student input factors,* which the student brings to the educational setting.
- These *student input factors* (first-language proficiency, second-language proficiency, or no proficiency; self-esteem; levels of academic achievement; and motivation to acquire the second language and maintain the first language) are in constant interaction with the *instructional program,* resulting in social integration and various academic, cognitive, and affective student *outcomes.*
- The *TWB program* gives high status to both groups of students and bilingual and nonbilingual teachers, integrates language and literacy, promotes the standards-based curriculum, encourages team teaching and action research, and includes a high level of parental involvement.
- Furthermore, the TWB program is primarily determined by *educational input factors* such as enrichment characteristics, fiscal resources available to the program, staff knowledge, skills, curriculum innovations, standards-based curriculum and assessment, experience, expectations and attitudes, and underlying educational assumptions or theories.

Figure 1.2 The Contextual Interaction Model

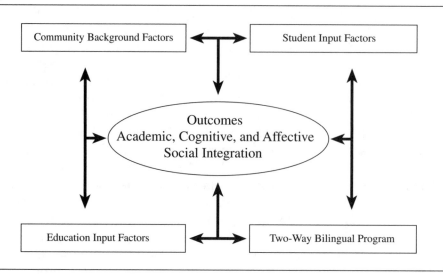

SOURCE: Adapted from Cummins (1979) and Cortes (1986).

In conclusion, the contextual interaction model accounts for the inter-action of the *community background factors* (majority-minority status, atti-tudes toward L1 and L2), which SLLs bring with them as *student input factors* to the TWB instructional program to meet their immediate needs: first-language proficiency, second-language proficiency, academic achievement, and psychosocial adjustment.

The Two-Way Bilingual Program as an Educational Reform Tool

Public school enrollments are being transformed by an increase in the number of English learners who bring the richness of linguistic and cultural diversity with them to school (Garcia, 2001). Education reforms have raised the bar so that all students, including SLLs, must finish school and participate in the economic and social world of the new century. These reforms place tremendous pressure on public schools across the nation; they are continuously challenged to meet the needs of a widely diverse population (Marcos, 1998).

TWB programs cannot be superimposed on existing structures or mind-sets (Calderón, 2001a, 2001b). It is not just your father's usual bilingual compensatory program. Since it is not a remedial program or a compensatory or subtractive one, it needs a whole-school reform setting. TWB programs need a new structure; schools and/or districts need to start all over. They need to have the following characteristics:

- Their goal is promote native-language literacy skills and balanced bilingualism.
- Their mission is to enrich with a quality program design for standards-based education while promoting bilingualism.
- Their mission is to educate first-class students who are able to achieve at the highest levels and who are bilingual. The programs need to be at the core of school and/or district efforts.
- They should be built on a new infrastructure and be well designed and integrated to make time for and do justice to the two languages and cultures.
- Their mission is to dispel the myth and mind-set as an "enrichment" versus "remedial" bilingual program before and during program implementation.

Researchers and policymakers also point to education reform to change schools in order to correct perceived social and educational problems and promote cognitive, academic, and linguistic development (Tyack & Cuban, 1995). The TWB program as a reform tool can focus on improving school performance and

> TWB programs cannot be superimposed on existing structures or mind-sets. Schools and/or districts need to start all over.

language enrichment. It can yield a procedural reform that introduces new and different socioeducational contexts for equitable language and academic education, with the goal to produce and sustain socioeducational change. The implementation of a quality TWB program can make a difference in the school community with concrete, short-term improvements. The program involves and supports teachers, principals, parents, and the community's efforts in a concerted effort to

- improve racial relations,
- refine classroom teaching and learning,
- reduce dropout rates,
- strengthen community/parent participation in the education of their children,
- apply research-proven curricula, and
- update staff development with the potential of sustained long-term changes.

The role of TWB programs can be pursued through reform implementation, refinement, and sustainability to build a capacity for change in the system and to lead the school toward sustained educational improvement.

Most analyses of reform are framed in a rather general fashion (Hess, 1999). The TWB program can offer quality education for SLLs based on a thorough and in-depth review of all aspects of schooling—curriculum, instruction, assessment, staff development, and organizational strategies—as well as other factors specific to the school or district. As an educational innovation, the TWB program has the potential to provide insights and analytical frameworks to spell out the theories supporting systemic reform (Montague, 1997; Sarason, 1996). In turn, the use of its individual components of reform can provide an understanding of the larger framework to conceptualize the school's or district's systemic reform (Johnson, 1996).

The TWB program as a reform tool can legitimize the overall performance of a school or district with a workable present and future of both structure and activity (Meyer & Rowan, 1991). The school requires time, focus, and the commitment of personnel who value student input factors. It may nurture school reform efforts with the goal to develop deep understandings of successful research-proven theories and applications for the improvement of teaching and learning (Hill, 1997). TWB program planning, implementation, and coordination in a multifaceted and integrated approach enable planners to alter instruction, curriculum, assessment, staff development, and other school organizational strategies (Greenfield, 1995).

> As an educational innovation, the two-way bilingual program has the potential to provide insights and analytical frameworks supporting the school's or district's reform.

Urban schools face many serious challenges in serving their students. With the proper implementation of a TWB program, progress can be made to meet these challenges and sustain them. The TWB program can be the connection between instructional processes and student outcomes, integrated curriculum and instruction, models of staff development, parental and community involvement, and organizational processes that sustain change (Sizer, 1996). Existing urban schools' reform efforts have already demonstrated that it is possible for schools serving large numbers of students placed at risk to help these students achieve levels of education far above those traditionally achieved by disadvantaged groups of students (Fashola, Slavin, Calderón, & Durán, 2000; Nadeau, 1996).

TWB programs represent a significant development in the evolution of bilingual and bicultural education and systemic reform (Calderón, 2002; Valdés, 1997). In a sense, TWB programs are the ultimate test of whether schools and districts can become meaningfully responsive to linguistic and cultural heterogeneity and can value students' languages and cultures and provide them with a successful schooling experience.

A goal of this how-to book is to demonstrate how the different TWB program components are used in the systemic reform. Individual components of school reform have been the focus of research at different times in isolated or smaller school systems, rendering incomplete pictures in making informed recommendations in policy and practice (Newmann, King, & Rigdon, 1997). A gap in the literature exists with respect to case studies on educational reform in urban, diverse, and larger contexts

(González & Darling-Hammond, 1997). A coherent examination of the conditions that foster this valuable reform is now needed.

The Two-Way Bilingual Program Promotes Language Development and Academic Achievement

Although the purpose of this how-to book is not to provide an extensive and in-depth review of the literature, we would like to present two theoretical frameworks that can help prepare us to deal with and understand the needs and strengths of SLLs. These frameworks are the threshold hypothesis and the dimensions of language proficiency.

The Threshold Hypothesis

Research on the relationship between bilingualism, academic achievement, and cognitive development carried out about half a century ago implied that bilingualism was a cause of language handicaps and cognitive confusion (Genesee, 1987; Lessow-Hurley, 2000). However, since the 1960s, a substantial number of studies have reported academic and cognitive benefits associated with bilingualism (Hakuta, 1986). These findings are not surprising when we consider that bilinguals have been exposed to more training in interpreting and analyzing language than monolinguals. As students develop high-level bilingual skills, they become "linguists" and are able to compare the grammars and vocabularies of their two languages (Bialystok & Hakuta, 1994; Lambert, 1984). They are able to express the same thoughts in two languages, as well as see their first and second languages as one system among many others as they become aware of their linguistic operations.

The level of bilingualism that students attain is an important factor in judging the effects of bilingualism on their educational development. The current research data have led us to believe that there are threshold levels of linguistic proficiency that students must achieve to avoid cognitive deficits and allow for the potentially beneficial aspects of becoming bilingual to influence cognitive growth. The threshold hypothesis assumes that those aspects of bilingualism that might positively influence cognitive growth are not likely to come into effect until students have attained a certain minimum of threshold-level proficiency in their second language. If bilingual students attain only a very low level of proficiency in one or both of their languages, their interaction with the environment through these languages in terms of input and output is likely to be impoverished (Cummins, 1981, 1984).

There appears to be two thresholds of bilingual proficiency. The attainment of a lower threshold level would be sufficient to avoid any negative cognitive effects. The attainment of a higher threshold level would be necessary for accelerated growth.

Figure 1.3   The Threshold Hypothesis for Two-Way Bilingual Programs:
Cognitive Effects of Different Types of Bilingualism

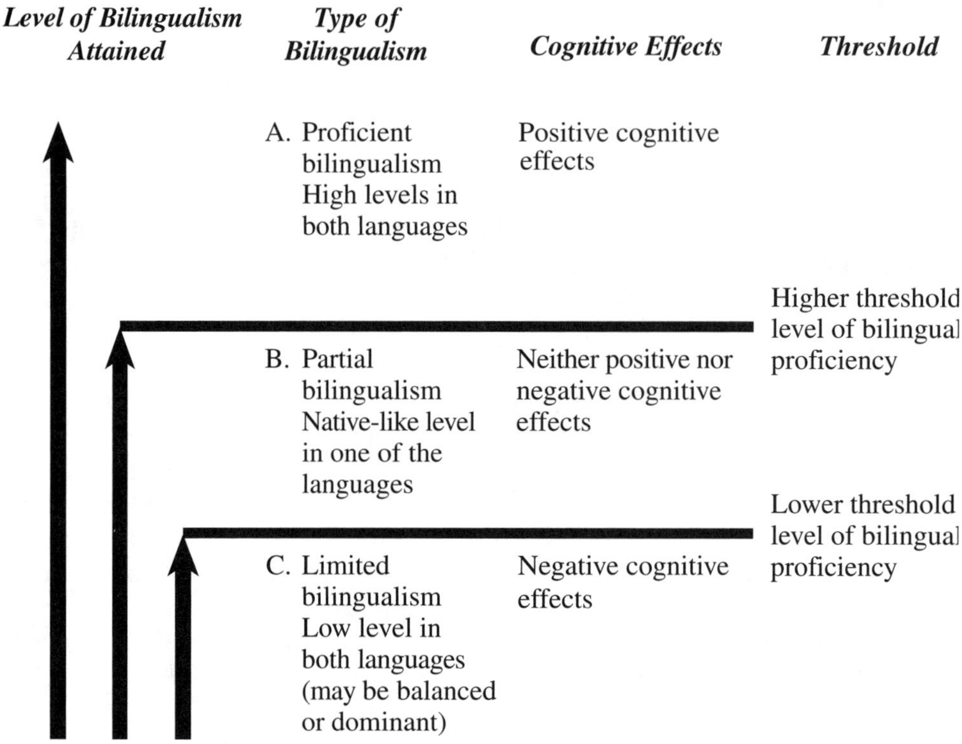

Level of Bilingualism Attained	*Type of Bilingualism*	*Cognitive Effects*	*Threshold*
	A. Proficient bilingualism High levels in both languages	Positive cognitive effects	
			Higher threshold level of bilingual proficiency
	B. Partial bilingualism Native-like level in one of the languages	Neither positive nor negative cognitive effects	
			Lower threshold level of bilingual proficiency
	C. Limited bilingualism Low level in both languages (may be balanced or dominant)	Negative cognitive effects	

SOURCE: Based on Cummins (1981, 1984).

- *Subtractive or limited bilingualism* (Type C in Figure 1.3) is the result of too little effort being made by the student and/or the program to maintain and develop the L1 while the L2 is being developed. Some English learners are limited bilinguals, and they do not catch up linguistically with native speakers of English and thus pay the price of limited or subtractive bilingualism. They experience academic difficulties, and their proficiency in both languages is less developed than among native speakers of each. This would also apply to all SLLs for their L2 development when full proficiency orally and in writing is not implemented.
- *Partial bilingualism* (Type B in Figure 1.3) is the intermediate step to proficient bilingualism. SLLs possess native-like levels in one of the two languages. If properly implemented, the instructional program offered to these students would aim at raising their level of bilingualism.

- *Additive or proficient bilingualism* (Type A in Figure 1.3) relates to positive consequences of bilingualism in SLLs with native or near-native proficiency in two languages.

In conclusion, bilingualism per se is not the cause of academic difficulties. When SLLs' first and second languages are strongly promoted by the instructional program, the resulting additive bilingualism appears to entail linguistic and cognitive benefits. In other words, there is a positive relationship between the degree of proficiency developed by bilingual students in both languages and academic achievement.

The Dimensions of Language Proficiency

Cummins (1981) has identified two major dimensions of language proficiency. These dimensions account for the differences between the linguistic and academic demands of the school and those of interpersonal communication contexts outside the school. All tasks requiring language skills may be placed along two continua, as presented in Figure 1.4.

The horizontal continuum describes the amount of contextual support available for expressing or receiving meaning.

- *Context-embedded communication* is less language dependent and more context dependent. Speakers and listeners can actively negotiate for meaning, while the language they use is supported by a wide range of contextual cues (nonlinguistic or paralinguistic cues such as gestures, body movements, voice intonation, visuals). It is the language typical of the everyday world's face-to-face communication.
- *Context-reduced communication* is more language dependent and less context dependent. Speakers and listeners rely exclusively on linguistic cues to extract meaning. Many of the linguistic demands of the mainstream classroom reflect communicative activities at this end of the continuum (class lectures, dictation, etc.).

The vertical continuum addresses the cognitive demands of the communication task or activity.

- The upper parts consist of communicative tasks in which the linguistic tools have become largely automatic. These tools have been mastered and thus require little active cognitive involvement for appropriate performance. Cognitive demands are easy (e.g., following simple directions, playground talk, simple yes-no responses).
- The lower parts of the vertical continuum consist of communicative tasks that have not become automatic and thus require active

Figure 1.4   Range of Contextual Support and Degree of Cognitive
Involvement in Communicative Activities

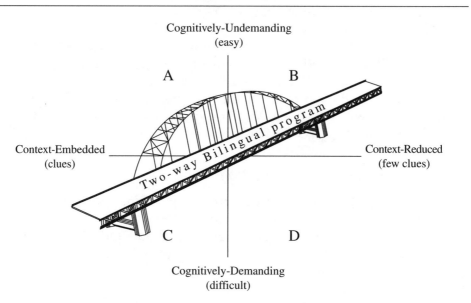

cognitive involvement for appropriate performance. Cognitive demands are difficult (e.g., describing a procedure, writing an essay, taking a standardized test).

Furthermore, activities in Quadrants B and D of Figure 1.4 require linguistic resources (grammatical, discourse, social, and the maximum use of strategic skills) to achieve communicative goals (e.g., a telephone conversation, translating in a store for a parent). In other words, cognitive involvement can be just as intense in context-embedded and context-reduced activities.

HOW CAN WE USE THESE CONCEPTS IN THE TWB PROGRAM?

Figure 1.4 illustrates how the TWB program can benefit from the concepts of contextual support and cognitive involvement across all four quadrants in a progressive manner.

1. First, the context-embedded and context-reduced distinction suggests reasons why SLLs acquire conversational skills in their second languages sooner than academic proficiency. The fact is that there are considerably more cues to meaning in face-to-face context-embedded situations than in typical context-reduced activities.

2.   Second, the aim of TWB schooling is to develop students' understanding of cognitively demanding and context-reduced tasks. The more initial literacy can be developed in a meaningful context (e.g., related to the student's background), the more successful it is likely to be. The same application holds true for L2 instruction: the more context embedded the instruction is in L2, the more comprehensible it is likely to be, and the more successful it should be in ultimately developing L2 skills in context-reduced situations.

Cummins (1981) stressed that one of the reasons English learners often fail to develop high levels of English academic skills is because their initial instruction has stressed context-reduced communication insofar as instruction has been through English and unrelated to their prior out-of-school experience. This would also apply to all SLLs whose background knowledge is needed to build their second-language proficiency. Cummins's proposals lead us to conclude the following: Language proficiency is the ability to use language for both basic everyday communication and academic tasks.

SUMMARY

This chapter has tried to demonstrate that TWB programs have the potential to promote a more equitable school climate in the context of school improvement and systemic reform. Based on the research literature of the past two decades, the chapter has provided a definition of TWB programs, an illustration of the benefits and a rationale for quality TWB programs, and a description of what a good TWB program is not. It has also examined the reasons and issues to develop a TWB program as a means for access and equity, educational innovation and reform, and program of instruction. Our challenge as educators, parents, policymakers, and researchers is to put in practice these concepts and become part of the educational transformation. These are tools to design and implement an innovative program to stimulate policy changes at all levels and sustain them: identifying the students; allocating time and curriculum for each language; facilitating ongoing professional development; developing curriculum, literacy, and assessment; involving parents; and evaluating programs. The chapters of this how-to book that follow provide a practical guide to develop TWB programs and implement existing ones.

2

Planning and Designing a Two-Way Bilingual Program

We know that the benefits of dual immersion are many. We also know that its planning, implementation, and evaluation can be quite complex. The focus of this chapter is to provide a path for the planning phase before implementation.

The planning phase should begin at least a year before implementation. There are several items to attend to, such as the following:

- Gathering information on program development and implementation
- Sharing this information with all stakeholders: teachers, administrators, parents, and the community
- Involving all stakeholders in the critical decisions

There are specific roles parents, community, teachers, administrators, and other stakeholders can play to promote and plan a quality program. Their role and commitment will hinge on the information and decision-making processes that are used. Let us examine each within the planning phase.

GATHERING INFORMATION ON PROGRAM DEVELOPMENT AND IMPLEMENTATION

The idea of implementing or converting a school into a two-way bilingual (TWB) school can come from anyone. It may be a handful of teachers who recently attended a conference and are excited about the potential benefits. It may be a group of parents who heard other parents bragging about their children's TWB education in a neighboring school. There are rare occasions, but very real nonetheless, when a superintendent, such as Dr. Anthony Amato at the Hartford Public Schools, urges schools to adopt TWB programs. Whenever there is a window of opportunity, the challenge should be taken.

The challenge begins with gathering information, summarizing key elements, and translating the summaries for parents who may not speak English. Chapters 1 and 2 summarize information that can be initially presented to all stakeholders. A list of additional sources and resources is included in Resource A. The National Clearinghouse for Bilingual Education publishes and distributes *Biliteracy for a Global Society: An Idea Book on Dual Language Education* (Lindholm-Leary, 2000) with frequently asked questions about TWB programs. Several Web sites have already summarized important information or provided in-depth studies. These Web sites are also included in Resource A. After gathering such information, the school or district might even consider putting a type of portfolio/folder or a booklet together with the information selected.

However, there is nothing as powerful as seeing it with one's own eyes. Visits to schools with TWB programs give everyone a wealth of information quickly and may serve to convince those who might be skeptical. There are more than 250 schools throughout the nation that have these programs. The Center for Applied Linguistics (CAL) updates a directory of these schools. The Success for All (SFA) Foundation also keeps a directory of all SFA-TWB schools (please see Resource A for contact information).

The local university can recommend researchers or experts in the field who can assist with information gathering, planning, or evaluating the program. They might even want to become involved in doing some research on the project and/or helping to secure additional funding through proposal writing.

SHARING INFORMATION WITH ALL STAKEHOLDERS

It is important to keep everyone well informed from the beginning. Teachers want specifics on curriculum and instructional program features, and parents want to be reassured of the benefits to their children. Central administrators, school board members, or funders will want projections of outcomes and expenditures. Principals want to know how best to staff these programs. The community wants to know the value of the programs to business and industry. Reporters will want to ask many questions, too. These are the audiences one must be prepared to address.

One- or two-page documents can be prepared for general audiences. Documents with more detailed information and videos will serve to address specifics. Local or national experts can be interviewed or asked to come to present additional information. Plan to conduct the same presentation two or three different times to reach as many people as possible. This chapter includes some of the most frequently asked questions and some brief responses to build on with the whole staff.

Checklist of Portfolio/Packet Contents

- Two to three pages with what you will anticipate as the *most frequently asked questions* and a short paragraph for each answer
- One- to two-page summary of program features (e.g., basic principles, designs, student evaluation)
- One-page summary of the research and benefits of TWBs
- One-page sample letter to parents that includes commitment criteria
- List of TWB schools to visit nearby or that contain the features you desire
- Anecdotes from your teachers, parents, and business community expressing support and need for the program
- Approximated costs/budget page and possible funding sources
- A press release or guest editorial

INVOLVING ALL STAKEHOLDERS IN THE CRITICAL DECISIONS AND THEIR ROLES

Once you have gathered printed materials and videos and identified experts on the topic, the next step is to begin conducting informational meetings. Small-group meetings are sometimes easier to handle. This will take up more of your valuable time, but there will be more opportunity for interaction and buy-in. Before conducting a large informational meeting, it is suggested that small-group meetings be conducted with the following groups:

- All potential teachers and principal
- Superintendent, curriculum specialists, bilingual director, foreign language specialist, principal, and teacher representatives from the school

- Parents, community members, principal, parent coordinator, bilingual teacher representative, and district administrator
- Business representatives or chamber of commerce representatives, principal, teacher representative, and two or three parents

Ideally, the Program Will Be Implemented Schoolwide. When everyone is involved, there is schoolwide ownership. Even if the plan is to implement only one grade level per year, it is still important to include all mainstream and bilingual teachers, librarians, and staff from the onset. Everyone must be given an opportunity to study the features, voice concerns, and assist in the overall design. Perhaps more important is the opportunity for all teachers to come together to analyze the details—"Who will I team-teach with? How will my classroom be changed? What type of schedule will I have?" Some answers will need to be suspended for later stages, but they should be recorded and not forgotten.

Administrators Want to Know the Logistics of Implementation. Programs differ in the way they select students. Some use a lottery system. Others offer priority status to existing students. Parental choice is also used in combination with the other two systems. Some have policies about admitting or not admitting new students after first grade. Some have tests to determine if the students should be admitted after first grade. The percentage of students representing each language has to be constantly monitored once a design has been selected. If this is not a whole-school design, how will the program be orchestrated within the whole-school instructional design? How will students be selected and placed within this framework? This nitty-gritty detail will avoid many headaches after the school is up and running.

Collaborating Partners	Roles
Parents	To influence the administration by expressing their commitment to the program
Bilingual and mainstream teachers	To plan and select the best design and identify the type of professional development that will be necessary
Community at large and business sector	Provide support and sponsorship for the program
Administration and school board	To ensure quality and compliance; to sanction and provide continuous support to the program

Most Frequently Asked Questions (FAQs)

- Why two-way immersion (TWI) programs? What are the benefits?
- What are the types of two-way bilingual/two-way immersion programs?
- Who can participate in these programs?
- How do we teach in two languages?
- What curriculum and assessment models are there?
- How do we develop biliteracy?
- How do we teach content?
- What staffing patterns are required?
- What type of staff development do we need?
- How do we get the parents to buy into the program?
- How do we evaluate the program implementation and outcomes?
- What type of governance is best for TWI/TWB?
- What is the cost of implementing a TWI/TWB?
- Where can we find a good model to visit?
- Who can assist us in developing a high-quality research-based program?

Suggestions to the most frequently asked questions are offered next as a point of departure. However, we recommend that staffs conduct their own research and select the responses that best fit their context and plans. For FAQ 1, we have synthesized the review of the literature in Chapter 1 and explained the benefits of two-way bilingual programs. In forthcoming chapters, we will also discuss curriculum models, biliteracy components, student assessment, and evaluation. Nevertheless, we attempt to synthesize the most common program features and variations for each FAQ.

FAQ 1: Why Two-Way Immersion Programs? What Are the Benefits?

Why TWI? Languages are the backbones of societies and global under-standing. Language is power. Language is understanding and being understood. Knowing two languages well and being biliterate opens doors to the technological world that is advancing more rapidly than we can keep up with. Literacy is the basis of technology. The more languages our children know, the greater their opportunities to participate in those advances.

Some Critical Benefits. Today's job market points to the need for a well-qualified bilingual workforce and translators. The country needs people with high bilingual competencies along with high technical and professional skills (Department of Labor, 2001). As Latino spending power reaches an all-time high of $400 billion a year in the United States alone, the business sector becomes more eager to learn Spanish. As more and more Spanish-speaking minorities enter the workforce, the importance of bilingualism becomes a critical need for everyone. Supervisors and middle managers are urgently seeking ways to learn Spanish (Adult Bilingual Curriculum Institute, 2002). As other minorities increase their presence in the United States, their languages will also become more and more desirable.

As the global market increases, the U.S. business sector must learn to communicate with new cultures and in new languages. As the world becomes more interdependent, we need ways of communicating effectively with all cultures. Cross-cultural understanding and multicultural competencies are needed for all Americans. "U.S. students still remain too isolated from people who are different from them, too insulated in their own cultures and languages" (National Alliance of Business, 1998, quoted in Lindholm-Leary, 2000, p. 12).

FAQ 2: What Are the Types and Features of Two-Way Bilingual Programs?

TWB programs have a variety of names: TWI, dual-language programs, dual-language immersion, developmental programs, or developmental bilingual education. In this book, we will use TWB and TWI interchangeably. These programs integrate language minority and language majority students for academic instruction that is presented separately through two languages. For both groups of students, one of the languages is their native language and one is a second language (Lindholm-Leary, 2000). The instruction is conducted through the two languages, but only one is used during predetermined periods of time. However, both native English speakers and native speakers of the target language are integrated for all or almost all instruction. In a sense, a quality maintenance bilingual program for English-language learners and a quality immersion program for Spanish learners are combined for TWI or TWB programs.

Grade-Level Articulation. The programs are typically implemented in elementary schools. However, they can be made available pre-K through 12th grade. Usually, the programs begin with kindergarten and add a grade level each year. One year at a time facilitates smoother implementation. The drawback is that it takes several years to begin to see the whole-school commitment to the program. Others prefer to implement a program in all grade levels all at once so that everyone becomes part of the program from the beginning. The drawback is that older students may or may not be proficient enough in two languages to handle dual instruction.

If a lot of time and effort are going to be dedicated to planning a program, one might as well consider a pre-K to 12th-grade implementation. A school might begin with at least two grade levels the first year. However, during the planning phase, early childhood centers and middle and high schools can be invited to participate. This way, they also benefit from having a year or more to get ready to receive the incoming students.

Language Distribution. The distribution of both languages is optional. The proportions for implementation vary by model, time, topic, and/or person. For example, three popular models are called 90-10, 80-20, and 50-50, and one is becoming very popular—70-30. Time blocks can be organized around topics, themes, and content areas or by the teachers' team-teaching schedules.

In the 90-10 model, 90 percent of the instructional day is devoted to content instruction in the target language (e.g., Spanish) and 10 percent in English in kindergarten and first grade. English time is devoted to oral language development and preliteracy skills. However, reading instruction is conducted in the target language for both Spanish- and English-dominant students. In second and third grades, students receive 80 percent instruction in Spanish and 20 percent in English. Formal reading instruction in English is conducted at the third-grade level. By fourth, fifth, and sixth grades, time of instruction in both languages becomes 50-50. Schools with this model sometimes experience the "second-grade parent panic," where English-speaking parents panic because their children are not receiving formal reading instruction in English. If teachers and administrators address this issue from the start and at the beginning of each year, the parents will feel reassured that in the long run, their children will be biliterate.

In the 80-20 model, the use of English is augmented from the beginning. In addition to oral language development and preliteracy, the children's learning centers may include more English activities. Another popular option is the hands-on science lessons conducted in "sheltered English," where manipulatives and simplified language are used to make the lessons comprehensible to non-English speakers.

In the 70-30 model, more English is used even in the early grades. Although the children begin reading in Spanish, more English as a Second Language (ESL) and sheltered English instruction are included. In addition, students begin their reading in English at the beginning of second grade. As one principal stated, "We need to introduce English much earlier because our students need to take state tests after 3 years in school."

In the 50-50 models, students receive half of their instruction in English and the other half in the target language from K–12, if desirable. Separation and distribution of languages usually involve half a day on one language and half a day on the other or one day each or one week each. Up to now, the distribution of instruction on literacy has not been

Table 2.1   Model and Instructional Time in Target Language

Grade Level	90-10 Program Model	80-20 Program Model	70-30 Program Model	50-50 Program Model
K	90	80	70	50
1	90	80	60	50
2	85	70	50	50
3	80	60	50	50
4	60	50	50	50
5	60	50	50	50
6	50	50	50	50
7	50	50	50	50
8	50	50	50	50

Table 2.2   The Alicia Chacón Model for Three Languages

Grade Level	Spanish	English	Third Language
K	80	10	10
1	80	10	10
2	80	10	10
3	60	30	10
4	60	30	10
5	45	45	10
6-8	45	45	10

researched, and there are many variations. At some 50-50 schools, students learn to read first in their primary language and then add the second language in first or second grade. In others, they begin all subjects, including reading, in both languages simultaneously. Our recommendation is that if the children are going to be exposed to any kind of print in the second language during the day, they should also receive instruction on the reading of that language. Fidelity to the 50-50 time-on-language is difficult to balance at first and must be monitored very closely. Once it is achieved, students derive great benefits.

Tables 2.1 and 2.2 show the sequence and how much time each model devotes to the target language (e.g., Spanish, Cantonese, Vietnamese).

There are no definite results on whether the 90-10 or the 50-50 model works best (Howard & Sugarman, 2001), nor is there sufficient research on the other models. Lindholm-Leary (2001) found modest differences in some components of each as follows:

- Both models, 50-50 and 90-10, promoted proficiency in two languages.

- Students in the 90-10 program models developed higher levels of bilingual proficiency than students in the 50-50 program.
- Students in both models developed equal proficiency in English.
- Students in the 90-10 model developed higher proficiency in Spanish than those in the 50-50 model.

Typically, students in TWB/TWI programs score at or above students in other bilingual programs on state standardized tests (Howard & Sugarman, 2001; Lindholm-Leary, 2001).

FAQ 3: Who Can Participate in These Programs?

Student Selection. Selection begins by studying the area's demographics and identifying the needs of parents and children in the community. Schools have several options for recruiting students:

- becoming a magnet school and recruiting students from different sectors of the school district;
- remaining a neighborhood school and recruiting only from the neighborhood; and/or
- implementing the program as only a strand within a school and recruiting from within the school.

Balance of Students. The student population should reflect an equal proportion of language minority students and language majority students. Where this is possible, each class should have a 50-50 balance. In some cases, schools ensure that there is at least a 33-67 balance. Criteria for accepting students into the program have to be determined by school staff, parents, and the community. The well-written criteria form part of the recruitment materials.

FAQ 4: How Do We Teach in Two Languages?

Equal Time and High Status for Both Languages. Language minority students are integrated with native English speakers, and the classroom environment values the language and culture of nonnative English speakers and vice versa. All students are respected and treated in an equitable fashion. Teachers are trained to have high academic expectations for all students and to teach importance and respect for diversity, languages, ethnicity, religions, and social class background.

Monolingual Delivery. Instruction should be conducted in only one language at a time. Translation methods and preview-review (preview in the native language, teach in the second language, and review in the native language) have not proven to be effective for second-language learning. The second-language learners wait for the explanations in their language and tune out the lesson in the second language. Therefore, separation of languages and delivery of instruction must be planned from the beginning, and all teachers must be asked to adhere to the decision. Different periods of time devoted to instruction in and through each of the two languages should be scheduled and monitored. If the first design does not seem to be working, the whole staff should redesign the delivery.

FAQ 5: What Curriculum and Assessment Models Are There?

Curriculum Components. Although the programs vary in sequence and time on language, all TWI/TWB programs attempt to have the following components addressed:

- Research-based instructional programs for reading, writing, language development, math, science, and social studies
- Articulation of all subject matter across grade levels
- English as a Second Language/sheltered English strategies
- Spanish as a Second Language/sheltered Spanish strategies
- Cooperative learning and interaction patterns
- Student-centered instruction; active, discovery, and research projects; and field-based-driven instruction in two languages
- Ongoing performance assessments, 8-week whole-school assessments, standardized tests assessments, and analyses of results
- Parent/family support services
- Early intervention programs such as one-on-one tutoring, family support, and afterschool programs

Curriculum and Assessment Models. One of the major tasks of choosing a program model is to research and select high-quality curriculum and materials. In some cases, these might have to be developed or translated. In others, a program such as Success for All/Éxito Para Todos provides all the training, materials, tutoring programs, and assessments for Spanish, English, ESL, and transition components. Ready-made programs such as these facilitate rapid start-up of program implementation, leaving time and energy for other priorities. They also help to create a shared language and shared values from the beginning of school (e.g., a spirit of relentlessness, high-quality instruction for all, early intervention). Whichever curriculum is chosen or developed, it must be articulated across grade levels. Another major task is to select student assessment instruments, teacher classroom tools such as rubrics, and observation instruments and to determine schedules for state-mandated and local tests. Chapters 3 and 4 present three models of curriculum and their assessment processes. The chapters on instruction—Chapters 5, 6, and 7—integrate assessment with the instructional components of oral language, reading, and writing. Chapter 8 discusses assessment further.

FAQ 6: How Do We Develop Biliteracy?

Literacy Instruction. The language arts/reading blocks can either bring students together or keep them separate. Three structures are widely used:

- Teach literacy in the native language first, separating students by their first language
- Teach literacy in both languages simultaneously, integrating students
- Teach literacy in the minority language first, integrating students

As researchers continue to look at these structures, more information will be made available about which combination works best. For now, the school might want to conduct its own pilot studies.

FAQ 7: How Do We Teach Content?

Content Area Instruction. The language and literacy objectives should be incorporated into the academic content areas (e.g., using past-tense verbs to discuss history and future tense to discuss science experiments, cause and effect, and comparing and contrasting for both). The content area instruction and materials need to be at the appropriate grade level. To ensure student comprehension, teachers need to be trained to use sheltered instructional strategies (e.g., "sheltered English" and "sheltered Spanish").

Cooperative Learning and Interaction Strategies. Learning content in a second language is facilitated by quality interaction. We learn something when we have an opportunity to discuss it with a peer. This is why cooperative learning is highly used in TWI. Although most teachers have attended workshops on cooperative learning, it is important to continue studying and looking at the communication within cooperative activities. Cooperative learning takes a new veneer in TWI. Students must be given the tools to be expert peers when their language is being used for instruction and to let other peers be experts during instruction in the second language. The duality of their roles takes more training and more practice. There is a multitude of cooperative learning methods, strategies, and techniques that can be used appropriately for TWI. Some of these are mentioned and referenced in Chapter 5.

FAQ 8: What Staffing Patterns Are Required?

Staffing. It is critical to have well-prepared, committed teachers for both languages of instruction. If there is a shortage of qualified teachers, an extensive and comprehensive staff development program can fill that gap. If a teacher needs further development in his or her target language of instruction, the school should require it at the onset and provide the means to reach that goal.

Team Teaching. Team-teaching configurations can take several forms. For example, one bilingual teacher and one mainstream teacher form a team, combine their students, and teach together in the same classroom all day. A team of two teachers might provide instruction for a combined class of 25 to 30 students. As one teaches, the other monitors the students. These teams can also trade students for 50 percent of the day or alternate days or weeks. Distribution can also occur by content area or thematic units. That is, one of the team teachers selects to teach science in one language while the other teaches social studies in the other language. All their students learn together during these blocks. Team teaching is challenging. As teachers are being selected for the TWB program, it is important to ask them if they are willing to team with another teacher and work effectively together. Professional development activities should include team-teaching strategies, problem solving, and cross-cultural communication if teachers have not worked together before.

FAQ 9: What Type of Staff Development Do We Need?

Extensive inservice training before the opening of school should include instructional methods, materials, assessments and procedures, program evaluation, family support activities, and early intervention strategies. Chapter 9 details the type of staff development topics and process that can sustain a quality implementation of the program. Successful students need successful teachers. The amount of staff development and follow-up support a teacher receives correlates with student outcomes (Calderón, 1991, 2002).

FAQ 10: How Do We Get the Parents to Buy Into the Program?

TWI programs are successful when parents of the target language are placed on an equal status with majority culture parents. While students learn each other's language, parents can also benefit from evening classes, workshops, or activities to help them learn a second language in the degrees they prefer. Multiple activities can draw parents into the school and into the program. Chapter 10 is dedicated to the discussion of these and other factors that facilitate parental engagement and collaboration.

FAQ 11: How Do We Evaluate the Program Implementation and Outcomes?

Before school begins, high academic goals, policies, outcome objectives for students from both language groups, and program evaluation indicators are established. As school begins, baseline data are collected for longitudinal studies to determine the effectiveness of the curriculum and instructional designs, teacher efficacy, and the appropriateness of support systems. Continuous analyses of data are employed by teacher-administrator-parent teams to discuss how these variables affect student progress and outcomes. The community at large, parents, reporters, and other schools will be knocking at the door constantly to see how the program is faring and to learn from everyone's experiences. Therefore, it is wise to always be prepared and have the latest test results, analyses, video recordings, professional brochures, and summaries of ongoing development.

FAQ 12: What Type of Governance Is Best for TWI/TWB?

Governance. Schools have some options for governance as well. They may choose to remain wholly within the district's governance or, as more and more schools are doing, to become a charter school. As a charter school, there are also varying degrees of involvement with the district's governing structures. Charter school initiatives and organizations such as the National Council of La Raza (www.NCLR.org) can provide ample information on existing variations and models.

FAQ 13: What Is the Cost of Implementing a TWI/TWB?

Funding Sources. TWB programs will generally cost more to implement than the mainstream program but about as much as any other bilingual program. The design might include additional teachers, teacher aides, or a teacher coordinator/facilitator. All classroom texts/library materials will need to be bought in two languages. A large portion of the funds will need to be set aside for professional development and follow-up teachers learning communities (TLCs) activities (see Chapter 9 for a description). Additional funding can be sought from the U.S. Department of Education, the State Educational Agency, private foundations (e.g., Annenberg), or local businesses that value a bilingual workforce. The National Council of La Raza receives funding from the Bill Gates and Walton Foundations to assist Latino TWB charter schools with planning and implementation of their programs.

FAQ 14: Where Can We Find a Good Model to Visit?

The CAL Web site (www.cal.org) keeps an updated directory of TWI/TWB schools. State and national conferences on bilingual education typically showcase successful programs.

FAQ 15: Who Can Assist Us in Developing a High-Quality Research-Based Program?

Your friendly neighborhood researchers at the local university are probably very willing to assist and even do some research in your school. Other researchers who publish on this topic will most likely be interested in your school, too. Resource A contains a list of sources to contact.

SUMMARY

Schools have many options for selecting the type of program, the sequence of implementation, and ways to design the program's curriculum components. Therefore, we recommend that the school spend at least a year exploring all the possibilities.

Summary of Program Options

- Type of school program: magnet, neighborhood, whole school, or strand within a school
- Language model: 50-50, 70-30, 80-20, or 90-10
- Language distribution: by time, topic, or teacher
- Initial literacy: native language first, both languages simultaneously, or minority language first
- Student population proportion: 50-50 balance, 67-33, or 33-33-33
- Implementation strategy: add one grade per year, begin with K–5, or implement from K–12 the first year

---

A quality program is achieved faster when the whole school staff buys into a philosophy, a way of teaching, and a way of nurturing student development and success than when only a portion of the staff is committed. A shared ethos is critical from the start. Some schools choose to begin implementation with one classroom per grade level, in hopes that the whole school will eventually want to participate. Unfortunately, many of these schools remain with partial implementation thereafter. Eventually, this partition can become a divisive tool in the school. At best, it will simply set the bilingual program apart from the mainstream, as bilingual programs have been historically.

Getting a whole faculty to buy into the program will take time and good planning. Completing well-conducted research on the type of program that is best for the school, listing the benefits that students and teachers will derive, and building a strong parental and administrative support system are precursors to convincing the school as a whole. As the planning proceeds, it is also important to keep in mind the conditions that enable successful results.

Conditions for Success of TWB Programs

1. Quality of the programs most evident in a comprehensive whole-school implementation
2. Systematic implementation at pre-K to 12th grade
3. Equal time and high status for both languages
4. Yearly high academic achievement for both language groups
5. Bilingual/biliteracy proficiency for all students and teachers
6. Positive intergroup skills, cross-cultural relations, and global understanding components
7. Continuous professional development and teachers learning communities
8. Carefully selected qualified teachers who are willing to become bilingual/biliterate
9. Parents, teachers, and administrators who make long-term commitments to stay and work hard for the program
10. Acceptance of being in the limelight and continuous evaluation and refinement

---

Strong support for the program by the school, the district, and the local board of education is evidenced by the structural and functional integration of the program within the whole school and the district. Strong principal support ensures a quality implementation through strong management and instructional leadership. Bilingual and mainstream teachers fully understand the program and have made a long-term commitment to help the program grow. Parental engagement becomes the basis of success for the program. Tips on leadership roles of all stakeholders are found throughout the chapters. Meaningful and deliberate home-school collaboration is discussed in Chapter 10.

The checklist that follows is intended as a tool for committees to initiate their planning stage. Once the planning is in full force, there will be a need to modify and adjust as necessary.

CHECKLIST FOR PLANNING

Stage 1: Information Gathering

- ☐ Identified collaborating partners
- ☐ Agreed on our roles
- ☐ Gathered the necessary information on TWB
- ☐ Scheduled meetings with all stakeholders
- ☐ Shared the information with all stakeholders
- ☐ Involved all stakeholders in the critical decisions
- ☐ Drafted portfolio contents
- ☐ Got feedback on portfolio and revised as necessary

Stage 2: What the Draft of the Program Design Should Include

- ☐ Student selection criteria
- ☐ Student proportions for each class
- ☐ Type of program (50-50, 90-10, other)
- ☐ Implementation strategy (K–5, K–1, K–12)
- ☐ Whole school or school within a school
- ☐ Governance
- ☐ Funding
- ☐ Facilities
- ☐ Curriculum for all subjects
- ☐ Literacy programs
- ☐ Student assessments
- ☐ Teacher selection criteria
- ☐ Team-teaching configurations
- ☐ Family support services
- ☐ Early intervention programs
- ☐ High goals and expectations for everyone
- ☐ Contract for parents
- ☐ Contract for teachers
- ☐ Professional development plan for Year 1
- ☐ Teachers learning communities plan for Year 1
- ☐ Program evaluation plan
- ☐ Dissemination plan

3

Comprehensive Curriculum Models for a Two-Way Program

Research on two-way immersion (TWI) has shown that the participating students acquire functional proficiency in both languages and demonstrate strong academic achievement (August & Hakuta, 1997; Christian, 1996; Genesee, 1999). Although these programs hold great promise for the academic achievement of English-language learners (Collier, 1998; Ovando & Collier, 1998), there are some concerns about the quality of instruction delivered in them (Valdés, 1997). Valdés (1997) questioned in particular the lower academic gains among English-language learners in comparison with English-dominant students in the same programs. The quality of instruction in Spanish is also questionable in most programs.

For these reasons, it is imperative that instruction in English and the target language be of high quality, offering equal opportunity for success for all students and their teachers. Through our national surveys and observations (Calderón, 2002), we have identified five widespread tendencies that limit equal opportunities for success:

1. When two-way bilingual (TWB) programs give more importance and resources to English instruction

2. When teachers are not proficient or literate enough to teach in Spanish

3. When teachers do not receive 20 to 30 days of staff development a year, including summers

4. When high levels of literacy are not developed in both languages in all students

5. When programs are not implemented schoolwide.

The main goal of TWB programs is to develop biliteracy to its highest levels. However, there is a tendency to spend a great deal of instructional time on oral language development and not enough time on the development of literacy in both languages. In the early grades, for example, instead of teaching initial reading and writing skills, programs spend too much time building vocabulary before exposing students to actual written texts. Teachers do most of the reading for children in kindergarten and first and second grades. These two well-intended practices hold students back in their reading and writing development. Second-language learners need to learn to use various forms and functions of print to attain high levels of academic achievement in the upper grades.

SCHOOLWIDE PROGRAM MODELS FOR TWO-WAY IMMERSION PROGRAMS

Whole-school implementation is not only desirable but also possible. Today, there are ample funding opportunities for TWB schoolwide implementation. Title I, Title III, and Comprehensive School Reform (CSR) funds can be used for this purpose. Implementing programs in all the classrooms also helps remove the problems of equal resources and training for all teachers. It equalizes teachers in every sense, as colleagues learning something for the first time and as equal partners in ensuring success for all the students.

While there are many effective and comprehensive TWB/TWI programs, which are richly described by other authors (see Center for Applied Linguistics at www.cal.org), we have selected three very different programs that emerged in the same region. They represent three approaches to whole-school models.

THE ALICIA CHACÓN MODEL

The Alicia Chacón elementary model, amply described in Chapter 2, has been one of the best home-grown comprehensive models we have seen. This 80-10-10 model has been crafted by putting together several curriculum approaches and philosophies. It has taken teachers and administrators years to refine their curriculum through experimentation and extensive professional development. While they are still working on improving reading and writing, they have grown accustomed to living with continuous improvement. There isn't a conference on TWB where one does not find the team of Alicia Chacón teachers avidly seeking more answers. It is this spirit of continued personal, professional, and programmatic growth that should propel all TWB programs.

AN EXAMPLE OF THE 50-50 MODEL

The TWB accelerated schools in the El Paso Independent School District created a 50-50 balance by using thematic units and dividing the delivery of the content areas into Spanish and English times. Their logo was a balance. Whenever an English math lesson was put on one side of the balance, a math lesson in Spanish had to be placed on the other. Every content area from the K–5 curriculum was balanced this way. However, they were not translations of the same lesson. They were separate lessons with separate objectives. Each lesson was correlated with the district's and state's curriculum mandates. Where the English lesson or unit left off, the Spanish lesson or unit picked up or vice versa.

Through its Title III grant, the district hired the TWB teachers the summer before starting the program. They received intensive training and developed their curriculum units. Each summer thereafter, they were hired to further develop and fine-tune the K–5 thematic units. These thematic units included the balanced lessons, all the materials necessary for each activity, the assessments, and the objectives met. The teams of teachers from each grade level met weekly with the teachers from the other grade levels to align and articulate the sequence of skills, content, and goals for each grade level. They also selected the children's literature for each theme and grade level so that the children would not complain that they had read that story the year before. During the school year, teachers gathered information from conferences and workshops for upgrading their units in the summer.

Team teaching consisted of a bilingual and a mainstream teacher teaching in the same classroom. Students were placed in teams of four: two English learners and two Spanish learners interacted all day long. This was highly beneficial because each teacher could see firsthand what the students were learning in the other language. More important, it also afforded a peer coach for each teacher. While one was teaching, the other would be taking notes to share with the teacher later on. They kept close tabs on the time allocation for each language through peer coaching, as well as ways they could improve their instruction each time. (For detailed descriptions of the curriculum and the teachers' peer coaching activities, see Calderón, 1999a, 1999b; Calderón & Carreón, 2000.)

Features of the Integrated Thematic Units

- Balanced time for each language
- Integrated curriculum and discourse
- No translations—each lesson developed in one of the target languages
- Content objectives (concepts and facts) articulated for the year and across grade levels
- Content language preselected for instruction by level of use and function
- Preselected language for learning processes (cooperative learning protocols) and thinking processes (debriefing content and process, think-alouds, self-correction)
- A variety of teaching and reteaching strategies that were carefully integrated into each unit
- Group investigation and team inquiry plus a variety of cooperative learning strategies that were integrated into the content lessons
- Bilingual cooperative integrated reading and composition that were used for the morning and afternoon 90-minute language arts blocks in English and Spanish

A COMPREHENSIVE SCHOOL REFORM MODEL DEVELOPED FOR TWB

Hueco Elementary School in the Socorro Independent School District, also in El Paso, selected a 70-30 model using the Comprehensive School Reform model, Success for All/Éxito Para Todos (SFA/EPT). Because there is a great interest throughout the nation in combining TWB with SFA/EPT, we include here how Hueco orchestrated its integration.

The teachers and principals selected the SFA/EPT model for TWB for the following reasons:

1. High levels of literacy are developed in both languages because the materials and programs are currently available for K–8. These materials are research based and develop the range of skills identified by Snow, Burns, and Griffin (1998).

2. Teachers of English and Spanish components receive the same materials, training, and support mechanisms (literature books, posters, manuals, DVDs, kits, cards, etc.).

3. Scripted materials help teachers when they are not adequately prepared to teach in Spanish.

4. SFA/EPT is always implemented schoolwide, with parental-family literacy and support activities such as tutoring, a facilitator for all teachers, follow-up training, implementation visits by experts, and annual conferences for networking and upgrading skills of teachers, principals, and parents.

5. The range of reading and writing skills, from phonemic awareness to high levels of comprehension and discussions, is distributed throughout the pre-K to Grade 8 SFA/EPT components.

6. In addition, there are other components, such as Older Roots/Lee Conmigo, for students entering SFA/EPT schools in the upper grades (e.g., Grades 2-8) who did not have an opportunity to develop their basic reading skills.

7. Teachers receive 24 days of staff development and follow-up support from the trainers.

At the beginning of the year, students are assessed and grouped across classes and grades by reading level. This gives teachers opportunities to work intensively with students at one reading level in each language. While students are being assessed for placement in their reading level, the teachers use a 2-week literature component to teach students the cooperative norms and protocols for working effectively in teams. Systematic assessments are administered every 8 weeks to ensure that students are making adequate progress and to help teachers determine if particular students need tutoring or family support services.

Reading instruction in the students' second language is introduced using the same routines, methods, and material formats that the students have used while working in their primary language. Hueco Elementary has distributed the languages across components and grade levels in the following manner.

Pre-Kindergarten and Kindergarten Components: Early Learning/Aprendizaje Inicial

In pre-K and K, teachers alternate the use of Spanish and English by days in what they call the 3-2 model. The students are immersed in listening comprehension, story elements, discussion, prereading, and emergent writing activities in Spanish for 1 hour a day for Days 1, 2, and 3. Two hours are spent in thematic centers and other activities in either English or Spanish. On Days 4 and 5, the pattern is repeated, but the focus language for literacy is English. In the second half of the school year, the students have "language of the week" for the literacy language. A brief description of these components follows.

Thematic Units

The pre-K and K programs emphasize oral language development using thematic units for the daily instruction organized around themes (e.g., dinosaurs, plants, community helpers, Kenya, Japan) and include art, construction, dramatic play, manipulatives, science experiences, writing, and listening through using media. The purpose of center activities is to provide the students ample opportunity to play independently and learn in a hands-on fashion the concepts that are presented in each thematic unit.

Listening Comprehension

This component is called Storytelling and Retelling/Contar y Recontar el Cuento (STaR/CyReC). The STaR/CyReC consists of a 15- to 20-minute series of activities that start out with the teacher reading a storybook for the purpose of modeling reading, discussing story elements (characters, plot, setting), and modeling "think-alouds" about comprehension strategies and deciphering meaning while reading.

Shared Big Books

Another 15- to 20-minute literacy activity is called Shared Book/Libro Compartido, in which teachers use big books so the students can see the print and pictures in the book easily. Big books are used to teach the students components of print (the structure and function of print). While the teacher reads from the big book, the students chime in and also learn the following:

- print directionality, as the teacher moves a hand or a pointer from left to right under the print in the story;
- that the teacher is reading words and that words are clusters of letters;
- that inflection and intonation are used to connect content and structure of the text; and
- that print is constant and that the same configuration of letters stands for the same word every time.

Oral Language Development

Focusing on vocabulary development and fluency of language, teachers use a kit called Book Corners/Puentes that structures language activities around the themes and the books students have read earlier in STaR/CyReC.

Phonemic Awareness

Phonemic awareness is introduced through Rhyme With Reason/Rima con Razón to develop the students' ability to recognize and manipulate the sounds that make up words. Teachers do not approach phonemic awareness with direct instruction on phonics but rather use poetry and nursery rhymes. The students learn to play with sounds in words and to understand the relationship between sounds and the printed word. Students also learn about their cultural heritages through traditional songs and nursery rhymes from the United States and various Latino cultures. The use of poetry, rhymes, and songs in both languages is also a way for the students to learn strings of discourse, with appropriate intonation and pronunciation in two languages. These activities usually range from 10 to 15 minutes or are used as transition points from one activity to the other. The teachers' thematic manuals contain the poetry, songs, and rhymes that go with each theme and the stories the students are reading with their teachers.

Letter Recognition

Based on evidence that knowledge of letters is one of the best predictors of future reading success, Letter Investigation/Investigación de las Letras focuses on exploring the physical features of letters of the alphabet and the role that letters play in everyday life. Letter Investigation activities are integrated into the themes and capitalize on the students' prior knowledge and interest in print. Learning the alphabet in this fashion prepares the students for becoming independent, fluent, and strategic readers and writers.

Emergent Writing

Teachers learn the stages of emergent writing so they can encourage student writing with respect to their initial stages of development and help students progress without pressure.

Initial Reading and Direct Instruction

During the second half of kindergarten, the students are introduced to formal reading through a series of 16 books called Kinder Roots/Kinder Lee Conmigo. These books allow students to read complex, engaging, and interesting stories even though they may only know a few letter sounds. The student sections use only the letter sounds and words that students have learned, a few key sight words, and readles (words represented by pictures). The teacher sections provide a context for the story and include predictive or clarifying questions that are answered in the student sections.

First-Grade Components: Reading Roots and Lee Conmigo

Language, reading, and writing components focus on developing phonics, meaning, and pleasure in reading in a balanced way, using children's literature and a series of interesting storybooks in which phonetically regular text is enriched by teacher-read text, similar to that used in kindergarten.

Storytelling and Retelling

The 90-minute cycle begins with 20 minutes of listening comprehension using the STaR/CyReC materials described earlier but at a first grade or higher level. More comprehension and reading strategies are modeled, and students are engaged in more complex story-related activities.

Teaching Reading Skills, Fluency, and Comprehension

Students read stories that build on previously learned letters, sounds, and words. More specific skills related to sharpening auditory discrimination, hearing sounds in words, identifying the sounds associated with specific letters, and blending letter sounds into words are developed in the Reading Roots/Lee Conmigo lessons. The lessons are structured around 50 shared books in Spanish and 48 in English that students can read with partners or on their own and take home to read to their parents. After partner reading and partner discussions, the teachers work with the whole class, using fast-paced lessons that incorporate games, puppets, sounds, chants, whole-class responses, and metacognitive skills training to build decoding and comprehension (e.g., use of context, self-questioning, summarizing).

Assessment, Placement, and Progress

The students are assessed in Spanish and English at the beginning of school and grouped according to their reading levels. From then on, teachers assess students every 8 weeks to determine their progress, move some to higher levels when ready, and provide tutoring to those who need extra help.

Second- to Eighth-Grade Components: Reading Wings and Alas Para Leer

In Grades 2 to 8, students develop higher order literacy skills, alternating 1 week in English (Reading Wings) with 1 week in Spanish (Alas Para Leer). Wings and Alas programs are built around 5-day cycles of activities that are designed around the school's existing novels, anthologies, trade books, and/or basal readers.

Listening Comprehension

The 90 minutes begin with 20 minutes of Listening Comprehension that is similar to STaR/CyReC but focuses on higher level skills. Novels are introduced as well as other genre. The teacher focuses on specific skills such as "irony" or "making inferences," which will later be transferred into the students' reading selections and follow-up activities.

Teamwork

The programs emphasize cooperative learning activities in which students work in teams to improve strategic reading and further their comprehension skills. They are designed to

- Promote oral language proficiency
- Develop fluency in reading
- Develop listening comprehension skills
- Encourage cooperative learning
- Teach strategies for reading
- Extend reading comprehension skills
- Enhance written expression
- Foster love of reading

Writing

Writing is emphasized throughout the week as a method for creative expression and responding to literature. Direct instruction on writing technique includes mechanics for writing sentences, paragraphs, and different types of writing. During the writing process, students plan, draft, revise, edit, and publish compositions with feedback from teachers and peers. The writing process is conducted in the language in which the students are reading.

The schedule of the main components of SFA is listed below, along with suggested ways of distributing the components by languages for the Hueco Elementary School's 70-30 model. The popular 90-10 model variations, which other SFA schools use, are also listed for comparison.

Other features of the program include an extensive set of noninstructional components that support student learning. Some of the key components are as follows.

Tutoring

One-on-one tutoring is used as an early intervention program for students who are experiencing reading difficulties in either language, particularly in first grade. Each tutor is trained to diagnose students' needs and tailor instruction to meet those needs.

School Facilitator

A full-time facilitator (certified teacher) helps faculty and staff implement the program. The facilitator at Hueco Elementary describes himself as an instructional leader who provides information, support, classroom visits, and coaching for the teachers. He also organizes meetings, data from the 8-week assessments, tutoring activities with tutors, and family support activities with the Family Support Team.

Family Support

The Family Support Team and integrated services are provided to help resolve nonacademic problems students may have. The team includes staff members (the principal, facilitator, social workers, counselors, attendance monitors, teachers) as well as parents. The team plans activities that involve parents in their children's education, such as workshops in Spanish or English on reading with their children or how to help their children with homework. The team also develops early intervention and prevention plans, closely monitors attendance, and integrates community resources such as providing eye exams and eyeglasses, as well as other needs.

Professional Development and Teachers Learning Communities

At the beginning of the year, teachers receive 3 days of training at the school. The trainers return to the school for three 2-day implementation visits during the year to help sustain a strong implementation. Teachers get together at least once a week in teachers learning communities to share their successes, do problem solving, study student progress, and help each other in their professional growth. Chapter 9 will describe the teachers learning communities in detail.

Hueco Elementary has been recognized as one of the top 10 schools by Just for the Kids, an educational research organization that is studying excellence in the state of Texas. The Texas (state) Educational Agency has also recognized Hueco as a school of excellence, based on the percentage of students who have passed the state-mandated assessments in reading, writing, and math.

SUMMARY

These models serve to demonstrate that schools have options in constructing or selecting models. What each illustrates is that when school organizational structure and curriculum components parallel in English and the target language, success and satisfaction can be obtained and sustained.

The balance of resources for each language also avoids the inequalities observed and documented in other TWB/TWI programs.

Table 3.1 on pages 49-51 lists the parallel components of one of the programs and how they can be distributed in three TWI models. Whether or not a school chooses the SFA/EPT, this table might serve to summarize how reading, language, and writing can be organized across grade levels and by program type.

Table 3.1   Success for All/Éxito Para Todos

Grade Level	SFA Component	70-30	90-10
Pre-kindergarten and kindergarten	Storytelling and Retelling/ Contar y Recontar el Cuento (STaR/CyReC): • Interactive reading • Story elements • Listening comprehension • Story retell • Extension activities Reading Roots/Lee Conmigo: • Oral language development • Phonemic awareness activities • Shared reading Thematic Centers/Centros Temáticos: • Reading • Writing • Science • Math • Dramatic plays • Art Music and physical education	Days 1, 2, and 3 are conducted in one language and days 4 and 5 in the other. The following week, the languages are alternated.	[90-10] CyReC and Lee Conmigo are conducted in Spanish; thematic centers and music and physical education are conducted in English.
First grade	STaR/CyReC: • Interactive reading • Story elements • Listening comprehension • Story retell • Extension activities Reading Roots/Lee Conmigo: • Direct instruction on sound-letter	90 minutes of Spanish CyReC and Lee Conmigo for a 3-day cycle; 45 minutes of StaR and	[80-20] 90 minutes of CyReC and Lee Conmigo; plus ESL, music, physical education,

(Continued)

Table 3.1 Continued

Grade Level	SFA Component	70-30	90-10
	correspondence, reading mechanics, and reading comprehension • Student reading • Writing activities	Reading Roots for a 6-day cycle.	and science in English.
Second grade	Reading Wings/Alas Para Leer: (1) Listening Comprehension • Direct instruction on genre, content, and story structure • Modeling of expressive reading and use of comprehension strategies • Understanding of author's craft (2) Reading Together • Direct instruction in reading comprehension • Silent and partner reading • Story-related activities • Writing meaningful sentences • Storytelling • Story-related writing • Two-minute edit (3) Book Club Activities • Independent reading • Sharing books through drama, reading circles, and other activities	45 minutes of Alas for a 10-day cycle and 90 minutes of StaR and Reading Roots for a 3-day cycle.	[70-30] 90 minutes of Alas; plus 45 minutes of ESL Roots, music, and physical education in English; science and social studies in Spanish.
Third grade	Reading Wings/Alas Para Leer: (1) Listening Comprehension • Direct instruction on genre, content, and story structure • Modeling of expressive reading and use of comprehension strategies • Understanding of author's craft	90 minutes of Wings for 1 week and 90 minutes of Alas for the following week. All subjects also alternate	[60-40] 90 minutes of Alas; plus 45 minutes of ESL Roots or ESL Wings, plus science, music, and physical

Table 3.1 Continued

Grade Level	SFA Component	70-30	90-10
	(2) Reading Together • Direct instruction in reading comprehension • Silent and partner reading • Story-related activities • Writing meaningful sentences • Storytelling • Story-related writing • Two-minute edit (3) Book Club Activities • Independent reading • Sharing books through drama, reading circles, and other activities	languages by week or thematic units.	education in English; social studies in Spanish.
Fourth through eighth grades	Reading Wings/Alas Para Leer: (1) Listening Comprehension • Direct instruction on genre, content, and story structure • Modeling of expressive reading and use of comprehension strategies • Understanding of author's craft (2) Reading Together • Direct instruction in reading comprehension • Silent and partner reading • Story-related activities • Writing meaningful sentences • Storytelling • Story-related writing • Two-minute edit (3) Book Club Activities • Independent reading • Sharing books through drama, reading circles, and other activities	90 minutes of Wings for 1 week and 90 minutes of Alas for the following week. All subjects also alternate languages by week or thematic units.	[50-50] 90 minutes of Wings for 1 week and 90 minutes of Alas for the following week; 45 minutes of Alas and 45 minutes of Wings for 10-day cycles. All subjects also alternate languages by week or thematic units.

4

Case Study

The Alicia R. Chacón International School

*I wish I had been here when the school opened. I think it might
have been difficult to get people interested in it. It took a few years
for the parents to begin believing that it could actually work and
that it was a good program.*

—Third-grade teacher

In this chapter, we describe the schoolwide two-way bilingual (TWB) and
bicultural program at the Alicia R. Chacón International School (hence-
forth Chacón School), a K–8 school in El Paso, Texas. Chacón School is a
whole-school TWB program that celebrates and practices linguistic and
cultural pluralism as a fact of school life. Chacón School students also take
a third language (Japanese, Russian, Chinese, or German). We envision
Chacón School as an important attempt in recognizing the validity and sig-
nificance of cultural and linguistic differences in the schooling process.
One significant inference is that the basic messages concerning proficiency,
achievement, punctuality, orderliness, and the individual as a unit of social
behavior are communicated through the two languages of the bilingual
school, plus an expansion in the third language. The linguistic and cultural
commonalities seem to be more impressive than the differences.

The Ysleta Independent School District's Web page (www.ysleta. isd.tenet.edu) describes Chacón School as a multilingual magnet school that focuses on language and cultural development and that offers a rigorous curriculum based on interdisciplinary units and critical thinking skills. The importance of the bilingual and bicultural program is not only in the language and academic areas inculcated and developed in Chacón School students but in the recognition and worth of cultural heritage other than that of Anglo America. In the long run, this seems to enhance functional intragroup relations since it removes significant static from the messages communicated in the Anglo cultural matrix to the culturally diverse students (Ovando & Pérez, 2000), though this is not the declared goal of Chacón School's TWB program.

Current and emergent TWB programs represent a significant development in the evolution of bilingual and bicultural education and public schooling (Calderón & Carreón, 2000; Valdés, 1997). They are in one sense the ultimate test of whether schools can become meaningfully responsive to linguistic and cultural heterogeneity and can foster a bilingual and bicultural experience and identity (Cazabon, 2001; Thomas & Collier, 2002). Such programs—and related research—attend to second-language acquisition, language and content teaching methodologies, differential learning styles, and school-parent interaction. There is a growing body of evidence-based research on these topics and significant ethnographic material from several fields and planes of knowledge (Tharp, 1999). Our focus on this chapter is, however, on the role of schooling processes in structuring and reinforcing a successful multilingual and multicultural experience.

SETTING

According to the 2000 census (U.S. Bureau of the Census, 2000), a surge in the Hispanic population in the United States over the past decade has paced its explosive growth with newcomers settling in the Midwest as well as traditional immigrant gateways such as Texas, California, and Florida. Texas has surpassed New York as the second most populous state, fueled by the growth of the numbers of Hispanics along its Mexican border. The Hispanic population in Texas grew by 54 percent, from 4.3 million in 1990 to 6.7 million in 2000, while the white population grew by 642,000, a 6 percent increase, to a total of 11 million (U.S. Bureau of the Census, 2000). El Paso, Houston, Dallas, and San Antonio have the largest single ethnic group. Mexican Americans, at 2.4 million, make up 11 percent of the state's population.

The Chacón School is a K–8 school in the El Paso metropolitan area on the Texas-Mexico border. The community's history has been shaped by economic developments to the north and cultural and linguistic ties to the south (Calderón & Carreón, 2000). Juárez is the twin city to the south. Both communities are seen as a single entity by more than 2 million people who live there (Calderón & Carreón, 2000). El Paso is a labor market for skilled and semiskilled workers and has become an attractive residential area for this economic group because of available and low-rental housing, and businesses thrive on low-wage employees. Over the years, El Paso, just as any border city, has attracted a large number of Juárez residents, part of the continuous immigration that characterizes the border area. Census figures indicate that this border community is among the poorest in Texas and the nation. The unemployment rate is twice the state and national average, and per capita income is three times lower than the national rate (U.S. Bureau of the Census, 2000).

According to the U.S. Bureau of the Census (2000), El Paso has 70 percent Hispanics (Spanish-speaking households). Its linguistic and cultural diversity is reflected in the seven school districts. Chacón School is part of the Ysleta Independent School District (ISD). Chacón School's 2001 report (www.ysleta.isd.tenet.edu) on racial and ethnic distribution of enrollment is as follows:

- Hispanic (95 percent)
- Others (5 percent)

Chacón School was named for Alicia R. Chacón, a Mexican American educator and community leader who dedicated her life to improve the general well-being of Mexican Americans in the region. Chacón School is a magnet school and brings a representation from all over the El Paso area. Chacón School students represent the ethnic, language, and economic backgrounds that dominate the city.

The Chacón School came into being in 1995, more than two decades after the 1974 Supreme Court decision, *Lau v. Nichols* (1974). The Court ruled that a school district's failure to provide non-English-speaking students with a program to deal with their language needs is in violation of Title VI of the Civil Rights Act. The Chacón School program predates the passage of Proposition 227 in California and Proposition 202 in Arizona, both state mandates to use only English in the schools as the medium of instruction (Tse, 2001).

The Chacón School's TWB program began as part of Project Mariposa (Spanish for *butterfly*), an interdistrict project effort that was funded by the U.S. Department of Education under Title VII (Bilingual Education) of the Elementary and Secondary Education Act in the early to mid-1990s. Chacón School started its TWB program with kindergarten and first, second, and third grades in 1995. Each year thereafter, a grade was added until Chacón School had its first eighth-grade graduates in 2000.

SITE SELECTION

Chacón School was chosen as the site because its TWB approach has been in operation schoolwide for 7 years. We wanted a school that had progressed beyond the initiation stage in program development. This would enable us to obtain data on characteristics and problems persisting over a period of time and on adaptations the school was making to legislative, judicial, state, and federal mandates as the needs arose.

The Ysleta ISD, with 61 schools, serves a heterogeneous student population, including a large number of Mexican Americans. Ysleta ISD is close and interdependently linked to *La Frontera* (The Border) and has a number of bilingual and bicultural schools. Twenty-two schools in Ysleta ISD are TWB programs; a school that has only a kindergarten level will grow to a K–6 school. Ysleta ISD's vision statement reads as follows:

> All students that enroll in our schools will graduate from high school fluently bilingual, prepared to enter a four-year college or university.

What makes Chacón School noteworthy, though, is that it was the only school in the district that decided to be a two-way bilingual school with a third language for instruction. Recently, its feeder high school, Del Valle High School, decided to implement Chacón School's TWB program model.

> Han egresado ya nuestros alumnos, están en el high school. . . . Estamos bien orgullosos porque vienen y nos dicen, "Ay, no, porque lo que aprendimos aquí nos ayuda." El Del Valle High School está siguiendo el programa. . . . Vinieron [los maestros] a observarnos. Estuvieron aquí una semana. Platicamos mucho. Tomaron unos talleres dados por nuestros maestros.

> (Our first cohort of students is already in high school. . . . We are very proud of them. They tell us, "What we learned here is helping us." Del Valle High School is following our program. . . . [Teachers] came to our school to observe us. They were here a week. We talked a lot. They took workshops given by our teachers.)

> — *Eighth-grade teacher*

FIELDWORK PROCEDURES/DATA GATHERING

We initiated fieldwork in October 2001. It was preceded by extended communications over 2 months' time—to seek authorization and discuss the proposal with district administrators and to obtain their permission to conduct the research. This case study was part of a much larger effort by Johns Hopkins University, which has conducted research at several other school sites for the past 12 years. The school principal was instrumental in presenting the proposal to the school faculty for review and approval. In total, the research design included several lines of inquiry to obtain data on the schooling experience. These included school administrators, teachers, parents, and students. The student survey and interview protocols for administrators, teachers, and parents are available on request. We attempt to describe the program in sufficient ethnographic detail so that one can draw one's own conclusions (Denzin & Lincoln, 2000).

THE CHACÓN TWO-WAY BILINGUAL SCHOOL AND PROGRAM

One of my dreams has been to have a school where both languages and cultures are valued . . . because we can learn both. Both languages are valued here, kindergarten through 8th grade, and we are working on K through 12, through the university. Kindergarten through life is what we talk about here to truly become bilingual, biliterate, and able to function in a professional capacity in English or in Spanish, in an English-speaking country or in a Spanish-speaking country.

— *Mr. Schulte, school principal*

The Ysleta ISD's stated goal for bilingual education is to develop literate bilingual-bicultural students who can function in two languages in the milieu of two cultures. Chacón School practices this goal with Spanish and English languages and adds a third language—Japanese, German, Chinese, or Russian. Mr. Schulte makes reference to the quality of bilingualism, biliteracy, and academic instruction in two languages plus a third language in a quality instructional setting, which yields positive academic results in Chacón School students:

Our goal reads "full literacy in English and Spanish and to the extent possible in a third language." This is our seventh year, and we have experienced kids with a high level of literacy. In fact, my German teacher was bragging about this particular student. . . . He passed the advanced placement test in German coming out of eighth grade for college credit. We have 31 out of 35 kids in eighth grade take it in Spanish and they received a 3 or a 4 or a 5. . . . So eighth graders got college credits for Spanish.

— *Mr. Schulte, school principal*

A balance is sought with regards to student composition per classroom: one-half monolingual English, one-half monolingual Spanish. We also learned of a few classrooms in the mid-elementary grades with a student population of one-third monolingual English, one-third monolingual Spanish, and one-third bilingual English/Spanish. Although it is 95 percent Hispanic, Chacón School students come with different levels of English and Spanish fluency and from different economic backgrounds. The teachers and administrators have developed a TWB program that is progressive and challenging and that addresses the needs of the whole student. We observed that they work as a team for the success of all students. Mr. Schulte corroborates our observations and states,

> In this kind of program, the need and the value of the language is there. . . . We take half English speakers, half Spanish speakers, put them in a classroom together and teach them to read and write in Spanish first. . . . So we've got role models of English-speaking kids and Spanish-speaking kids. Both languages are valued here throughout . . . kindergarten through eighth grade.
>
> The perfect classes have one-third monolingual English, one-third monolingual Spanish, and one-third bilingual. So, the kids help each other.
>
> Me encanta el concepto y he visto éxitos académicos como sociales, que se aceptan los niños como son sin segregación o separación, los de habla inglés con los de habla español. El concepto es lo que nos ha dirigido. . . . It's something we buy into.
>
> (I love the concept and I have seen academic as well as social successes, that children are accepted as they are without segregation or separation, those who speak English and those who speak Spanish. This concept is what has directed us. . . . It's something we buy into.)
>
> — *Kindergarten teacher*

Student recruitment is done via word of mouth, yearly advertisement, and community meetings at Chacón School. The school is open to all El Paso–area students. A lottery system is also in place for Spanish- and English-speaking student candidates. The priorities for future students also include siblings of students in the school. We also learned that most of the faculty and administrators have their own children attending Chacón School.

Chacón School is a TWB program that combines native speakers of Spanish, the target language, with native speakers of English so that there will be cross-learning of the two languages. Native speakers of English are offered an immersion program, and native speakers of Spanish are offered a bilingual maintenance program. Since the entire school is a TWB program, native Spanish speakers and native English speakers are integrated for instruction throughout the school day. Table 4.1 illustrates

Table 4.1 Instructional Approach and Design

	Grades								
	K	1	2	3	4	5	6	7	8
Percentage of time that Spanish is used with native Spanish speakers and English speakers	80	80	80	60	60	45	45	45	45
Percentage of time that English is used with native Spanish speakers and English speakers	10	10	10	30	30	45	45	45	45
Percentage of time that the third language[a] is used with native Spanish speakers and English speakers	10	10	10	10	10	10	10	10	10

a. Chinese, Russian, Japanese, or German.

Chacón School's instructional approach and design schedules, which represent the actual time allocations for each language from kindergarten through eighth grade. Furthermore, as we will describe later, students change classrooms and teachers for instruction whenever the second- or the third-language component is designated.

The Chacón School instructional program model emphasizes individualized instruction implemented through the use of curriculum management systems. These are essentially systems of standards-based curriculum objectives to be used with each student, primarily in the areas of reading and mathematics. The demand these systems place on teachers' time is formidable. Their widespread use determines to a great extent the kinds of experiences students are having. These systems are mandated by the state and provide the content of learning experience and also the structure and sequence of behaviors required to reach a learning goal. A practical consequence for students is the opportunity to learn how to manage a group-oriented academic environment.

Chacón School has one principal and no vice principals. Instead, it is divided into four families to match the four third languages offered, and each family has a coordinator: the Chinese family coordinator, the Japanese family coordinator, the German family coordinator, and the Russian family coordinator.

> Nosotros en lugar de tener subdirector tenemos los coordinadores que vienen a funcionar como subdirectores. Pero algún problema que tenemos en el salón, es más rapido resolver porque cada uno de nosotros tiene una persona inmediata a la cual recurrir. Entonces no hay que esperar hasta que el director esté libre y éso nos ayuda mucho. Cada uno de los coordinadores está a cargo de 5 ó 6 maestros.

> (Instead of having vice principals, we have coordinators who have the role of vice principals. Any problem that arises in the classroom, we solve it quickly because each of us has an immediate person to go to. We don't have to wait until the principal is free and that helps us a lot. Each of the coordinators is in charge of five or six teachers.)

> — *Second-grade teacher*

The Chacón TWB program's duration is 8 years. The program focuses on academic achievement for both groups. The lesson delivery is monolingual, either in Spanish or English. However, Spanish is used for emergent literacy instruction in K–2. English literacy is taught in third grade for both language groups. The separation of languages for instruction is done by subject area. The program promotes a positive and reciprocal instructional climate and a strong home-school collaboration. It nurtures high-quality instructional staff and raises the minority status not only of Spanish but also of Spanish speakers. All students spend 30 minutes a day in the third language and also have activities such as karate, kung fu, ballet, and soccer twice a week. It used to be 45 minutes daily for the third language, but physical education had to be included into the program.

Program Design for Kindergarten and First and Second Grades

Subjects taught in Spanish for all students: Mathematics, reading, writing, and science.

Subjects taught in English: English language development based on the social studies curriculum, which continues through the eighth grade. Varied themes are introduced throughout the year.

Program Design for Third and Fourth Grades

Subjects taught in Spanish for all students: Mathematics, reading, writing, and science.

Subjects taught in English: The social studies curriculum continues as a foundation for instruction for English-language development. Formal instruction of English literacy begins in third grade. Students begin to experiment with the written language. Formal lessons in phonics, syntax, grammar, and other parts of speech are taught. Further development of literacy continues in fourth grade.

Program Design for Fifth and Sixth Grades

Subjects taught in Spanish for all students: Mathematics, reading, writing, and science.

Subjects taught in English: The social studies curriculum continues as a foundation for formal instruction for English-language development.

Club time: Club time offers students the opportunity to choose from a variety of specialized academically based classes such as golf, fine arts, or drama. These classes may change from one semester to another. Club time may be taught in English or Spanish.

Program Design for Seventh and Eighth Grades

Subjects taught in Spanish for all students: Mathematics, algebra, reading, writing, science, pre–Advanced Placement Spanish, and literature/language.

Subjects taught in English: The curriculum for English language arts and social studies continues as a foundation for formal instruction for English-language development. Pre–Advanced Placement curriculum begins in seventh grade, and Advanced Placement begins in eighth grade.

Electives are offered during the two semester sessions for both seventh- and eighth-grade students. State-mandated electives include fine arts, physical education, technology, and health. Other elective classes are also offered to students. Classes may be taught in either English or Spanish. Table 4.2 on page 62 summarizes the TWB program design and instruction in Spanish, English, and a third language.

English-Language Development

English-language development is offered to all Chacón School students with the following specifications:

Table 4.2   Language of Instruction for All Students

Subjects	Grades K, 1, 2	Grades 3 and 4	Grades 5 and 6	Grades 7 and 8
Literacy	Spanish	Spanish and English	Spanish and English	Spanish and English
Literacy	Spanish	Spanish and English	Spanish and English	Spanish and English
Pre–Advanced Placement	—	—	—	Spanish and English
Mathematics	Spanish	Spanish	Spanish	Spanish
Algebra	—	—	—	Spanish
Science	Spanish	Spanish	Spanish	Spanish
Social studies	English ELD	English ELD	English ELD	English ELD
English language arts	—	Begin formal English instruction	Continue English instruction	English formal instruction
Third language	30 minutes a day	30 minutes a day	30 minutes a day	30 minutes a day
Electives	—	—	—	English or Spanish
Club time	—	—	English or Spanish	—
Physical education	Spanish	Spanish	Spanish	—

NOTE: ELD = English-language development. Third language = Russian, Mandarin Chinese, German, or Japanese in related activities such as karate, kung fu, soccer, or ballet. Electives = fine arts, physical education, technology, and health, among others. Club time = golf, fine arts, and drama, among others.

- Kindergarten and first and second grades
    45 minutes daily
    Oral language development through literature, themes, and holidays
    As part of the social studies curriculum

- Third and fourth grades
    120 minutes daily
    Begin formal English reading through literature and language arts
    As part of social studies curriculum

- Fifth through eighth grades
  175 minutes daily
  Literacy development through literature and content areas

Third-Language Development

Third-language development is offered to all Chacón School students with the following specifications:

- Students choose one of the four languages:
  Mandarin Chinese
  Japanese
  German
  Russian
  30-minute lessons three times a week

- Special activity classes
  Kindergarten to sixth grade = 30 minutes twice a week

- Concentration is on oral language development
  Level of difficulty increases by grade level

Worth mentioning is the fact that team teaching (as opposed to self-contained classrooms) is the mode at Chacón School. Each grade level has both a Spanish component section taught by a bilingual teacher and an English component section taught by another bilingual teacher.

Furthermore, Chacón School practices a complex system of classifying and assessing a student's bilingual profile, following district guidelines. We can legitimately consider Chacón School as a multilingual and multicultural life situation. To be sure, ethnic proportions are heavily skewed toward Latino students: 95 percent are of Mexican American origin, and 5 percent are white, non-Latino, African American, Native American, or Asian American. Seventy percent of students qualify for the free or reduced lunch program.

But traditional Anglo values are strongly reflected in schooling processes and in the socialization goals of the teachers. As a school, Chacón is infinitely more complex than a regular monolingual school. It is viewed here both as an academic organization with internally generated social norms, role expectations, and patterned behavior and as an instrument of multicultural transmission and socialization for the parental constituency, the community, and the state.

WHAT MAKES CHACÓN SCHOOL A SUCCESSFUL TWB PROGRAM?

We turn now to an examination of schooling processes and the multicultural experience. We will draw primarily on data from observations; administrator, teacher, parent, and student open-ended interviews; and student surveys. These data helped us to find out the following:

- How Chacón School sustained the quality of its multilingual and multicultural program
- Whether the presence of three languages in the curriculum affected in observable ways school or classroom services, teacher behavior, and teacher values
- How leadership roles were shared between the administration, teachers, and parents

We will address these issues around the title of this section, "What Makes Chacón School a Successful TWB Program?" We start with the observation that Chacón School parents, faculty, and administrators play important additional roles as socialization agents and models in this multilingual and multicultural setting. We will, therefore, preface the examination of Chacón's schooling process with principal, teacher, parent, and student data relating to schooling and attitudes toward the multilingual and multicultural program. Throughout our interviews and communications, we used both English and Spanish and encouraged all those interviewed to choose a language to respond to our questions.

We observed a number of important features at Chacón School that have proven to be successful features for quality TWB program implementation (Cazabon, Lambert, & Hall, 1993; Lindholm, 1990). What follows is a brief summary of selected components with a focus on salient Chacón School features.

- *Common philosophy and camaraderie shared by school administrators, teachers, parents, and students.* All those interviewed reiterated to the researchers their belief in the program, in bilingualism. They expressed ownership and pride in the program and celebrated diversity. A selection of interview transcripts follows to reflect outstanding features:

> It is important to have people, the principal for one and all of the teachers, to be able to articulate what are the goals of the program, what are the expectations that we have for the children so that parents are not upset or confused. Sometimes we have to convince the parents. We are familiar with the Virginia Collier studies. This kind of program takes longer; you can't learn everything in 1 year or 2 years.
>
> — *Third-grade teacher*

- *School climate.* This is represented by observable and stated harmony among teachers, hard work, commitment, and readiness to defend the program:

> El éxito se debe a nuestro entusiasmo y al hecho de que queremos trabajar como burros.... No nos limitamos. Cuando se empezó la escuela, no había techo. Cuando llovía, nos inundábamos; no había piso. Era una cosa increible. Sin embargo, sin saber qué, cómo, cuándo, qué iba a pasar. Nos dieron entrenamiento y comenzamos con el modelo que se tuvo que modificar después. Estamos en proceso de definir básicamente la dedicación de los meastros; es una entrega total. O nos ayudamos todos o nos hundimos juntos.

> (Our success is due to our enthusiasm and the fact that we want to work like donkeys.... We do not limit ourselves. When we started the school, there were only building structures. There was no roof. When it rained, we flooded; they were dirt floors. Unbelievable.... However, we started without knowing how, when, what was going to happen. We had some training and we began constructing the model. Many things had to be changed later. Basically we defined the teachers' dedication; it is a complete dedication. We work together; otherwise, we would all sink together.)

> — *Fourth-grade teacher*

- *Strong language and academic development.* This includes Spanish-language development, English-language development, and third-language development:

> It is a long process, a lot of oral language development. It is immersion in Spanish in kindergarten. We do not read in English. It's 80-10-10. We do a lot of oral language in English and we expose them to print but we are not guiding them to do reading, just certain types of reading strategies in English like tracking, but not specifically phonics or sight words or anything like that.... But in Spanish we do a tremendous amount of oral language development. We use lots and lots of modeling, visual aids, lots of picture books, manipulatives, always contextual. We try to make it as meaningful as possible.

> — *Kindergarten teacher*

> During my first year teaching, I had the great opportunity to go to China with my fourth graders and there is where I realized they were learning a third language. We were at a store, a mall, and I was trying to buy a pair of sneakers. I was impressed that my students had to help me. It was not a sophisticated conversation, but they were able to communicate. The more languages a person knows, the more skillful she or he is.

> — *Fourth-grade teacher*

- *Strong literacy component.* This includes approaches to reading and writing, literature, transition to the other languages, and reading readiness:

> We always teach Spanish reading and writing or literature in the content areas. . . . We start literature in Spanish in kindergarten. We don't separate the groups, we don't translate. . . . First grade is an extension of the phonics that they are taught in kinder. They start introducing basal reading. Basically the approach in kinder is you learn to read. Once that is established a few months into first grade, you read to learn about a subject. The kids are given literature pieces, whether it is basal or something else to learn about a topic. So there is more cognitive learning. . . . It is really a holistic way of teaching.
>
> — *School coordinator*

> We teach twice the amount of English that the second-grade teachers do. First to second grades is 45 minutes, and in third grade it is 90 minutes of English. And we do introduce more formal language, reading, and writing activities. . . . We are trying to make an effort not to interfere with the Spanish literacy at that level. When they come to third grade, most of the students have a very solid foundation in Spanish literacy, and that's when we transition them to English. Since I taught second also, you see it with the majority of the students. They make a natural transition somewhere toward the middle or the end of second grade. They start to read in English all by themselves. They pick up a book in English and say, "Hey, I can read!" Of course they need directions; they are not going to be fluent readers by themselves.
>
> — *Third-grade teacher*

- *Separation of languages for instruction.* Teachers model one of the languages for instruction, and students associate the language with the teacher who uses it:

> Generalmente los niños no mezclan el inglés con el español porque cambiamos de maestra. Los niños de inglés no saben que yo hablo español y mis niños de español no saben que yo hablo inglés. Entonces cuando ellos ponen una palabra en inglés, les digo, "No entiendo. Necesitas preguntarle a alguien." Entonces ellos van a un compañerito y le preguntan, y luego vienen y me dicen.

> (Generally, the children do not mix English with Spanish because they change teachers. The English-speaking kids don't know that I speak Spanish, and my Spanish-speaking kids don't know that I speak English. Then when they say a word in English, I say, "I don't understand. You need

to ask somebody." Then, they go to ask a classmate and afterwards they come to tell me.)

— *First-grade teacher*

Se me hace ideal como lo tenemos ahorita. En la mañana tenemos todo lo de español. Vamos, comemos y entramos. Al entrar en la puerta ya saben que se cambian de canal; cambiamos del español al inglés. Ahorita se van al tercer idioma y alla se cambian de canal. Este horario se aco-moda muy bien.

(It is ideal the way we have it now. In the morning, we have everything in Spanish. We go eat and come back. When we enter, they know we change the channel; we change from Spanish into English. Right now, they are going to the third language and they change the channel. This schedule fits very well.)

— *Fourth-grade teacher*

• *Teachers learning communities.* Teachers learn from each other, create and improve the program together, and continue ongoing professional development. The Chacón School faculty is composed of relatively young individuals (average age in the mid- to upper 30s) with mostly a Mexican American background. There are 47 teachers: 41 women and 6 men. Teachers interviewed feel they work at Chacón School because they teach effectively within the program. They staunchly believe in the value of maintaining two, three, or more languages. They also agree in the program's organizational aspects (e.g., the amount of time Spanish-dominant students spend in English instruction, the necessity for Spanish-only and English-only classes). The teachers at Chacón School exemplify a "learning community" philosophy. Each teacher within each grade and across grades has something to contribute and something to learn from every other member (Calderón, 2001a, 2001b). Task collaboration has shown to be quite power-ful in improving learning environments (Crandall & Loeb, 2000):

We do a lot of training. Although we don't have a choice to attend the district's inservices and staff development, we do have a lot of opportu-nities to go to training on reading, math, science. The teachers in this school are very good about sharing with the rest of the teachers because not everyone can go to the inservice. So maybe one teacher from each level will go, and that person shares it with the grade-level teachers. We do take time during our planning meetings to share. Each group, grade level meets roughly once a week, maybe twice if everyone agrees. We have 1 hour for planning, a 1-hour conference every day. Usually 1 hour a week is for grade-level meetings, and we have an alternating schedule for faculty meetings. Every second Friday, we have a full staff-faculty meeting, and on the alternating Fridays we have the vertical meetings. Students usually have an extended PE schedule with the coaches on Fridays.

— Third-grade teacher

• *Staff development.* There is a high interest on behalf of the teachers for continuous learning. We observed a sustained support for professional development from the school principal. He had no qualms about letting three teachers attend an international conference on gifted education in Juárez, Mexico.

• *Parental involvement.* We observed full participation of Chacón School parents and a strong sense of ownership in the education of their children. The school's open-door policy to parents allowed them to participate in the educational process not only at home but also at school. Examples of practices include information exchange, decision sharing, volunteer services for school, home tutoring or teaching, and child advocacy. Parents strongly support the program:

By knowing Spanish, he [my son] was able to help himself. He reads [in] English better than he reads in Spanish. I asked him, "How did you do it?" "With the Spanish that I know I could figure out what the word is." He tested in reading in English. He reads at the high second-grade level. For someone who has never had English, it's great!

— Parent of a third-grade student

• When their children are selected to attend Chacón School for the first time, parents need to sign a parent agreement contract with the school. The agreement consists of 22 items, which can be summarized under the following topics:

Minimum requirement of 4 hours of volunteer time a month
Long-term commitment as a volunteer (8 years if the child is starting from kindergarten)
Child's special needs communicated prior to registration
Completion of homework/weekly reading log
Mandatory regular student attendance
School-parent partnership with discipline
Understanding of Chacón School's trilingual concept
Rigorous curriculum
School of choice
Adherence to contract and evidence of child progress
Parent Center
Parent classes in general educational development (GED), English as a Second Language (ESL), and U.S. citizenship

Work with parent/teacher coordinator
Abiding by the year-round calendar
Providing children with school uniforms and cultural arts activity
uniforms

• *Teachers and parents working together.* Teachers believe in the importance of parental involvement for the students' language and academic success. What follows illustrates the kinds of activities teachers perform to involve parents to support their children's schooling. Teachers set up monthly family projects for parents, siblings, and relatives to work together:

> Hay un contrato desde kinder en el que los padres tienen que ayudar a sus hijos a poner horas de voluntarios en alguna actividad que sea provechosa para sus hijos. Aparte, el diario de lectura que los padres lean con sus hijos. Por ejemplo, nosotros en segundo, tenemos el proyecto familiar cada mes. Mandamos como grupo un proyecto de familia donde el padre va a tener que ayudar al estudiante y los dos van a tener que hacer investigación o ponerse de acuerdo cómo lo van a hacer. Y así se ve que el papá está interesado en la educación de su hijo y cómo se ayudan. Por ejemplo, el libro de familia donde tienen que poner fotografías y eventos desde que nacieron hasta el presente. Entonces los papás escriben sus vivencias y experiencias, escriben juntos y luego tienen que presentarlo al salón. Siempre se presenta oralmente. Eso le da validez al niño de su trabajo y al niño también.

> (There is a contract from kindergarten that parents have to help their children and to volunteer hours in activities for the benefit of their children. In addition, there is a reading diary for them to read with their children. For example, in second grade we have a monthly family project. We send a family project where the parent will help the student; both will have to do research and agree on how they are going to do it. In that way, we see how the parent is interested in the education of his or her child and how they help each other. For example, there is a family book where they have to put photographs and events from birth to the present. Then the parents write their experiences; they write together and have to present it to the class. Parents always make presentations. This gives validity to the child's work and his or her self-esteem.)

> — *Second-grade teacher*

• Teachers use strategies such as the following to help parents' lack of English- or Spanish-language proficiency:

> Tengo algunos padres que no hablan inglés pero los conecto con padres que hablan inglés y español para que puedan trabajar con las tareas. Tengo

padres muy accesibles que les dan el teléfono a los padres que tienen dificultad con el español para ayudar a sus hijos en la tarea. Entonces lo que hago es comunicarlos por si tienen una duda o también puede comunicarse conmigo. Muchas veces he tenido a padres que vienen al salón a aprender español o a escribirlo.

(Some of my parents don't speak English, but I connect them with parents who speak English and Spanish in order for them to work with their children's homework. I have very accessible parents who give their phone numbers to parents who are having difficulty with enough Spanish to help their children with homework. So I connect them in case they have any doubts. They can also communicate with me. Many times I have had parents who come to the classroom to learn Spanish.)

— *First-grade teacher*

• Teachers help parents feel comfortable with their decision to bring their children to a TWB school and to collaborate with the school:

A mí se me hace que todos los niños que vienen a esta escuela están aquí porque sus papás conocen el programa y les gusta el programa. Ellos decidieron, "Yo quiero que mi hijo estudie aquí, que sepa más de dos idiomas." Ya con ese hecho ayuda que los papás estén involucrados en la educación de sus hijos. Trabajamos todos juntos, niños, padres y maestros.

(I have the feeling that all the children who come to this school are here because their parents know and like the program. They decided, "I want my child to know more than one language." That fact helps the parents be involved in the education of their children. We work together, children, parents, and teachers.)

— *Second-grade teacher*

• Teachers and parents give their time generously:

Los padres siempre nos han apoyado. El año pasado hicimos dos viajes fuera de la ciudad. Estábamos con el tema de las estrellas, del espacio, los planetas. Fuimos a las montañas, son tres horas de aquí más o menos. Casi el 90 por ciento de los padres fueron acompañándonos a ese viaje. Los padres están involucrados . . . un apoyo bastante fuerte.

(The parents have always been supportive. Last year we made two trips out of town. We were studying the topic of the stars, the planets, universe. We went to the mountains about 3 hours from here more or less. About 90 percent of the parents came with us on that trip. . . . Parents are involved . . . a very strong support.)

— *Second-grade teacher*

WHAT DO CHACÓN SCHOOL PARENTS THINK OF THE TWB PROGRAM?

I like the ambiance of the school. It is very receptive to parent input. The parents are able to participate in any way that they are able to. Of course, you are required to dedicate 4 hours a month. But if you are able to participate more, you are welcomed to do so.

— *Parent of a third-grade student*

The following parent interviews illustrate how parents view the TWB program. Throughout these conversations, parents demonstrated in-depth knowledge of the school and ownership in what it offered, as well as its organization, strength, and implementation of its goals and objectives. We have selected portions of transcriptions from the two focus group interviews of about 1 hour for each interview, with a total of six parents (two men and four women). Parents were asked to choose to respond in English or in Spanish. Faithful translations into English of the portions selected have been provided. Furthermore, brackets and parentheses indicate language added.

• *The program works.* Chacón School parents expressed satisfaction, admiration, and support for the program in different contexts. They are convinced that the TWB program works. They relate the TWB program success to language learning, bilingual competence, and transfer of knowledge from one language to the other and vice versa. Their support for instruction in and use of Spanish literacy is reiterated throughout their conversations with different topics:

The funny thing—it's not funny—that they might have learned Spanish since kinder[garten] and all of a sudden, they start reading in English without anybody to help them. Right now [my son] started the third grade. I was amazed! I asked him to read a book and he read everything, from page one to the last page, everything. Right now what he has to learn is to spell in English. But he already knows how to read it and . . . comes automatically.

— *Parent of a third-grade student*

• *True bilingualism.* Chacón School parents also value bilingual competence as a tool for celebrating linguistic and cultural diversity and maintaining and valuing the minority language. They express how satisfied they are with the program, compare it with other school settings, and believe that the program will work for their children:

Yo estoy super satisfecha [con el programa]. No hay adjetivos. En mi casa mis cinco niños, mi esposo habla inglés y yo hablo español. Pero yo me di cuenta que a los tres más grandes se les empezó a olvidar el español cuando estaban creciendo. Y ahorita no quieren hablar el español. Ya están hablando casi todo en inglés. Y lo que tiene esta escuela es que siguen hasta el ocho con el español. Es más difícil que se les olvide cuando están más grandes. Tengo ahorita una niña en el siete y ella habla muy bien el español y lo escribe muy bien, y una niña en segundo y también habla muy bien el español y lo escribe. A los grandes ya se les olvidó y no lo saben escribir. La escuela va a ayudar a las dos chicas porque los grandes no pudieron entrar aquí. Esta escuela es nueva, es joven, tiene 6 años apenas. Entonces los grandes están en high school y no alcanzaron a entrar aquí. Yo pienso que las más chiquitas van a tener más oportunidad de ser completamente bilingües por esta escuela.

(I am super satisfied [with the program]. There are no adjectives. . . . At home with five children, my husband speaks English and I speak Spanish. But I noticed that the three older sons were beginning to forget Spanish when they were growing up. And right now they don't want to speak in Spanish. They are speaking almost everything in English. And what this school has is that the children continue with Spanish up to Grade 8. It is more difficult for them to forget it when they are older. Right now I have a daughter in Grade 7 and she speaks and writes in Spanish very well, and a daughter in second grade, and she also speaks Spanish very well and she writes it well. The older ones forgot it and do not know how to write in Spanish. This school is going to help my two daughters because my older ones could not attend this school. This school is new, 6 years only. My older sons are in high school and could not attend this program. I believe that my young girls will have more opportunity to be completely bilingual in this school.)

— *Parent of seventh- and second-grade students*

• *The school respects the home culture.* Most Chacón School parents are Mexican American. They have close ties to Mexico. They have continuing contacts with Mexico through regular trips across the border to shop or visit relatives. Chacón School parents use this context to express strong support for the program. They perceive their children are having a great experience in the school much different from their own. Often, the value parents place on Chacón School's program has its genesis in their schooling experience as members of ethnic minorities in an Anglo-dominated society, as illustrated with the following statement:

Ninguno de mis tres hijos sabía español cuando entraron aquí porque mi esposa y yo hablamos puro inglés en la casa. Entonces cuando yo los traje, por esa razón los metimos a esta escuela porque tengo mucha familia en Méjico. Yo quería que mis hijos se pudieran comunicar con la familia.

Mi mamá ... mi familia toda es de Méjico. La de mi esposa, toda es de aquí [El Paso] y hablan muy poco inglés. De cualquier modo, yo soy mejicano ... Es una tristeza no saber las dos lenguas porque a mí me han servido más bien mucho hablar los dos idiomas en los trabajos que he tenido. Es una oportunidad para que nuestros hijos aprendan.

(None of my three sons knew Spanish when they came here because my wife and I speak only English at home. That was the reason we enrolled them in this school because I have a lot of relatives in Mexico. I wanted my sons to communicate with the family. My mother ... all my family is from Mexico. My wife's family is from here [El Paso] and they speak a bit of English. Anyway ... I am Mexican. ... It is sad not to know the two languages because to me, speaking two languages has helped me a lot. I have used them in the jobs I have had. This is an opportunity for our children to learn.)

— *Parent of third-, fifth-, and sixth-grade students*

- *Academic success.* Chacón School parents offer comparisons of academic success between the Chacón School TWB program and other schools in the same district and/or city. Their support for instruction in and use of Spanish is reiterated throughout their conversations with different topics:

La comparación es una de las cosas que uno tiene por naturaleza. "A ver cómo está mi hijo comparado. ..." Y estos niños de aquí están muy avanzados. Hay algunos aspectos que se atrasan por decir así en el inglés. Pero ya cuando van al seis, ya casi están al nivel de los demás en inglés más los otros idiomas que por decir así el tercer idioma y el español que lo llevan más que en otras escuelas. Y se ha comprobado. Nos estaba platicando una señora de una niña que ya no quiso estar aquí en el ocho, que se quiso ir a la middle school. Y dice que es la más avanzada. Que quiere decir que este sistema está trabajando más bien que en las otras.

(Comparisons are things that one does by nature. "Let's see how my son is doing compared. ..." These students here are more advanced. At first, there are some aspects in which they lag behind, let's say in English. But when they go to [Grade] 6, they are up to par with the others in English, plus the other two languages ... the third language, and Spanish, which they have more of than in the other schools. And it has been proven ... I was talking to a mother of a student who went to another middle school and she is doing better than those students there. This means that this system is working better than the others.)

— *Parent of a sixth-grade student*

- *Preparing for the real world.* The expectations parents have for their children's schooling at Chacón School reflect their judgment and the instrumental motivation about what kind of education is functional in a world in which bilingualism and multiculturalism are still a continuing reality:

Ahorita en el mercado de trabajo, el que es bilingüe... tiene oportunidad. Incluso a la gente que es bilingüe, le pagan un poco más en cualquier rama—en la inmigración, en la escuela. Como dicen, "El que es bilingüe vale por dos." Ayuda mucho en la comunicación porque es bonito comunicarse en los dos idiomas.

(Now in the job market the one who is bilingual... has a chance. Bilingual people earn a bit more in any job—in immigration, in the schools.... As they say, "A bilingual is worth two." It helps a lot for communication because it is beautiful to speak in two languages.)

— *Parent of an eighth-grade student*

• *Positive relationships with teachers.* Parental attitudes about the Chacón School program are presumably affected also by the quality of interpersonal relations among faculty, staff, and parents. Parents characterize Chacón School as "very friendly," a judgment that is informed by their sense of ownership of the program and the increasingly significant role they play in the life of the school and the national, regional, and state visibility they give to the program:

[Me gusta el programa] porque tienen el open-door policy. Podemos entrar a las clases y hablar con las maestras. También podemos agarrar los resultados de nuestros niños, no esperar que nos hablen, que nos manden una notita. También ofrecemos ayudar a los maestros.

([I like the program] because they have an open-door policy. We can enter into the classrooms and talk to the teachers. We can also ask for the test results of our children and not wait until they send us a written note home. We also help the teachers.)

— *Parent of an eighth-grade student*

• *Parents learning in their children's classrooms.* Chacón School also considers parents who have special emotional needs, allowing them to help all children, not just their own:

[Me gusta el program] la convivencia con los niños. Yo nada más tengo este niño. Se me hacía mucho dejarlo en la escuela. Se me hacía mucho que algo le iba a pasar. Entonces cuando entró a esta escuela, que aquí me pude quedar todo el día. Perfecto! Estoy viendo que me he encariñado con los niños. Yo venía por el mío, pero ahora estoy viendo a todos. Tengo muchos hijos adoptivos. Y es una de las cosas que me gusta, que uno tiene la facilidad de entrar y salir cuando uno quiera, cuando uno pueda, el contacto con ellos. Nos dan la oportunidad a veces hasta en el salón. Como ahora voy a empezar con la maestra un programa que ya ellos tienen en literatura.

([I like the program because of] the cohabitation with children. I only have one son and it was difficult to leave him at school . . . that something was going to happen to him. Then, when he entered this school, I found out that I could stay all day. Perfect! I see that I am getting close to the other children. I used to see to my son, but now I see to all. I have many adopted children. And that is something I like, that one can come in and leave when one wants, when one can, contact with them. They give us opportunities in the classroom. Like I am going to start a literature program they have.)

— *Parent of a fourth-grade student*

- *Parents as trainers.* Chacón School parents are also trainers of other parents and have shared their knowledge of literature and language arts with other parents and staff from other schools at state and national conferences.

Nosotros los padres presentamos en NABE y TABE de literatura, como ayudarlos a los niños a escribir y entender la literatura. Ahora la maestra quiere que lo que presentamos, paso a paso, en NABE y TABE también lo vayan a hacer con los niños, con el propio libro que están leyendo ahora ellos. Y luego haremos un mural de todo.

(We, the parents, presented at NABE [an annual conference of the National Association for Bilingual Education] and TABE [an annual conference of the Texas Association for Bilingual Education] literature on how to help our children to write and to understand literature. The teacher now wants us to do in the classroom, step-by-step, what we presented at NABE and TABE, with the book they are reading now. Then we make a mural of everything.)

— *Parent of second- and seventh-grade students*

- *A principal who values parents.* Under the leadership of Robert Schulte, Chacón School's charismatic principal, there is an active classroom volunteer parent program. They share the ownership with him. There is also support, respect, and admiration in the parents' statements about him:

Mr. Schulte is our principal. We believe in his values and ideas because they work. We try to back him any way we can.

— *Parent of a sixth-grade student*

- *Parents' active roles.* Parents contribute to the Chacón School's academic success through an active classroom volunteer program:

[Funciona el programa de voluntarios?] Sí, necesariamente. El año pasado yo era la coordinadora de los voluntarios. Se les da un papel que proporciona la escuela para marcar el tiempo de voluntarios cada mes. No necesariamente tiene que estar presente en la escuela. Por ejemplo, los niños que están en la familia de ruso, de chino, llevarlos a alguna actividad, ya sea el ballet, eso ya cuenta como voluntario. Ya eso cuenta como una hora. Voluntaria es actividad del desarrollo de los niños. También puede ser en la casa, leyéndoles a los niños. Tenemos que firmar el papel. Es bastante trabajo. Una mamá del salón está encargada de recoger las horas que le dan a la maestra. Ella se trae a su casa y saca las horas. Por ejemplo esta mamá puso por decir 80 horas; ese padre sólo 4 horas. Entonces ella tiene que reportar, "Estas son las horas que metieron los de la maestra _____." Es mi papel como coordinadora. Funciona porque nos quedamos en el "Top 10" del distrito.

([Does the volunteer program work?] Yes, it's necessary. Last year I was the coordinator of the volunteer program. You give each parent a paper to indicate the volunteer time per month. The parent does not have to be present in the school. For example, take the children who are in the Russian family . . . to an activity, to the Russian ballet. That counts like volunteer time. That counts like 1 hour. Volunteering is an activity on behalf of the children's development. It could also be at home, reading to the children. We have to sign the paper. It is a lot of work. A classroom's parent is in charge of picking up the volunteer hours. She brings them home and does the math. Let's say this parent gave 80 hours; that parent gave just 4 hours. Then at the end of the month, she has to report, "These are the hours that the parents gave in Ms. ___'s classroom." That is my job as coordinator. It works because we are in the district's top 10 list.)

— *Parent of a fourth-grade student*

• *Parents and homework.* Chacón School parents are also able to explain how they help their children with homework and to elaborate on their children's literacy and academic development. In a participatory way, they become teachers, and their participation does not seem restrained by any preconceived notion of school boundaries:

Mis hijos leen mucho y eso es bueno para la escuela. Porque hasta los problemas de matemáticas tiene uno que leerlos para resolverlos. Vamos a la biblioteca. Por ejemplo, los maestros escogen un tema por mes. Por ejemplo, este mes están con los insectos. Entonces vamos a la biblioteca y buscamos libros que hablen de insectos y los estudiamos. Así es cómo los ayudo. De acuerdo al tema que están tratando, vamos y buscamos en la biblioteca y es lo que leemos. Los temas son por salón, por grado tienen un tema.

(My children read a lot and that is good for them and the school. Even the math problems, one has to read them to solve them. We go to the library. For example, the teachers choose a monthly theme like this month it is about insects. Then, we go to the library and look for books that talk about insects and we study them together. That is the way I help. According to the theme of the lesson, we look for it in the library and read the books. The themes are by classroom, by grades; they each have a theme.)

— *Parent of third-, fifth-, and sixth-grade students*

• *Parents and change/improvement.* Also of importance is the fact that parents have the authority and the power to recommend and evaluate changes and improvements in the school's academic and extracurricular program. The quality of parental involvement is shaped in these roles. They become knowledgeable in a great number of school-centered topics about which they have to make a judgment. Furthermore, they exercise their right to give opinions on how to better or strengthen the program and the school:

[Qué cambiaría en el programa?] Yo no pienso que tendría que cambiar pero si reforzar el tercer idioma porque se nos está yendo. No hay suficiente dinero, no sé lo que pasa. Por ejemplo, la familia china ahorita no tiene personas que están dando chino. No sé si es cuestión del distrito que no tiene más dinero para traer a alguien más de un tercer idioma. En el tercer idioma, antes tenían 1 hora y ahora tienen 45 minutos. Lo han estado recortando. Que debería ser al contrario, aumentar más el tiempo. Cortaron la hora porque ya metieron PE. Tenían que cortar de algún lugar. Fue un requerimiento del estado que no tenían aquí. Tuvieron que llamarle educación física.

([What would you change in the program?] I do not think a change is needed, but the third language needs to be reinforced. There is not enough money. I don't know what is going on. For example, the Chinese family does not have people who are teaching Chinese. I don't know if it is a matter of the district that has no more money to bring somebody else for a third language. . . . In the third language they had 1 hour before and now they have 45 minutes. They have been shortening [the schedule]. It should be the other way, increase the time. They cut the hour because they introduced PE. They had to cut from somewhere. It was a state requirement that they did not have here. They had to call it physical education.)

— *Parent of an eighth-grade student*

I believe it is a long-term program, a long-term commitment because my children were English dominant. When they came to kindergarten, they had a very hard time because they did not speak Spanish. Being that 80 percent of the curriculum is in Spanish, 10 percent in English, 10 percent in Japanese, if I were to pull them out, say, in first grade or in second grade, I feel they would be at a disadvantage at another school, since they have been focusing in Spanish. I have contemplated taking a job outside of

El Paso. That is the only thing that would hold me back because they haven't learned English like the other children. But in the long run, it is going to even out. They are going to rank higher and become more knowledgeable than other children. It is a commitment. You can't have the children 1 or 2 years and pull them out because it won't work. They [school administration] want you to keep the child at least 5 or 6 years. . . . There was an instance in the meeting last year. A lady pulled her children and took them to another school and they got behind. What happened? They stayed there all year and came back to [Chacón] school.

— Parent of third-, fifth-, and sixth-grade students

WHAT DO CHACÓN SCHOOL STUDENTS THINK OF THE TWB PROGRAM?

Este programa me ha cambiado la vida para lo mejor y estoy orgulloso de haber estado en esta escuela. . . . Hemos estado juntos como siete años aquí. Casi somos hermanos, somos como familia.

(This program has changed my life for the better and I am proud of studying in this school. . . . We have been together about 7 years here. We are almost brothers, we are like family.)

— Eighth-grade student

We interviewed groups of students and administered a survey to 19 Chacón School students from fourth through ninth grades. As with the other participants interviewed, students had the opportunity to choose the language to respond to the survey (written in English and in Spanish) and during the interview. When students were asked why they liked studying at Chacón School, they asserted that it was because they learn languages. A selection follows.

Student Responses

- The dual-language program has proven that it works and that students can learn in this environment.
- The students learn three languages in all modes—writing, reading, and vocabulary.
- The students learn different languages and have opportunities to go to different countries.
- The program teaches students things that other schools don't and provides an opportunity to do more when they begin to work.

In summary, the students interviewed feel that the conditions for success at Chacón School have the following characteristics:

- It is an additive bilingual program for both groups of students at no cost to the primary language of either group of Spanish speakers or English speakers.
- Teachers, administrators, parents, and students know the benefits of bilingualism.
- Students are grouped together for literacy.
- Conversational language is present from interaction with peers in both languages.
- Academic language is present from interaction with teachers and parents.
- Careful adherence is given to the program design.
- Early entrance at kindergarten or first grade is important.
- Classrooms are balanced linguistically.
- Program duration is 8 years.
- Instructional staff is of high quality.

All of Chacón School students interviewed expressed the instrumental value of bilingualism and their desire to continue learning the languages when they leave for high school. They expressed how pleased they are with the program. When asked if they taught languages to anybody at home, they responded positively:

[I teach] my dad . . . like how to say long sentences in English. He is Spanish dominant and he knows very few words in English. I teach him like how to say basic sentences so we can communicate in English. . . . I teach my dad because when he wants to pronounce something in English, he says it wrong. I correct him. The first time he came here to the U.S. like a little kid, he didn't know anything but Spanish. And then his dad left and he had to help his mom with work. He was not able to learn English. Now I am helping him.

— *Sixth-grade student*

Chacón School students also expressed their role as multilingual translators and confidence in their linguistic skills in three languages:

[I translate] when my brothers and sisters don't understand English at home and in the market because sometimes they speak to them in English and they don't know what they are saying.

— *Fifth-grade student*

I helped my mom when we went to China. She didn't know what they were saying. We went to a shop. She was asking me to tell her what they were saying. They understood me. They sort of spoke too fast in China.

My teacher . . . we went to a store with her in China, she wanted to buy these shoes. The lady was speaking in Chinese and my teacher asked me to tell her what they were saying. I would tell her because she was putting the prices too high. She got the shoes for a low price.

— *Sixth-grade student*

Chacón School students also reflected on the TWB program and attributed its success to many contributors:

[Who is behind the program's success?] I think they have to be the administrators. They have done a good job with the school. They deserve most of the credit. But a lot of it goes to the parents because without their support, I mean . . . I live far. Without their support, I wouldn't be able to come here. I could walk to the other middle school, but Dad drives me here. My sister is in sixth grade and my brother is in third grade here also.

— *Eighth-grade student*

Chacón School students also socialize with Spanish-speaking and English-speaking peers. They cooperate with each other in class:

[How do you like being with kids who speak Spanish?] Pretty fun. They like to play soccer and football. They help me sometimes in Spanish. In English class, I help them a little bit. . . . Pretty much fun.

— *Fifth-grade student*

Chacón School students also voiced their aspirations to become professionals and be able to use their multilingual skills:

I want to be a teacher. . . . Because I want to teach children and prepare them for higher grades. I could teach them a second language, like if they learn in Spanish only.

— *Sixth-grade student*

Creo que voy a ir al colegio. Pues quiero estudiar la política y a lo mejor soy un embajador a Alemania.

(I think I am going to go to college. Because I want to study politics and maybe I can become an ambassador to Germany.)

— *Eighth-grade student*

The responses to the students' survey also revealed the following:

- *They expressed confidence in the knowledge of English and Spanish.* Of those students surveyed, 74 percent indicated they knew how to speak, read, and write Spanish very well, and 53 percent indicated they knew how to speak, read, and write English very well.

- *They used their bilingual skills in and outside of the school.* Thirty-seven percent indicated that they spoke with their classmates in Spanish in and outside of the school, and 58 percent indicated that they spoke with their classmates in English in and outside of the school.
- *They are able to use their bilingual skills at home as well.* Sixty-three percent indicated that they spoke Spanish at home with all members of their family, including the extended family. There was a balance in the percentages when they spoke English at home with their extended family (35 percent), siblings and all members of the family (25 percent each), and the father (15 percent).
- *They are able to study content areas, such as mathematics, in both languages.* Seventy-nine percent indicated that they could study mathematics in both languages.
- *They can read in both languages evenly.* Fifty percent indicated they prefer to read in both English and Spanish.
- *They can write in both languages also.* Forty percent indicated they prefer to write in both English and in Spanish; however, 47 percent indicated that they prefer to write in Spanish.
- *They are avid readers in both languages.* Fifty-three percent indicated that they had read from two to five books in Spanish in the past 2 months, and 47 percent indicated that they had done so in English.
- They were unanimous in their statements (100 percent in each) that they want to continue learning in English and Spanish and using both languages for instruction.
- To strengthen their bilinguality, they indicated that they needed help from their teachers in conversation (33 percent) and mathematics (33 percent), followed by vocabulary and writing (22 percent each).
- Specific areas of needed improvement in Spanish are vocabulary, reading, and writing.
- Specific areas of needed improvement in English are writing, vocabulary, reading, and conversation.

SUMMARY

We have tried to do justice to an exemplary TWB program and have presented only a few examples of Chacón School's strengths. To understand the role of administrators, teachers, parents, and students, we must view the program as a cohesive TWB program in which its curriculum system and extra-classroom activities play a role in structuring and reinforcing a multilingual and multicultural experience. The Chacón School model assumes the continuing importance of trilingual competence and developing needs of the students. At every grade, students can express themselves in the language that provides them with the most meaning. The constant availability to students of their first language affords them a more open relationship with teachers and more freedom to adapt to a multicultural environment. Of more importance, Chacón School's TWB program affirms the equal worth of ethnic backgrounds and the inseparability of language and culture.

Part II

Implementing
Effective Instruction

5

Instructional Techniques and Activities for Second-Language Learners

Two-way immersion (TWI) classrooms will have second-language learners all the time. During English instruction time, the Spanish-dominant students will be second-language learners in need of English as a Second Language (ESL) techniques. During Spanish instruction time, the English-dominant speakers will need Spanish as a Second Language (SSL) techniques. Some of the best ways to teach second-language learners are to focus on strategies that make any language comprehensible, such as hands-on activities, peer interaction, small-group learning, and technology. These activities enable students to hear, see, speak, and analyze new information in various ways and give them automatic practice with the new learnings. However, the teacher plays a critical role in setting a safe context where the students are willing to take risks with the new language and are actively engaged in learning all the time. The teacher's delivery of information or instructions can either be a hurdle or a clear path to student success.

WHAT IS SHELTERED INSTRUCTION?

Sheltered instruction refers to the concept of comprehensible subject matter teaching (math, science, social studies, etc.), with the second language (L2) as the medium of instruction. Sheltered instruction can function in two-way bilingual (TWB) programs as a bridge or transition between the first- and second-language class as a means of facilitating comprehension of and responses to content instruction. In TWB programs, the aim is to provide both language (listening, speaking, reading, and writing) and academic instruction to students so that they do not fall behind in grade-level content learning.

STRATEGIES FOR INSTRUCTIONAL DELIVERY

The teacher's delivery of instruction can be made comprehensible despite the difficulty or complexity of the reading material, the information being presented, and/or the instructional model being used. The instructional strategies and techniques proposed here will complement any instructional approach used by the teachers. They can be used to teach any content: math, science, social studies, or language arts, reading, and writing.

Teacher Speech

Teachers can facilitate comprehension, regardless of the difficulty of the text or subject matter. Teachers can use a combination of the following strategies to help second-language learners comprehend without having to resort to translation:

Slower but natural rate of speech and clear enunciation, being careful not to raise volume

Simpler and shorter sentences to explain a process or a concept

Frequent communication strategies such as rephrasing, repetition, and clarification when presenting new material, explaining tasks, or conducting interactive reading of literature books

Verbal emphasis or writing new vocabulary, idioms, or abstract concepts on the board to facilitate comprehension during interactive reading or provide explanations to students who are at the beginning stages of comprehension in L2

Contextualization

Teachers can make abstract concepts more concrete by using examples that are already well known or can be easily understood when providing visual reinforcement. Meaning becomes clearer when teachers use the following:

Pantomime, gestures, or exaggerated facial expressions

Props, *realia* (real objects)

Pictures of the objects or sets of pictures for a concept

Blackboard sketches as the teacher explains

Films, filmstrips, videotapes, slides, and transparencies before, during, and after reading complex text

Demonstrations and role-plays (for social studies or science)

Hands-on interactive tasks during an explanation or afterward to check for understanding

Use of graphic organizers on the board, such as story maps and word webs during storytelling or retelling

Computer graphics by the teacher and students

Computer vocabulary activities as a follow-up to sustain vocabulary development

Giving Directions

Teachers have found the following techniques useful for giving directions in ESL or SSL that will avoid translating, mixing languages, or doing preview-review in the other language:

Break down complex tasks into simpler steps with specific instructions such as, "Look at the story map. Point to the author box. Now point to the first event box. . . ."

Interrupt the lesson with questions to the students. This is a natural way to check for comprehension throughout the lesson.

Ample Opportunities for Student Interaction

Teacher talk needs to be balanced with student talk, no matter how limited the students might be in L2. One way is to stop every few minutes and ask students a question, who then turn to their partners and "buddy buzz" until they come up with a good answer. The types of questions to ask students periodically are as follows:

What do you think will happen?

Do you have any questions so far?

Please summarize up to here.

Please clarify for your partner. . . .

Teach each other. . . .

Ask students to "buddy buzz" or "put your heads together and see if you have any questions," "summarize," "clarify," "tell me more," and "teach each other" as frequently as possible.

Checking for Understanding

The teacher should verify comprehension of each instructional unit by checking for understanding frequently. This will help students start their tasks right away since they understand the "what and how" of their task. Some techniques for checking understanding are as follows:

"Tell us the first step, Laura. What is the second step, John?"

"Wh___" questions (who, what, where, when, whose)

"Proof" questions ("How do you know that?")

"Funny" questions ("So, the head of the United States is called a king, right?")

Confirmation checks ("Do you mean. . . ?")

"Tell me more" (when clarification is needed)

Error Correction

To prevent students from withdrawing or feeling embarrassed and thus refusing to "try to use the second language," teachers and student partners should use the following guidelines:

- Error correction must be minimal at the beginning. Let the student feel safe in the new environment.
- Teacher and student peers should recognize that language errors are a necessary part of second-language acquisition.
- Teacher and student peers should concentrate on the message the students communicate, not the correctness of the message (function before form).
- When correction is done, a "restatement" form (positive modeling technique) can be used:

> Student: "Does she has a pet?"
> Teacher: "Does she have a pet? Yes, she does. She has a pet."

Interdependent Dialogue

- To foster conversation, teachers should use a rich discussion instead of a straight lecture or instructions because this builds comprehension and fluency. Dialogue where meaning is negotiated works best. Teachers can foster conversations with and between L2 learners by asking referential (open-ended questions) rather than display (closed-ended) questions; in the former, the teacher seeks new information ("What do you think this looks like?"), but in the latter, the teacher already knows the answer ("Where is the boy?").
- Teachers should give examples that are personalized rather than impersonal (e.g., "Let's say that Juan took that trip into the jungle" rather than "We took a trip into the jungle").

TEACHING TECHNIQUES
FOR VOCABULARY BUILDING

The most urgent need for second-language learners is to rapidly acquire a large enough vocabulary to be able to express ideas and feelings, as well as to master the material being taught. Therefore, time needs to be set aside for vocabulary building before, during, and after each lesson. At first, teachers may feel guilty spending so much time on vocabulary building, but the benefits to students will become evident soon, and there are major losses for students if they don't. Even fluent speakers of English suffer when vocabulary- and background-building activities are not conducted. One of the major reasons second-language learners do not progress quickly is that not enough time is spent on vocabulary development even when they are reading and writing in the second language. Time should be added as needed throughout the lesson using the techniques described below.

Techniques for Vocabulary Building

In addition to presenting the vocabulary word list, the choral reading, and definitions, some vocabulary-building techniques that can be interspersed throughout the week's activities are as follows:

- Having necessary vocabulary, concepts, and messages written and hung *all over* the classroom (print-rich environment)
- Labeling drawings and pictures to help students make the connection between oral and written English and pointing to these visuals to clarify meaning when these words are encountered
- Using the word wizard
- Using the students' ideas as the starting point and elaborating on them to clarify meaning (this allows the students to contribute to the

meaning process and enhances their self-esteem when their ideas are accepted)

- Repeating incorrect utterances correctly in an unexaggerated manner and encouraging the students to try again, without them feeling embarrassed or criticized

- Incorporating role-playing activities to allow students to employ vocabulary and learn new concepts through personalized physical activities, which give meaning to new vocabulary.

Strategies When Previewing a Selection

Vocabulary is first introduced as the teacher previews a story in the language of instruction by doing the following:

- Writing additional key words on the board or chart tablet and asking students to read with you
- Writing "kid-friendly" definitions after each word and asking students to repeat the words and definitions after you
- Pointing to pictures in the book or to paragraphs where the words are found
- Making predictions by discussing the title, pictures, and vocabulary along with the students' predictions
- Skimming to determine main ideas
- Scanning to find specific details of interest

Mapping and Graphic Organizers

Semantic maps are very effective in building vocabulary. Using semantic maps, webs, diagrams, or any cognitive (graphic) organizer engages students in a mental activity that activates prior knowledge and provides multidimensional contextual clues to the new vocabulary and concepts. It also gives students more vocabulary for talking about new knowledge or new words. First, model on the board techniques for mapping. Second, have small groups of students work on their maps. This preliminary practice will provide the students with patterns to replicate. Encourage students to use drawings for those words not yet in their repertoire. Some graphic samples are presented in Figures 5.1 through 5.7.

Grouping/Classifying

This technique is similar to mapping. Classifying or reclassifying vocabulary and concepts into meaningful units will make them easier to remember. Categories or groups can be based on the type of word or concept, such as the following:

(Text continued on p. 93)

Figure 5.1 Word/Concept Web

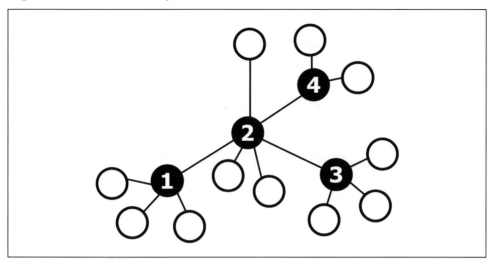

Figure 5.2 Timeline

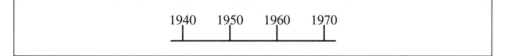

Figure 5.3 Flow Chart

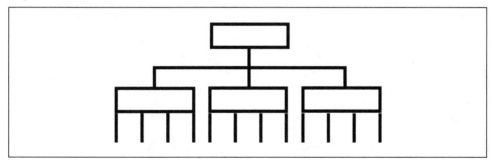

Figure 5.4 Character Map

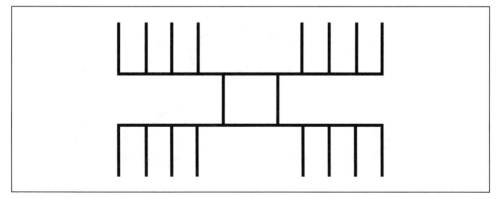

Figure 5.5   Story Line Creative Map

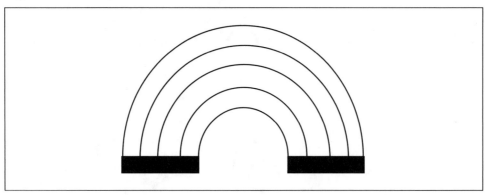

Figure 5.6   Venn Diagram

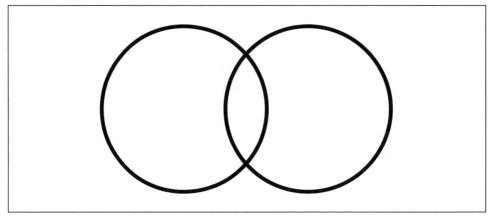

Figure 5.7   Semantic Map

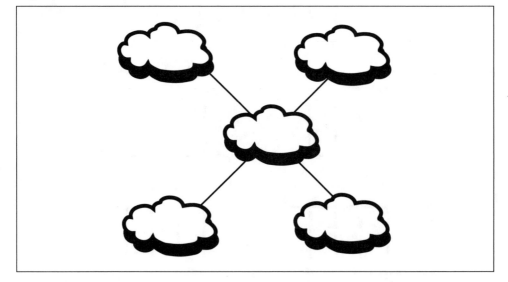

Figure 5.8 Grouping/Classifying

	Number of Wheels			Powered by		Travel by		
	1	2	4	foot	motor	land	water	air
Bicycle	−	+	−	+	−	+	−	−
Car								
Airplane								
Boat								

- Nouns, adjectives, or verbs
- Topics and subtopics (words about plants, communities)
- Practical function (parts of the computer; joining words)
- Linguistic function (words for requesting, apologizing, demanding, or denying)
- Dissimilarity or opposition (friendly/unfriendly, dangerous/safe)
- Synonyms

Word Banks

Words generated from the prior activity can be written on color-coded cards to represent the different groups. These cards can also become the word bank of the student. The cards can be used for peer-learning activities in which students drill each other for meaning, concept mastery, or spelling. These cards can also be kept in envelopes or in a key-ring binder, or they can be hung on strings from the ceiling for easy consultation during writing activities.

Imagery

Visual images are a potent device to aid recall of verbal material. This is particularly so for the large proportion of learners who have a preference for visual learning. The students can be asked to picture in their minds or make a manual drawing of the meaning of an association or a sequence. Even the mental representation of the letters of a word is helpful.

Cognates and False Cognates

Students can be asked to identify a familiar word in their own language that sounds like the new word (e.g., *discussion* and *discusión*). This

Figure 5.9 Word Bank

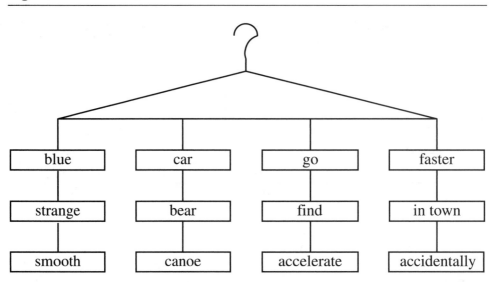

becomes an auditory link to meaning. The sound can also accompany a visual image to strengthen recall. However, some words may sound the same but may not mean the same—for example, *library* and *librería* (bookstore). Remind students that these words sound alike but do not mean the same thing. Here is a small sample:

Cognates	False Cognates
Exponente (exponent)	*Atender* (assist)
Cámara (camera)	*Asistir* (attend)
Cafetería (cafeteria)	*Librería* (bookstore)
Cable (cable)	*Biblioteca* (library)
Director (director)	*Embarazada* (pregnant)

Physical Response

Students can physically act out a new expression or idiom, such as "pouring the poison into his ear," "going into a frenzy," and so on. They can also relate a new expression to a feeling or sensation, such as *freezing, lukewarm, heavy,* or *bumpy.* Abstract concepts such as *trial, betrayal,* and so forth can be scripted out, rehearsed, and role-played.

Sentence Elaboration

Writing complete and elaborate sentences can be practiced through activities for defining, identifying negative and positive examples, using sentence expansion strategies, and webbing words and phrases to develop meaningful and correct sentences.

Dictionaries and Thesauruses

Sentence elaboration activities are also one way of teaching students the use of dictionaries and thesauruses. But dictionary exercises should be done only once in a while. Often, we see these take the place of all other vocabulary-building activities. Initially, the students can work with a "buddy." They look up words, write elaborate sentences with the different meanings of word, and then learn spelling or meanings together. This can also be done in teams.

Think Aloud or Metacognition

ESL students need to learn to develop a plan to solve problems on their own and use learning strategies. The teacher says aloud any thinking or decision-making she or he is doing during a procedure. Next, the teacher describes his or her actions step-by-step while doing a task. Finally, the teacher goes back to Step 1 and says the whole procedure all over again. When a procedure or plan does not succeed, the teacher and students can retrace their steps to investigate another way to solve the problem or improve the product. Chapter 6 shows posters for metacognitive strategies for writing. These can be constructed for reading and other subjects by teachers and students.

Highlighting

Second-language learners sometimes benefit from highlighting vocabulary or a key concept with the help of other students or as a whole-group activity with the teacher through the following:

Dramatic use of color	<u>Underlining</u>
bold type	*Italics*
CAPITAL LETTERS	Initial Capitals
BIG WRITING	*stars*
Text Box	circles = ©
Shadow	dingbats ✂📖•

Learning Logs

Learning logs can be used as personalized concept organizers, vocabulary dictionaries, and learning tools for recording the following:

- Words and their definitions
- Assignments
- Personal goals and objectives
- Words students hear or read and want to learn
- Summaries of what they read or hear
- Records of errors they want to work on
- The reasons they think they are making those errors
- Strategies that are helping them learn the content

TEACHING TECHNIQUES FOR READING SUBJECT MATTER TEXTS

As students begin to read in their second language, they will need some initial assistance to ensure development of the appropriate reading strategies for content texts.

Reading and Listening Comprehension

- Model reading content area text (e.g., math explanation or problem; a history paragraph) before they begin reading the selection on their own. When you model reading aloud, demonstrate and elaborate many of the important subtle techniques such as pronunciation of words and whole sentences, as well as dramatic voice inflection to add meaning and emotion to the written word.
- Model how to ask comprehension questions or "think aloud" as you are reading, so they can learn metacognitive devises during their silent reading.

Partner Reading

ESL students are partnered with an English reader during English time. SSL students are partnered with a Spanish reader during Spanish time. The reader is taught how to help the second-language student through the partner reading process. At first, it is vital to ask partners to read alternate sentences aloud. Later, they can move on to paragraphs. As they are reading, ask them to stop and discuss portions of the reading, and then summarize at the end what they have read.

Echo Reading

The teacher reads a sentence and students repeat it, following along with their books.

Shadow Reading

A more fluent reader reads a sentence and the partner repeats it, following along in his or her book. After a few pages, the new reader attempts to read each sentence on his or her own, and the partner helps only when necessary.

Whisper Reading

Whisper reading is done in triads. While two students are partner reading, a new reader sits between them and whispers along with each partner. The students read the same segments again, but this time the new reader reads during his or her turn aloud. Partners assist only if necessary.

Silent Reading

Silent reading can occur after partner reading because it helps students reinforce their reading and anchor their understanding.

Sponge Activities

While partners are waiting for others to finish reading or a task, they can do any of these sponge activities to reinforce their learning:

- Discuss what they learned
- Map out main ideas or critical elements
- Find word meanings they don't know
- Work on their word banks
- Give each other pretests on pronunciation, spelling, and meaning
- Practice the answers missed
- Work on the pronunciation of new words
- Write in their journal or learning log

INSTRUCTIONAL TIPS FOR DIFFERENT STAGES OF LANGUAGE ACQUISITION

The California English-language development (ELD) standards are very helpful in identifying the stages of oral language proficiency in a second language. These standards are synthesized here, along with tips for addressing the individual student's instructional needs at his or her level (for additional information on the ELD standards and curricula, please contact the California State Department of Education or any county office of education).

Stage 1: Beginning

The student begins to speak with a few words, answers simple questions, uses common social greetings and repetitive phrases, and demonstrates comprehension of simplified language.

- Provide a lot of opportunities to model all new vocabulary and allow students to listen to the rhythm, sounds, and patterns of English by using

  Songs, chants, and simple poems
  Pairs or teams of preproduction students with more advanced speakers
- Provide background knowledge through contextual clues such as

  Emphasizing picture clues
  Using total physical response (TPR) movement during all activities
  Encouraging use of art, music, pantomime, and other forms of creative expression
- Listening centers are stocked with songs, taped versions of stories, riddles, new words, simple questions, and so on.
- Speaking activities begin with mimicking songs, whisper reading, and working cooperatively with puppets to perform a story students just read.
- Show students how to respond by using signals, pointing, gesturing, nodding, or drawing.
- For emergent writing, ask students to copy words and/or represent an idea in pictures or drawings.

Cooperative Learning Strategies for Stage 1 (see pp. 101-105)

- Team-building activities (logo, team name, banners) and simple team products
- Draw around
- Team TPR
- Buddy Buzz, Turn to Your Partner

Stage 2: Early Intermediate

The student begins to be understood with inconsistent grammar, asks or answers questions with simple sentences and vocabulary, retells familiar stories using some gestures, and recites familiar rhymes, song, and stories.

Stage 3: Intermediate

The student is understood when he or she speaks using standard grammar and pronunciation, but some rules are still missing; asks or answers instructional questions; actively participates in conversations; retells stories; and uses expanded vocabulary and paraphrasing.

- For emergent writing, ask students to label objects or pictures, copy phrases or sentences, and write in their journals through a combination of drawing and labeling; invented spelling is OK.
- Continue to provide the following:

    Modeling and peer learning opportunities
    Listening opportunities
    Context clues
- Partner SLL with dominant-speaking student (DSS). Model with a student on how to help the partner.
- Begin peer choral responses or shadow talk:

    DSS states answer to a question.
    SLL says answer *with* DSS.
    SLL says answer *without* DSS.
- Check SLL performance after each activity. Ensure 80% to 100% mastery of vocabulary and understanding of the task and protocols before moving on. Unmastered little items turn into big learning blocks!
- SLLs may write using words they have learned during this lesson plus a few *sketches* or *readles* (pictures representing a word).

Cooperative Learning Strategies for Stage 2 and Stage 3

- Team-building activities
- Team products in which students use drawings and one-word labels
- Roundtable for recall of vocabulary
- Buddy Buzz, Turn to Your Partner, and Think/Pair/Share
- Numbered Heads Together
- Team books
- Concept cards
- Tea Party

Stage 4: Early Advanced

> The student is understood when he or she uses consistent Standard English grammar, pronunciation, and intonation with random errors; asks or answers instructional questions with more detail; actively participates and initiates conversations on unfamiliar topics; retells stories in greater detail; and recognizes appropriate ways of speaking.

- Since the focus at this stage of development is on comprehension and communication, ask open-ended questions and help the student describe, explain, compare, expand, restate, enrich, and retell small portions of the story.
- Provide more opportunities for students to create longer oral narratives, story retell, and written responses to text questions and writing prompts.
- Ask for complete sentences and improved punctuation and spelling. However, correctness is still not the most important issue to stress; connected discourse and more extensive vocabulary are the goal at this stage.
- Focus on teaching and practicing reading comprehension strategies.

Cooperative Learning Strategies for Stage 4

- Team-building activities
- Team products with more narrative
- Roundtable for brainstorming
- Buddy Buzz, Turn to Your Partner, and Think/Pair/Share
- Numbered Heads Together
- Team books
- Concept cards
- Tea Party
- Simple jigsaw

Stage 5: Advanced

> The student is understood when speaking, using consistent standard grammar, pronunciation, and intonation; negotiates and initiates social conversations; and uses idiomatic expressions and appropriate ways of speaking that vary by purpose and audience.

- Structure more student team discussions.
- Encourage increased levels of accuracy and correctness in oral, reading, and writing activities.

Cooperative Learning Strategies for Stage 5

Any cooperative learning strategy or method is beneficial for Stage 5 students.

COOPERATIVE LEARNING STRATEGIES FOR SECOND-LANGUAGE LEARNING

Cooperative learning strategies are most important for second-language learning. They provide opportunities for students to practice their new language in safe contexts. Cooperative learning is basic to the development and use of communicative skills and social interaction skills. Combined, they help produce higher academic gains (Sharan & Sharan, 1994, 1997; Slavin, 1997). The list of cooperative learning strategies included here can be used as a starting point. More comprehensive models include group investigation, group inquiry, team games and tournaments (Sharan & Sharan, 1997; Slavin, 1997), and the bilingual cooperative integrated reading and composition (BCIRC) model (Calderón, 1991; Calderón, Hertz-Lazarowitz, & Slavin, 1998).

Buddy Buzz, Think/Pair/Share, or
Turn to Your Neighbor and Say/Write/Draw

During or after reading a selection or a math problem, students turn to their neighbor and ask questions regarding what they have read. The teacher can also give the following directives for a Buddy Buzz. To vary the process, sometimes ask for oral responses; other times, ask for a list of three words or a complete sentence. These responses can be requested in writing or with quick drawings.

Check your answers.

Find the main idea.

Describe the main character.

Make a prediction about. . . .

Tell your neighbor the questions at the end of the story.

Provide a new title and a new ending for the story.

Show your neighbor the sentences you wrote with the new vocabulary words and check each other's sentences.

Discuss with your neighbor the questions at the end of the story.

Discuss with your neighbor what you want to write about.

Draw a simple graph to illustrate the concept.

Write a three-sentence description of. . . .

Provide an alternative method for solving a problem or an inquiry question for the science project.

Brainstorming in Groups

Students brainstorm as many answers, ideas, or facts about a particular topic as they can. They (1) record their ideas, (2) prioritize, and (3) reach consensus on the best choices.

Havruta

In pairs, one student takes the role of the teacher and explains different story elements to his or her partner, who takes the role of the learner. For the next selection, they reverse the roles, and the learner becomes the teacher and vice versa.

Numbered Heads Together

In this strategy, groups of four students first select their team name. Each team member is assigned a number (1, 2, 3, or 4). Teams discuss a given question for 2 minutes. Students must make sure that everyone in the group is prepared to answer the question. The teacher then randomly picks a number and a team name out of a "hat." One student from that team answers for the group. Then, the teacher selects another question, and after 2 minutes another number and team name is called. One way to vary this activity is to call a number and have all the team representatives with that number stand, with each student giving a different point of view.

Learning Buddies

During an experiment, a math process, or the reading of a selection, teams of students meet with three or four students from other teams in different corners of the room for 4 to 5 minutes to

Clarify information

Review answers to questions

Review for tests

Practice meaning, spelling, or vocabulary words

Roundtable

Students sit in a small circle. Only one paper and pencil are used. After one student writes a response, the paper and pencil are passed to the student on his or her right. The next student writes a response and passes the paper and pencil to the right. They continue this process until the teacher calls time-out (usually 2 minutes). This strategy can be used for

Writing the names of the states, presidents, chemical elements, and so on

Brainstorming adjectives to describe a particular character

Writing words that come to mind when students hear a word such as *democracy,* knowing that this is a key word in an upcoming chapter

Writing one word or sentence to describe their feelings after they have finished reading a selection

Write Around

This strategy is basically the same as Roundtable, except that all students have their own paper and pencil and need about 7 to 8 minutes because the students write in full sentences.

Students retell a story they just read and then edit each one.

Students create their own stories based on the story they just read.

Students summarize chapters. Each student writes the first line of the summary; the paper then goes around the table, and each student adds a line. The group ends up with four summaries.

Freewriting of a creative story. All students start with an open-ended sentence, finish that sentence, and pass it on. They keep adding to each other's stories until they wind up with four separate stories. The team can select one of the stories, edit and revise it, add a powerful conclusion, and then read it to the class.

Character Mapping

Students work in groups of four to complete a graphic organizer or a character map. Students choose a character from the story that they have just read and identify basic traits or attributes for that character. Students then make a picture of the character and use key words to describe the character. For second-language students, pictures can be drawn when the vocabulary words are not yet in the students' repertoire.

Story Mapping

Each team is assigned a different story or chapter. The map includes the title of the selection, setting, main characters, main idea, events, and ending or conclusion of the important facts from a social studies chapter. Then each group presents its map to the rest of the class.

Story Retell/Chapter Retell

Students sit with a partner, face-to-face, and take turns retelling the story (or information from a chapter) with as much fidelity and detail as possible. Partners learn to probe or cue one another as they take turns telling the story or important information from the chapter.

In-House Jigsaw

Each of the four students in a team is responsible for reading one part of a chapter or story and then teaches the information to the rest of the team. In this way, the jigsaw puzzle parts become a whole. Other examples of jigsawing include the following:

Lists of questions to answer

Mastering mathematical or scientific processes

Putting together a team project

Tea Party

For this strategy, the class is first divided into two groups. The groups form two concentric circles in the middle of the room and face each other. Students in the outer (or inner) circle get a list of questions related to a selection just read. Each pair of students then answers the first question, and the students in the outer circle move one step to the right. They face a new partner and work on a new question. Students continue to move to other partners until they answer all the questions. There are other variations for using this strategy. For example, the inner circle is given the definition of the words while the outer circle is given the vocabulary words. Sometimes, both work on the answer. When there isn't sufficient space, two or three concentric circles are formed in different areas of the class.

Team Product

After reading a story, or as a culminating activity to any lesson, students can select a topic of interest they want to investigate further. Each team works on a different product and presents it to the class.

Team Books

In teams, students write creative stories that are based on certain elements of a story just read. After prewriting, writing, revising, and editing their stories, each team makes a creative book to publish their story. The books can be shape books, big books, tiny books, box books, accordion books, or any type of creative books.

Team Practice and Drill

Students drill each other for 10-minute periods on specific skills, content, or preparation for state-mandated tests. They work in pairs, then do a round-robin in which all four members take turns answering a question or memorizing a fact.

Concept Cards

Give a pretest on vocabulary, meaningful sentences, and so on.

Students create color-coded cards on the words or problems each one missed. Each student on the team has a different-colored card.

Students tutor each other with the cards. Tutors hold up the card. The tutee reads the question (answer is seen by tutor only), and the tutee attempts to answer. If the answer is correct, the card is "won back" by the tutee; if not, it is placed on the bottom of the deck to be repeated. When the tutee wins back all his or her cards, the tutor and tutee roles are switched.

Students take a practice test.

Repeat the practice and testing if necessary.

Give final test, scoring, and recognition.

Tear-Ups

Each team will tear two sheets of different-colored construction paper into creative pieces. The members will study the pieces and imagine what figures the pieces represent. The team writes a group story and pastes the pieces beside the story portions that match. The teams share their stories.

SUMMARY

This chapter highlights the importance of oral language development in the first language (L1) and second language (L2) and ways of using a variety of instructional strategies that can be integrated into any lesson. Researchers such as Biemiller (1999) remind us of the importance of vocabulary and oral fluency. Biemiller suggested that students learn roughly 1,200 root words per school year, or 6 per school day, prior to Grade 4.

Bringing a child to grade-level language comprehension means that the child must acquire and use grade-level vocabulary plus some post–grade-level vocabulary. Lack of knowledge of vocabulary can ensure failure. A child's maximum level of reading comprehension is determined by the child's level of listening comprehension and vocabulary development. Therefore, teachers need to do much more than they do now to develop language in L1 and most certainly in L2. If a monolingual child is expected to learn 1,200 root words a year, does that mean that TWI programs need to develop twice as many in 50-50 programs? What is the range of vocabulary development proposed in your program? How can your program ensure that no SLL will lag behind mainstream speakers of that language in vocabulary? Are the books that have been selected controlling the development of vocabulary? Overloading the minds of the students? Are the teachers' delivery styles controlling or overloading vocabulary? These are some questions the school's curriculum committee might want to discuss extensively and then take the appropriate actions to make sure that teachers and materials do have a positive impact on language development and comprehension.

6

Literacy in Two Languages

The Importance of Research–Based Instructional Models

Instructional models do make a difference in student outcomes (Joyce, Weil, & Showers, 1992). A model is the way instructional strategies, methods, and techniques are put together. But not all models are effective. Unless they have been studied and proven effective, a set of instructional strategies may only turn out to be the popular trend for the moment. The reading field has also realized that reading instruction must be based on research, incorporating factors that make up a comprehensive reading program. Particularly for students who lag behind during the first few grades, a comprehensive reading program can improve their reading significantly. Better yet, early prevention of reading difficulties is overwhelmingly accomplished through research-based programs (Chall, 1996; Curtis & Longo, 1999; Snow et al., 1998).

A model should have the following criteria: effectiveness and replicability. A program model is considered to be effective if evaluations that compare students who participated in the program with similar students in matched comparison or control groups find that the program students perform significantly better on measures of academic performance. Once the program model is tested, it should be replicated to ensure validity and viability for wide use. The best evidence that a program is replicable is if it in fact has been replicated elsewhere and found to be effective in sites beyond its initial pilot locations (Slavin & Fashola, 1998).

TYPES OF INSTRUCTIONAL MODELS

There are several families of models: information processing, social, personal, and behaviorist (Joyce et al., 1992). Some of these apply to content-area learning such as science and social studies in a second language, such as the cooperative learning, inquiry, and concept attainment models. However, the field of second-language learning has also developed its own models. Some of the most popular ones include total physical response, Suggestopedia, audio-lingual, the natural approach, and many eclectic versions that combine listening, speaking, reading, and writing activities (Ovando & Collier, 1998). For the most part, these focus on oral language development, as outlined in Chapter 4. They are rarely integrated with the teaching of reading and writing, which is also a vital part of learning. We read to learn. Second-language learners need extensive reading to learn. Teaching in two languages is a fairly new field that is also in need of model testing. However, comprehensive reviews of the literature on the development of language, cognitive, and social skills for K–12 students point to the strong evidence that all these skills, measured in a variety of ways, can be significantly improved with effective teaching.

TRADITIONAL MODELS
FOR TEACHING READING

Instead of using a research-based instructional model of bilingual reading, most schools still use basals to guide instruction. Allington (1990) found that most lessons offered in teacher basal guides were designed more to assess student recitation proficiency than to improve that proficiency. The lessons focused more on immediate recall of the information than on the development of thinking while reading. The teacher guides were full of activities, but most were "mindless, useless activities" such as recall questions for oral interrogation, written end-of-chapter questions, worksheets with crossword puzzles, hidden word searches, vocabulary definition tasks, and other such busy time killers. The lessons and tasks simply assessed whether students could adequately respond to low-level questions, rarely tapping higher order thinking and comprehension skills.

Although most basals have modified their approaches since 1990, they still leave many gaps in the students' bank of reading, writing, and oral skills. More current studies (Elmore, Peterson, & McCarthy, 1996; Pressley, Rankin, & Yokoi, 2000; Turner & Paris, 1995) show that in the typical classroom, the tasks assigned as "reading" overwhelmingly emphasize copying, remembering, and reciting a few low-level items on what the students read individually. The situation for struggling readers seems even more dire (Allington, 2001; Johnston & Allington, 1991). Researchers consistently report that lower achieving readers spend little of their instructional time on comprehension tasks of any sort. Struggling readers simply read less often in their classrooms, with limited tasks on comprehension. Instead, for these students, the lesson focus is often on words, letters, and sounds through phonics, drills, or recall questions on worksheets. The typical pattern of interaction during the reading of texts has been the IRE pattern of instruction: initiate, respond, and evaluate. That is, the teacher initiates interaction with a question, one or two students respond to the question, and the teacher evaluates that response by usually saying "good" or "that's right." This type of instruction rarely generates rich discussion, language acquisition, student thinking, and equal turns for all students.

EFFECTS OF LITERACY INSTRUCTION IN THE PRIMARY LANGUAGE

Considerable evidence shows that readers use knowledge of their native language as they read in a second language. Second-language learners transfer skills between Spanish and English for phonological awareness, word recognition, oral discourse skills, vocabulary, comprehension strategies, and writing (August, Carlo, & Calderón, 2002). The higher the threshold level of literacy in Spanish, the easier it is to transfer those skills into English (August & Hakuta, 1997; Cummins, 1981). When reading comprehension is explicitly taught, it affects all learning (Pearson & Fielding, 1997; Pressley, Johnson, Symons, McGoldrick, & Kurita, 1990). Research with native English speakers indicates that small-group instruction focusing on building basic skills in phonological awareness, orthographic processing, phonics, decoding, and fluency is the basis for higher comprehension skills.

Vocabulary and comprehension strategies are critical as learners become more skilled readers. Therefore, it is imperative that explicit instruction be used to teach these skills. In some cases, it will be more beneficial for the student to receive this instruction in the primary language (L1); in other cases, the student might be ready to be instructed in the second language (L2). If a student is assessed and found to have a high threshold level of literacy in the primary language, that student will be able to develop literacy in L2 in a much shorter timeframe than a student who tested at a low level in L1. This is possible because skills first taught in L1 transfer into the second language (L2) and facilitate faster learning of L2 (August et al., 2002).

EMERGING MODELS OF READING FOR TWO-WAY INSTRUCTION

Two-way bilingual (TWB) models of teaching can be constructed by putting together effective components that had been previously tested or were tested in the implementation of a TWB. The models reported here center on reading. These biliteracy models attempt to integrate oral language proficiency, reading, writing, and cooperative learning methods, strategies, and techniques that have been proven effective. They also lend themselves for content-area reading, rich discussions, and descriptive and informative types of writing. They adhere to basic principles of first- and second-language learning and teaching. An effective model of teaching and the training of instructors for that model(s) begin by establishing high expectations for the students.

Expected Outcomes for L1 and L2 Learners

- High scores on standardized tests
- Peer collaboration and social skills
- Personal responsibility for learning and teaching their peers
- Abilities for problem solving, informational text comprehension, and writing
- Motivation, independence, and persistence in accomplishing learning goals
- High degrees of L1 and L2 proficiency and literacy

Basic Principles of an Effective Instructional Model

Effective literacy instruction requires changes in the way second-language learners (SLLs) in bilingual or English as a Second Language (ESL) programs have been traditionally taught. Now that all SLLs will be integrated, a different approach must be taken to ensure that it is not a sink-or-swim situation for any of them. While the major challenge is changing traditional instructional practices, we have identified other changes that need to take place to ensure a context for student success.

In this book, we use the terms *English learners* and *Spanish learners* as examples for the different languages currently used in two-way immersion (TWI) programs (Cantonese, Japanese, etc.). Our purpose is to simplify the reading, but it is our hope that TWI becomes more and more a multilingual approach.

Effective TWB Instruction

- English learners (ELs) and Spanish learners (SLs) need to be immersed in text.
- ELs and SLs need to receive many demonstrations of how texts are constructed and used.
- Larger blocks of uninterrupted teaching and learning time are needed.
- Instead of individual desks or long tables, the classroom should be furnished with tables for teams of four.
- Instead of multiple copies of a single text, have four copies of multiple texts from a variety of genre.
- Each teacher owns an extensive repertoire of reading strategies (from decoding to comprehension).
- Teacher mediation and peer support are used in the development of reading for meaning, especially the problem-solving strategies that undergird independent reading.
- Literacy development, including the learning of strategies, should occur during functional, meaningful, and relevant language use.
- Risk taking is an essential part of language learning. Learners should be encouraged to predict, share prior knowledge, argue a point, make mistakes, and self-correct.
- Careful placement of students must ensure they have the appropriate reading material that challenges but does not frustrate them.
- Opportunities to practice and apply the skills learned as they read extended text should follow any text reading.

Comprehensive Reading Model Components

The 10 components listed below are used by current reform models and are recommended by the National Research Council (Foorman, Francis, Fletcher, & Mehta, 1998; Slavin & Madden, 2001b, 2001c). These components can become part of a comprehensive literacy instructional model that can be conducted in both languages, using any of the programmatic models described in Chapter 5. Students are expected to engage in several activities that involve working with the instructor, with their teams, with their partners, and independently throughout the week. The purpose of this type of comprehensive reading is to teach language and comprehension strategies—how to read materials that become progressively more difficult and how to write using a variety of composition techniques.

1. *Background and vocabulary-building* strategies are used to introduce concepts and key vocabulary, as well as create interest in the reading selection.

2. *Listening comprehension/teacher reading aloud* is a selected body of texts having features that lend themselves for the teacher modeling of appropriate reading behaviors, as well as knowledge of language and content.

3. With *shared reading, guided reading, echo reading, partner reading,* and many other reading strategies, instructors and students work together on fluency and comprehension of text at a reading level slightly above the students' level.

4. *Direct instruction of reading skills* will range from decoding to comprehension, from phonemic awareness to pronunciation, from orthography to composition, and from simple responses to rich discussion protocols.

5. *Independent reading* offers a range of material at the students' reading level. This includes student self-selection as well as book club activities.

6. *Extensive guided conversations and discussions* on the content of the text probe students' insights and debrief the learning that is taking place. This includes rereading and extension activities.

7. *Vocabulary instruction* is explicit. Students are exposed to new vocabulary through in-depth and extensive experiences while listening to and talking about stories read to them, as well as learning words through fun activities.

8. In *interactive writing,* the instructor and students work together to compose the variety of texts relevant to the adult learners' writing needs. This includes the use of technology for the written products.

9. In *independent writing,* students are given time to plan, draft, revise, edit, and publish or present their own writing.

10. *Instructor's assessment and follow-up* measure students' growth as readers, as well as their ability to handle a range of increasingly difficult text as a vehicle for learning and applying new skills. The instructor's role is to listen, take notes, and plan for follow-up teaching or reteaching.

SEQUENCING INSTRUCTION FOR READING

On the basis of the current knowledge base and research about reading, the National Research Council (NRC) agreed on the following premises about reading (Snow et al., 1998):

- Reading should be defined as a process of getting meaning from print.

- Reading requires using knowledge about the written alphabet.
- Reading assumes knowledge about the sound structure of oral language for the purposes of achieving understanding.
- Reading instruction should include direct teaching of information about sound-symbol relationships to children who do not know about them.
- Reading instruction must maintain a focus on the communicative purposes and personal value of reading.
- The key to preventing reading difficulties is excellent instruction.

For two-way bilingual programs, excellent instruction in reading means that a teacher is well prepared in either or both target languages to teach phonemic awareness, phonological awareness, decoding strategies, comprehension strategies, vocabulary, background knowledge, communication strategies, spelling, and composition. We do not advocate putting too much emphasis on one component (e.g., phonics) over another (e.g., teacher read-alouds).

Summaries of the NRC report (Bickart, 1998) intertwined with our own studies (Slavin & Calderón, 2001) are given below to help plan a balanced curriculum and its professional development components. Later in the chapter, we present examples of instructional strategies, methods, and techniques that address the NRC recommendations.

Pre-Kindergarten and Kindergarten

Curricula include activities to do the following:

- Stimulate verbal interaction
- Enrich children's vocabulary
- Talk about books
- Practice the sound structure of words
- Develop knowledge about print
- Recognize and produce letters of the alphabet
- Become familiar with basic purposes and mechanisms for reading

Although there is a popular belief that the NRC promotes mainly a phonics approach to reading, it is important to highlight its emphasis on oral language development. The NRC stresses that these elements should be found in every kindergarten classroom:

- Oral language activities
- Language play
- Teacher read-aloud times and discussions with children
- Use of big books, predictable books, and rebus books

- Language experience activities
- Play-based instruction

Listening to stories read aloud by the teacher in L1 and L2 is a way to provide receptive and expressive vocabulary in addition to modeling reading. Pre-K and K teachers can use Spanish and English trade books to

- Introduce children to the characteristics of stories (plot, characters, setting, problem, solution, author's craft)
- Extend vocabulary, depth of knowledge, and background building
- Vary activities often to lengthen attention spans
- Create an atmosphere of pleasure related to languages and books in different languages
- Allow children to focus on the language and story line without doing the work of reading
- Provide children with literary models of writing
- Provide children with multicultural awareness and respect for other cultures through multicultural literature selections
- Provide a way to introduce science and social studies topics
- Provide opportunities for story retell through dramatic retellings, sequence cards, and other partner activities

Increasing letter knowledge (the ability to distinguish and identify the letters of the alphabet) and phonemic awareness (understanding that spoken words are composed of smaller units of sound) helps children begin to understand how the English or Spanish alphabets work. *This does not mean teaching phonics through drills.* It means teaching through research-based activities, such as the following:

- Learning poetry and songs that are alliterative or rhyme
- Finding objects in the classroom whose names begin or end with the same sound
- Doing clapping activities to identify the syllables in words
- Analyzing each other's names to make discoveries about letters and sounds
- Making charts about letter/sound discoveries

First-Grade Reading

Poor instruction in first grade may have long-term effects.... The primary job of first-grade teachers is to make sure that all of their students become readers.

— *Snow et al. (1998, pp. 26, 194)*

Effective first-grade teachers build on the activities described in the excellent kindergarten classrooms. First-grade teachers continue with listening comprehension activities, adding more complex strategies for deriving meaning. In addition, the teacher-directed instruction on reading should be designed to develop the following:

- Enriched vocabulary
- Greater awareness and practice with the sound structures of language
- Increased familiarity with spelling-sound relationships
- Conventional spelling of basic words
- Sight recognition of frequently used words
- Independent reading

Direct instruction on reading comprehension should include discussions for the following:

- Summarizing the main idea
- Predicting what will happen next
- Drawing inferences
- Checking whether ideas make sense

Second- to 12th-Grade Reading

While the challenge of first grade is to decode text and find meaning in it, the challenge of second and third grade is to develop the ability to analyze, critique, abstract and reflect on text so that by the fourth grade children can absorb new information efficiently by reading.

— *Bickart (1998, p. 10)*

Fostering independent and productive reading in second grade and beyond builds on the decoding and comprehension skills developed in kindergarten and first grade. If a second-grade student arrives at school without the rich instruction provided in K–1, it will be necessary to begin with the development of those basic skills before placing the student in second-grade instruction with other children who have those skills. The same strategy applies to older students who enter in the third, fifth, or ninth grades without a solid literacy base in L1 or L2. This does not mean, however, that middle and high school students should suffer through phonics drills. A carefully crafted age-appropriate program should be developed or adopted for middle school TWB programs.

Once the foundation for the alphabetic principle (phonemic and phonological awareness) is developed, along with basic decoding and comprehension skills, the students at a 2.0 reading level and beyond will benefit from the following in L1 and L2:

- Exposure to a variety of reading materials
- Engagement in thinking about the text through self-questioning strategies
- Increased reading fluency
- Spelling lessons to promote phonemic awareness and letter-sound/sound-letter relationships
- Emphasis on comprehension and word recognition skills
- Writing techniques, conventions of print (e.g., capital letters, punctuation, grammar, spelling), and composition

STRUCTURING COMPONENTS FOR INTEGRATING LISTENING, SPEAKING, READING, AND WRITING

Each of the components described below can be adapted to teach listening comprehension, verbal production, reading, and writing. A school faculty can use these components to combine prereading, reading, postreading, and writing activities sequentially by grade level. The process for planning, testing, and refining the process is through action research by the teachers involved. This process is explained in Chapter 9 on teachers learning communities.

1. Background and Vocabulary Building

Materials Selection. One cannot stress enough the importance of identifying material that will challenge, but not overchallenge, the students and that is relevant to their needs. There are three types of text to select: (1) texts for the teacher to read to the students for listening comprehension and to model reading strategies, (2) texts at the level where students can read them with about 90 percent accuracy (with teacher support and an introduction), and (3) texts at an easier level for independent reading. The genre should include children's literature from different cultures, fiction and nonfiction, poetry, songs, chants, theater selections, newspapers, and other environmental print.

Although there are many popular children's literature trade books and basal selections, not all lend themselves to second-language reading. Some are too difficult (e.g., too many idioms, cultural background too different) and take too much time to explain. Others are too simplistic and do not elicit rich conversations or have good story elements.

The following are questions to guide selection of texts:

- Is it interesting and relevant to the students' content needs?
- What is the readability (lexile) level?
- Are the text's features appropriate: length, layout, cohesiveness, and places for segmentation and analysis (where the teacher can stop and ask meaningful questions)?
- Does the text offer opportunities to highlight certain comprehension strategies?
- Does the text offer opportunities to problem solve?
- What are five high-frequency words that need to be introduced before reading?
- What are five other high-frequency words the students will need for vocabulary development?

The introduction to concepts, words, or language patterns needs to be brief (5-7 minutes). This introduction includes the following subcomponents: developing concepts, creating interest, introducing vocabulary, establishing the purpose for reading, and modeling the reading comprehension skills the students will need when they read similar texts independently. The teacher can select two or three different strategies that are most appropriate for a reading selection. The following checklist or poster can help the teacher vary the election of introductory activities.

Instructional Strategies Before Reading

- Motivating
- Activating prior knowledge
- Building text-specific knowledge
- Relating the reading to students' lives
- Preteaching vocabulary
- Preteaching concepts
- Prequestioning
- Predicting
- Direction setting/purpose for reading
- Suggesting comprehension strategies

Motivating, Activating Prior Knowledge, and Building Text-Specific Knowledge. The teacher connects the new concepts with the students' previous experiences or readings. Visual props may be needed to build background experiences. Concepts can be built through discussions centering on the title, illustrations, personal experiences of the students, films, pictures, maps, or other audiovisual displays. Misconceptions or hazy understandings are clarified.

Creating Interest and Relating to Students' Lives. Student interest and motivation can be established from the beginning through the enthusiasm exhibited by the teacher and by merging prior knowledge with active participation such as brainstorming, group discussions, team discussions, or Turn-to-Your-Partner conversations. The teacher can use the same strategies as those in concept development or choose to read a short portion of the selection with some prediction questions or cliffhangers (see details for making predictions).

Vocabulary Introduction, Preteaching Vocabulary, and Concept Development. The brief introduction of vocabulary deals only with those words or idiomatic expressions that are critical and unlikely to be understood without some introduction. The teacher has five words written on the board or chart paper with short ESL- or SSL-friendly definitions for each. The teacher pronounces each word and reads the definition or the word in context. Then, the students do a choral reading of each. This is not the time for drill or word-attack skills. It is only for giving students oral familiarity with selected words. Later in the week, students will write sentences with these words and be tested on spelling, pronunciation, and meaning.

Establishing the Purpose, Direction Setting, and Suggesting Comprehension Strategies. The teacher sets the purpose for reading the selection by stating, for example, "We are going to read to find information about bats before we go to Carlsbad Caverns," or "Today, we are going to read to find examples of irony and how the author uses irony." A reading comprehension objective can also be stated, such as, "Today we're going to read to find examples of 'cause and effect' and apply it to our lives."

Assignments that require students to read the text and answer questions at the end of the selection without these introductory elements will probably not foster students' engagement with text and may even turn them off reading and learning. ELs and SLs need to be provided the kind of learning experiences that allow them to integrate their prior knowledge and interest with a purpose for reading, guide them as they read, and enable them to synthesize and evaluate the information they glean from the text. The first step in learning is by exposure to daily modeling of listening comprehension.

2. Listening Comprehension/Teacher Reading Aloud

Listening comprehension (LC) is an approach designed to facilitate building understanding of text ideas. It is used to teach the story grammar of narratives or to analyze the main concepts of expository text. This strategy is particularly useful when a reader's comprehension is limited by knowledge of certain word meanings or knowledge relating to the topic of the text, or if the text itself is ambiguous or lacks clear connections between ideas or concepts (Anderson, Reynolds, Schallert, & Goetz, 1977; Beck, McKeown, Worthy, Sandora, & Kucan, 1999; Pearson, Hansen, & Gordon, 1979). Reciprocal teaching (Palincsar & Brown, 1984) and listening comprehension (Slavin & Madden, 2001b, 2001c) encourage teachers to assume more active roles in teaching, modeling, and practicing the strategies used by proficient readers as they read and think aloud to students. This helps emergent readers learn how to actively search for meaning in any given text. At least 20 minutes of daily LC should be integrated into lessons.

Teacher Preparation and Segmenting Text for Listening Comprehension. Everyone is engaged in constructing meaning by going back and forth between the teacher reading small segments of text and discussing the ideas encountered. Decisions about where to stop reading a text and the type of question to use or reading strategy to model require preparation. Through *Read and Think Aloud,* teachers can model confusion, identify problematic language and difficult ideas in a text, and teach students how to reread for meaning, how to self-correct, and how to ask questions that focus student thinking. Teachers write the questions, strategies, or difficult vocabulary on Post-its and place them strategically throughout the text. Sometimes, a single sentence will be sufficient to emphasize meaning or a reading strategy. Other times, it takes three or four sentences or a whole paragraph.

The Process of Instruction. The teacher selects a variety of text genre: a newspaper, procedure manual, memorandum, flier, literature selection, poem, letter, or biography. Through oral reading to the students, the teacher can demonstrate how an experienced reader sometimes stops and questions what is being read to make sure that comprehension is occurring, how background knowledge can help us understand a text, how different markings on a page can affect meaning, and how to "read between the lines" for some hidden meaning.

The purpose of all these methods, techniques, and strategies is to provide students opportunities to observe the instructor modeling how proficient readers and speakers of English maneuver through texts and acquire information. The more strategies a teacher models, the more tools the students have to apply in the next set of activities as they engage in their own reading, thinking, and discussions of texts. Good readers first develop comprehension by listening to a teacher read aloud and model comprehension strategies. Some "think-aloud" techniques to model a variety of comprehension strategies are as follows:

Comprehension Strategies During Reading

- Determining which information is most important
- Self-questionning
- Summarizing
- Inferring
- Predicting
- Interpreting
- Imaging
- Skimming
- Decoding unfamiliar words
- Deriving meaning from context clues
- Using prior knowledge
- Monitoring own reading
- Having a positive attitude and interest in reading

The Think-Aloud Process

During a think-aloud, the instructor verbalizes her or his thoughts while reading aloud.

- Select a passage that has at least three long paragraphs. Read the first paragraph aloud. The students can have a copy to follow along, or they can just listen.
- The passage should have points that will pose some difficulties, such as ambiguity and unknown words.
- Model your thinking. When you come to a trouble spot, stop and think through it aloud while students listen. "I wonder what they mean here? Could it be. . . ?"
- Model self-correction. Make a mistake reading a word. Back up and blend sounds or syllables together. Reread the whole sentence fluently.
- After you have completed the passage, ask the students to tell you what you were doing or saying.
- Pair up students and have them practice the procedure with the second paragraph. Each can take turns reading and responding to the other.
- Have students use the procedure with the third paragraph as they read silently.
- Debrief the activity: What did we do? Why? How? What did you learn about yourself?

Select other passages each time to illustrate other comprehension strategies. The more strategies you model in your read-alouds, the more that students will use when they read.

- Read with exaggerated fluency, adding a sense of the dramatic, as you create voices for different characters, different procedures, rules and regulations, and so on.
- Vary prosodic elements of pitch, volume, phrasing, and rate.
- Model asking yourself questions about what you read after each paragraph.
- Model summarizing each paragraph.
- Debriefing questions: What parts stood out for you? Why? Did any parts need clarification? Which strategy helped you remember more of what I read? What strategies will you use?

The Process of Creating Imagery/Mind Movies

Imagery is used to aid understanding, remember detail, construct inferences, and make predictions.

- Select a brief passage that contains much description so that students can see how words help form mental pictures.
- Read and stop two or three times to model how you are forming images in your mind as you read (e.g., "This reminds me of the beach in Hawaii during Christmas when the lights. . . ." or "I can see the long arms on that machine and I can hear it crying in pain as its arms bend with so much weight. . . .").
- Provide students with guided practice. Continue reading the passage or another passage and invite students to tell about their images.
- Either pair or group students and give one member a passage to read silently. After preparing, ask the student to read it aloud to the team members and to talk about the mental images she or he is forming. Invite other students in the team to share their images and to explain what caused them to form the particular image.
- Debrief the activity. Have a couple of students share their images. How did this help you create meaning? Why will you remember those details?

Variation of Imagery/Mind Movies. You ask the students to follow along as you read orally and to stop you to ask about what you are thinking at a given time with questions such as the following: How did you figure out "x" word? How did you clarify what the writer is saying? How would you summarize what you read? What kind of mind movie were you making?

The Process for Directed Listening Thinking Activity (DLTA)

DLTA is used as the teacher reads aloud, stopping at appropriate points along the way to engage students in ongoing discussion or meaning making through predictions. You'll need an interesting passage, such as a chapter from an easy-to-read novel, a biography, or a hot newspaper article. Select the pages or sections where you will stop and ask questions. Write the question on a Post-it and put it on the page. You can use one color of Post-its for predictions and a different color for other types of questions.

- Before reading the text, begin by relating the topic to the students' lives.
- Invite students to make predictions based on the topic, the title of the selection, or a picture it might contain.
- Read the text aloud as the students listen. Stop at designated points to confirm or change predictions and to make new predictions or ask a question about what is happening up to this point.
- Read to the next logical point, and again confirm, question, discuss, and make new predictions. Say, "We are now going to continue reading to find out what causes that" or "Let's see if our predictions are on target; let me continue reading."
- When you are finished, ask students to summarize the main idea, the problem, the solution, the procedure, the lesson to be learned, and what they read between the lines.
- Debriefing questions: What did you learn from DLTA? How will you use those strategies?

Predictions

Making Predictions

Ask students to make predictions and to tell "why" they think that. All predictions are accepted. Be careful not to confirm or dispel predictions. Don't tell a student "that's right" or "that's not a good prediction." All predictions are hypotheses and therefore must be tested as we read on.

Testing Predictions

Do all the students make predictions?

Are the predictions wild and random?

Are the predictions based on the logic of the text?

Can they give reasons for their predictions?

Variation of DLTA. Students can preread the questions about the text and listen to the teacher read a portion of the text. At the end of the section, students can discuss if their questions have been answered.

Using Typographical Signals During Reading

Typographical signals help readers better understand the message. Commas, for example, signal when to pause to create the intended meaning. See the following table, for example.

Signal	Meaning	Example
Comma	Need for pause; placement affects meaning	Kay, my friend is as smart as you. Kay, my friend, is as smart as you.
Period	Need a longer pause	The desert is beautiful.
Question mark	Need to raise intonation at the end of a sentence	Will you really? The desert is beautiful?
Exclamation mark	Need to read with a certain emotion	It's a wonderful surprise!
Underlined, enlarged, and/or italicized print	Need for special stress	This is what <u>I</u> believe. <u>This</u> is what I believe.
Combination	Used to emphasize meaningful units	The El Paso desert is <u>SO</u> beautiful! Beauty *is* Sara.

- Select a passage where you can dramatize the effect of signals.
- Read it first in a monotone.
- Reread the sentence or sentences, using all typographic signals.
- Ask the students to point out the differences. Which reading interested them more? Did emphasizing different words and pausing on others give them a better understanding of the passage?
- Show the passage to the students. Point out the signals.
- Select passages where a variety of moods or emotions can be conveyed (e.g., excitement, joy, anger, love). Give each team a different passage for them to practice reading aloud to each other.
- Debriefing questions: How do signals help us understand what we are reading? What emotion were you trying to convey when you were reading?

Teaching Sequencing

The instructor or the students write several sentences on sentence strips that either were or were not in the text. Pictures or drawings can also be used for sequence activities. The students decide which events did happen and then arrange the order. They can do this activity in teams of four, where each team works with a different text. All teams share results.

3. Different Types of Shared Interactive Reading

Shared Reading

The purpose of shared reading is to review and teach the conventions of print by talking about the title, authors, introductory page, appendix, table of contents, and so forth.

- Introduce a variety of texts, pointing out their unique features. Point to and explain the features, asking questions such as the following: Which have a hard cover, and why? Which do not have authors, and why? What about this small print?
- Invite students to discuss how each of these formats conveys what type of message.
- Read portions from each.
- Continue discussion about messages and formats.
- Debriefing question: What did we discover about print?

Choral Reading/Readers Theater

Choral reading involves groups of students orally reading one text together, usually to make a meaningful and enjoyable performance. It is an excellent way to build teamwork during reading and to help the reluctant readers feel confident about their performance because it allows all readers to be successful.

- Select a text to be read as a group in unison. Poems, fables, short stories, and ritual text such as the Pledge of Allegiance are good choices.
- Model choral reading by first reading the text aloud to students.
- Discuss with the group how you use your voice to express meaning.
- Read the text chorally a couple of times over several days with students until they are comfortable performing by themselves.
- Ask them to bring texts they would like their team to use for choral reading next time.
- Debriefing questions: What did you like about choral reading? What did you learn?

Variations to Choral Reading/Readers Theater

- Line per person—each one reads a line at the appropriate time.
- Antiphonal reading—students are divided into two groups, and each group reads assigned parts alternately.
- Unison—the entire class reads together.

Echo Reading

In echo reading, the instructor, a mentor, a tutor, or more capable peer provides support, or *scaffolding,* for the reader. Echo reading is used when there are several struggling readers in the class. It helps to boost their confidence in reading.

- Select a simple text with short sentences.
- Model the process. Read one sentence, and the student rereads, or echoes, the same text.
- After modeling, assign partners.
- Students should choose their own texts, or you provide the easy texts.
- Ask students to find a comfortable spot in or outside the class to do their reading.
- Debriefing: Please share with us about your reading experience.

Partner Reading for Fluency

- Give students a simple passage that you know they will be able to read at least 80 percent with ease.
- Model partner reading with a student. Let that student correct you as you make an obvious mistake when it's your turn.
- Ask your students, "How did he help me?" and discuss polite ways of helping one another.
- Ask students to read the whole passage aloud, alternating sentences.
- Debriefing question: What are the benefits of partner reading?

Partner Reading for Comprehension

- Give students a simple but complete passage with a beginning, middle, and conclusion.
- Ask students to read aloud, this time by small paragraphs. As one student reads, the other listens and prepares to (1) summarize what the partner read, (2) think of a question the instructor might ask about that content, and (3) think of a question he or she might want to ask the instructor for further clarification or background information.

- Students alternate roles and read, synthesize, and analyze the next paragraph.
- After reading, ask the students to share their questions.
- Save their questions to use as a review quiz for the next class.

Question-Answer Relationships (QARs)

You can teach students how to formulate questions by using question-answer relationships such as the following:

- "Right there" are questions whose answers are explicitly stated in the text.
- "Think and search" are questions that have ideas stated in the text but in different places.
- "Our own" are questions that have answers that are not stated explicitly in the text.
- You can also give them a copy of Bloom-type question stems for questions at the recall, basic comprehension, application, analysis, synthesis, and evaluation levels of comprehension (see Figure 6.1).

Popcorn Reading

Students pop up from their seats and read their favorite sentences, paragraphs, or poems to others or to the whole class.

- Invite students to look back through something they have read previously and to find a favorite portion. They can use fiction, non-fiction, magazines, comics, and so on.
- Ask students to rehearse or practice their reading at home.
- Ask for volunteers to read their passages.
- The instructor can read his or her favorite passage, too.
- Debriefing questions: Why did you choose that passage? What did you do to prepare?

Variations of Popcorn Reading. For phonemic awareness, pronunciation, and intonation, use poetry and/or songs.

- Provide students with poems or songs.
- Discuss and emphasize the rhyme and rhythm of each as you read.
- Reread the whole poem once more.
- Provide time for students to rehearse in pairs.
- Ask for volunteers to share their reading.
- Debriefing question: What did you learn from this type of reading?

Figure 6.1a Bloom-Type Questions

CONOCIMIENTO	¿Qué pasó después…? ¿Quién fue…? ¿Puedes nombrar el…? Describe qué pasó… ¿Quién habló para…? ¿Puedes decirme por qué…?
COMPRENSIÓN	¿Podrías escribir con tus propias palabras…? Escribe un breve esquema… ¿Qué piensas que podría pasar la próxima vez…? ¿Quién fue…? ¿Cuál fue la idea principal…? ¿Quién fue el personaje principal?
APLICACIÓN	¿Conoces otra situación en donde…? ¿Podría pasar esto en…? ¿Podría reunir por características como…? ¿Qué factores cambiarían si…? ¿Podrías aplicar el método usado con tus experiencias? ¿Qué preguntas tendrías de…?
ANÁLISIS	¿Cuál evento no podría pasar si…? ¿Si…ocurriera, ¿cómo podría terminar? ¿En qué fué similar a…? ¿Cuál fué el tema principal de…? ¿Qué pudiste ver como otro posible resultado…? ¿Por qué…acontecieron cambios?

SÍNTESIS	¿Puedes diseñar un…para…?
	 ¿Cuál es la posible solución para…?
	 ¿Qué pasaría si…?
	   Si tuviste acceso para todos los recursos, ¿que
	     ofrecerías con…?
	 ¿Cómo podrías desviar tu propio camino para…?
	 ¿Cuántos caminos puedes…?

EVALUACIÓN	¿Hay una mejor solución para…?
	   Juzgar el valor de…
	   Defender tu posición acerca de…
	 ¿Piensas que…es una cosa buena o mala? Explica
	     por qué.
	 ¿Cómo podrías haber manejado…?
	 ¿Qué cambios para…recomendarías? ¿Por qué?

Figure 6.1b Bloom-Type Questions

KNOWLEDGE	How many…? Who was it that..? Can you name the…? What is…? Which is true or false…? Who was it that..? What happened after…?
COMPREHENSION	Do you know another instance where…? Could this have happened in…? Can you group by characteristics such as…? What factors would you change if…? Can you apply the method used to some experience of your own…? What questions would you ask of…?
APPLICATION	Can you write in your own words…? Write a brief outline… What do you think could have happened next…? What was the main idea? Who was the main character? Can you distinguish between…?
ANALYSIS	Which event could not have happened if…? If…happened, what might the ending have been? How was this similar to…? What was the underlying theme of…? What do you see as other possible outcomes? Why did…changes occur?
SYNTHESIS	What is a possible solution to…? What would happen if…? If you had access to all resources, how would you deal with…? How would you devise your own way to…? How many ways can you…? Can you create new and unusual uses for…?
EVALUATION	Is there a better solution to…? Judge the value of… Defend your position about… Do you think…is a good or bad thing? Explain. How would you have handled…? What changes to…would you recommend? Why?

Rapid Retrieval of Information (RRI)

Skimming to locate specific information requires students to distinguish relevant from irrelevant information.

- Provide a simplified version of a text with critical information.
- Ask students to read it silently.
- Present each student with a task to find specific information. Write several prompts on individual cards—for example, a prompt that proves a given point, asks students to find a phrase that defines a specific word, describes a certain step in a process, or allows students to compare two things. Or ask questions such as, "How did that person feel? Find a couple of sentences that support your answer."
- Ask students to read their task to the class, their findings, and the supporting text.

Learning and Literature

Teachers and parents can direct this activity. A book is read by a parent or a teacher. The students learn about plot, setting, and characters. Students then go to a table with a parent to continue working with the story. Then a discussion follows, guided by a mural that contains the responses of the students. The parents use a frame to elicit more discussion around the *observations, connections, questions, and moral values* the students found in the story:

Observations	Connections	Questions	Values & Morals
I noticed that . . . • •	It reminds me of… • •	¿ ¿ ¿	• • •

Observaciones	Conecciones	Preguntas	Valores y Morales
Me dí cuenta que… • •	Me recuerda que… • •	¿ ¿ ¿	• amor • respeto

They also start a list of new vocabulary found in the story. After the chart is finished, the students write a similar story containing some of the characteristics on the chart. They can be persuasive, narrative, or descriptive stories.

Literature Circles

Literature circles are small, temporary discussion groups that choose to read the same story, poem, book, or magazine.

- Students choose their own reading materials.
- On the basis of these choices, small temporary groups are formed.
- Different groups read different texts.
- Regular times are scheduled so that students can meet and discuss what they've read.
- Readers are encouraged to use notes, Post-its, or study guides as they read from different perspectives or stances.
- Discussions are student led and are intended to be natural and open, affording digressions, personal connections, and open-ended questions.
- Teachers are facilitators and monitors of the groups but not participants.
- Students are expected to play rotating roles in the group, including introducing topics, issues, and questions for discussion. Other roles include illustrator, connector, discussion director, character captain, and vocabulary/word master.
- When books are finished, the readers share with classmates, and then new groups are formed.
- Evaluation involves a mix of observations by the teacher, portfolios, other informal procedures, and various forms of student self-evaluation.
- Playfulness and fun are seen as key elements.

4. Independent Reading

The objectives of independent reading are to (1) provide students with a quiet time to practice their silent reading, (2) provide students with models of good silent reading behavior, (3) increase students' abilities to sustain silent reading for longer periods of time, and (4) show children that the teacher trusts them to select their texts and engage in reading for pleasure. Students will not be asked to report on what they read.

Reading at Home

Another form of independent reading is conducted during the 20 minutes of reading students are required to do every night for homework. For this, teachers usually require that students and parents keep a "reading log" with titles, commentaries, and signatures from the parents to certify that the child has read for 20 minutes at home.

Book Club

The book club is another variation of student choice reading. In this case, they are expected to share with other students what they read.

5. Vocabulary Instruction

The strategies described in Chapter 5 apply to reading. In addition, students will need direct instruction in word analysis because word analysis is the basis of good decoding and spelling skills.

SUMMARY

Enhancing SLL reading comprehension and language capabilities is essential in TWI. Reading aloud and discussing what is read helps children develop fluency, comprehension, and metacognitive strategies. But there are gaps and discrepancies between common practices and research-based practices. Even read-aloud practices often focus on simply retrieving information from a text instead of constructing the meaning of ideas and developing rich vocabulary and fluency in speaking.

Students who are not exposed systematically to a variety of texts, reading strategies, and activities to develop comprehension will develop reading difficulties for life. Implementation of effective literacy in L1 and L2 is not a simple matter. Substantial teacher preparation is required for teachers to become successful at teaching decoding, fluency, comprehension, and love of reading.

7

Using Writing to Promote Reading and Oral Language Development

Writing is a social process for second-language learners (SLLs) just as it is for any other writer. Writing is communication, collaboration, and creativity. Writing can be a very difficult task for SLLs when they experience failure, or it can be an exciting and rewarding experience as they become acquainted with their new language and culture. The balance between feeling successful and meeting standards in writing hinges on the instructional process and the classroom climate.

Moll (1992) suggested two principles of literacy instruction. First, literacy instruction should center on understanding and the communication of meaning. The teacher's role is to support students as they carry out meaningful literacy activities, often chosen by the students themselves,

> Writing is a means of meaningful communication in a new language, and it must be standards driven.

involving the full processes of reading and writing. Second, literacy instruction takes place in the context of a rich and challenging curriculum.

If we apply Moll's principles to a writing curriculum, we can say that writing is a means of meaningful communication in a new language, and it must be standards driven.

Recent research and emergent promising practices have helped us point out that the balance between student-centered meaningful instruction and standards-based instruction can be attained through four key principles: (1) writing can be taught earlier than once believed, (2) explicit instruction of the skills necessary for writing must not be overlooked, (3) vocabulary and oral language development are an integral part of writing, and (4) writing flourishes in a safe community of learners and with culturally responsive instruction.

TEACHING WRITING FROM THE START

Reading and writing are part of language development for SLLs (Au, 1993; Rigg & Allen, 1989). This means that students should be involved with reading and writing right from the start, whether or not they can speak English or Spanish fluently. Rigg and Allen (1989); Slavin, Madden, Dolan, et al. (1996); and Calderón (2001a, 2001b) have suggested that teachers read a variety of literature aloud to English as a Second Language (ESL)/ Spanish as a Second Language (SSL) students, so that students can become acquainted with the structure of narratives in their new language and as a basis for proficiency in writing. Well-written, high-interest literature provides models for good writing. After the teacher reads a story in the target language in a way that is comprehensible to the students, extension activities help students internalize new vocabulary and story elements.

EXPLICIT SKILL INSTRUCTION
TO MEET THE STANDARDS

Standards identify what students should know and be able to do. They reflect the major concepts, essential ideas, attitudes, and skills that students must reach and develop through explicit instruction. Sometimes, teachers who adhere to constructivist models of teaching are reluctant to provide students with explicit skill instruction because they don't want to appear authoritarian (Delpit, 1988) or because it goes against their philosophy of teaching. However, Delpit (1988) warned that not making skills and requirements explicit to students of diverse backgrounds may put them at a serious disadvantage. She has found that "some process approaches to writing create situations in which students find themselves held accountable for knowing a set of rules about which no one has ever directly informed them" (p. 287). She described how these students feel cheated because they believe that knowledge has deliberately been withheld from them. She also implied that, in some instances, the absence of explicit instruction may be viewed as one means by which the dominant culture seeks to place subordinate-group students at a disadvantage. In two-way bilingual (TWB) programs, parents often feel this way if their children's reading and writing skills are limited in either language.

VOCABULARY AND ORAL LANGUAGE FOR WRITING

On one hand, the strategies teachers used with mainstream students are not appropriate with two-way immersion (TWI). Therefore, adaptations to the teaching of the writing process need to be made by including more oral language development, explicit teaching of new vocabulary words each day, and direct teaching of writing skills. On the other hand, we know from research that SLLs typically have few opportunities for acquiring a rich vocabulary because their language use is limited to some basic functions of classroom discourse, what they pick up through listening, and some reading of simple text. These early delays in language development come to be reflected in low levels of reading comprehension, limited writing ability, and resulting low levels of academic success (Bear, Invernizzi, Templeton, & Johnson, 1996; Biemiller, 1999).

A COMMUNITY OF WRITERS

The concept of a community of writers has been emphasized by Graves and Graves (1983) and others. Teachers learning communities (TLCs) have also emphasized writing as a powerful mechanism for a teacher's continuous reflection and professional development (Calderón, 1998, 2001a, 2001b). When both of these concepts are combined, a more powerful learning community can emerge through writing. Students and their teachers have the opportunity for learning through a variety of joint literacy activities. The arrangements for learning can be varied and adjusted to provide support for all learners. The classroom becomes a context where teachers and students co-construct knowledge and meaning to the art of writing. Learning communities use a talent development approach. Teachers set out to deliberately identify individual talents as students work in heterogeneous and homogeneous group combinations. In these small and large communities, the students share their individual talents without fear of experimentation or trial and error. All members have a responsibility to assist one another and to contribute their talents. This type of participation also gives students the motivation for being in school every day. Teachers also meet in their own communities of learning to discuss their students' writing, assessment issues, problems, successes, and ways of improving writing instruction.

CULTURALLY RESPONSIVE INSTRUCTION

As part of culturally responsive instruction, teachers may explore with their classes the ways in which students and their families use literacy at home and in the community (Au, 1993) or in their former schooling experiences. For instance, well-educated Mexican students will start a narrative with long sentences filled with flowery language. To them, it is an insult to start with a succinct topic sentence. The topic is not typically approached until the elaborate introduction is complete. Korean students tend to use more inductive logical structures, putting details first and working up to a conclusion. Their style may appear indirect and unconvincing in their arguments to teachers unfamiliar with such a rhetorical approach. Arabic students, who also love long descriptions, may be seen as digressing. The Vietnamese students focus more on setting the scene than on developing the plot (Trumbull & Sasser, 2000). These cultural mismatches might raise false impressions about the students' writing abilities. Thus, teachers who are unfamiliar with cultural variations such as these might want to begin with class activities to discover the variations in class. An ample variety of multicultural literature will motivate students to write and can serve as templates for writing.

SETTING A CONTEXT FOR TWI WRITING

Writing is an essential skill for SLLs, but it has been perceived as much more difficult to master than listening, speaking, and reading. It is not, however, necessary to delay until students have mastered these. In fact, the sooner students begin writing, the faster they will make connections with both languages. In our studies and classroom observations (Calderón, 1999a, 1999b) of English-language learners in Success for All classrooms and other effective classrooms, we have learned that certain practices help establish a successful context for writing right from the start. These practices that apply to TWI instruction are as follows:

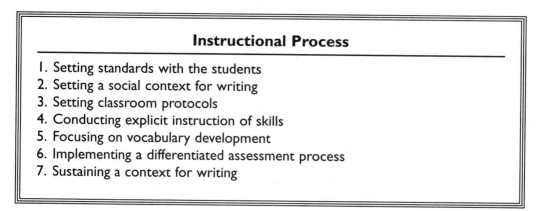

Instructional Process

1. Setting standards with the students
2. Setting a social context for writing
3. Setting classroom protocols
4. Conducting explicit instruction of skills
5. Focusing on vocabulary development
6. Implementing a differentiated assessment process
7. Sustaining a context for writing

Setting Standards

The first step in creating success for English learners (ELs)/Spanish learners (SLs) is to convey to them the high expectations, standards, and support they will have to meet these goals. The instructional sequence and process are summarized below.

Setting Standards

- Set high standards for writing.
- Display standards and tools for writing.
- Display rubrics and criteria for students' portfolios.
- Grade only those elements that have been explicitly taught.
- Students use checklists to review completed work.

Setting a Sociocultural Context

A community of writers is like any other community; its success hinges on trusting relationships and agreed-on norms and protocols. SLLs coming from diverse backgrounds and home environments need a sense of community and structure. Most of all, they need the type of relationships with their peers and teachers that afford them continuous and rapid learning in a new language and culture.

A teacher can set a positive climate for learning and writing by establishing procedures for each phase of the writing process: exploration, planning, drafting, revising, editing, publishing, and presenting. Each phase has specific norms of interaction and tasks. Unless they are explicitly taught, presented, and modeled, it will be very difficult for students to "guess" the intent and scope of each phase.

A positive "social context" begins with team-building activities for building trust and relationships. In cooperative teams, students can be directed to create team names, posters, or games based on book titles, character descriptions, or lines from their favorite poetry that will be used for further writing. After the team building, a discussion can highlight the cooperative norms, peer interaction protocols, and speech patterns. If possible, in a 50-50 program, the primary language can be used to convey all these important concepts and attract the SLLs into the wonderful world of writing. Their love for writing and writing accomplishments in their native language will sustain them through their struggles in the second language. All the skills learned through the writing process in the primary language will transfer quickly into the second language.

Setting the Social Context for Writing

- Build trust with team-building activities.
- Build passion for a topic by hands-on exploration of topics.
- Build passion for writing by helping students find their real audience.
- Set expectations for writing.
- Model and explain how to give and receive feedback.
- Model and discuss setting goals and making a plan for writing.
- Model and discuss self-reflection.
- Focus on the ideas the student has rather than the ones he or she lacks.
- Focus on the message the student is trying to convey, not on the form.
- Emphasize language repertoires rather than right answers or correct grammar.
- Encourage interaction with peers to seek feedback, question, analyze, discuss, and write down.
- Provide continuous differentiated assistance.

EXTENSIVE GUIDED CONVERSATION AND DISCUSSIONS FOR WRITING

The Role of the Teacher as Facilitator of Discussion

For productive writing, all students must be actively engaged in talking and thinking. Teachers use carefully crafted and organized verbal interactions with their students as they read aloud to them and point out the writer's craft. This is called *scaffolding*. Scaffolding is a process that enables a novice to solve a problem, carry out a task, or achieve a goal that would be beyond his or her unassisted efforts (Graves & Graves, 1994). Teachers ask higher order questions and guide their students to respond to these, contribute their ideas, respect everyone's ideas, and use these ideas in their writing. This type of teacher modeling and pointing out the author's craft are accompanied by a conversation that we might have with our friends when we tell them a story, argue a point, ask to have something clarified, and interrupt to ask for more information. Students are expected to transfer these discussion skills into reading and into their writing.

The Purpose and Benefits of Peer Discussion

Student contributions involve collaborating with one another to construct meaning, get ideas, and learn information from a text. One way to do this is to use Buddy Buzz or Think/Pair/Share (see Chapter 5) whenever possible in the writing process. Isabel Beck and colleagues (1999) described an approach for enhancing student engagement with text as Questioning the Author (QtA). This same process can be used when the students do their own partner, team, or individual writing and want feedback on what they have written.

Types of Questions for Feedback and Discussions

☐ What is the author trying to tell us here?
☐ What is the author's message?
☐ What is the author talking about now?
☐ What does the author mean here?
☐ Did the author explain this clearly?
☐ Does this make sense with what the author has told us before?
☐ How does this connect with what the author has told us here?
☐ Does the author tell us why?
☐ Why do you think the author tells us this now?
☐ How do things look for this character now?
☐ How has the author let us know that something has changed?
☐ How has the author settled this for us?
☐ Given what the author has already told us about this character, what do you think he's up to?

Teacher's Strategies for Rich Discussions

As stated previously, the role of the teacher is that of mediator of learning, scaffolding, and orchestrating a context in which students feel comfortable to express their views, regardless of the fluency and richness of their vocabulary. For this purpose, the following strategies can be used.

Marking. Acknowledging the importance of a student's idea by restating or rephrasing it and highlighting its importance within the discussion.

Turning Back. In this strategy, responsibility is turned back to students for thinking through and figuring out ideas. The teacher expresses confusion and turns back to the students for clarification by probing for elaboration, encouraging students to connect their ideas with the ideas of other students, connecting scattered concepts, and drawing unrelated or forgotten information together, especially when students debate an issue that can be easily clarified by what the author has explicitly presented.

Revoicing. Paraphrasing or revoicing occurs when students have constructed ideas but are struggling to express them. The teacher revoices their ideas so that they can become part of the discussion.

Modeling Between Discussions. An attempt is made to show how writers actively interact with ideas in the course of drafting. The teacher uses think-alouds to show appreciation of the author's craft (humor, irony, play on words, how an effect is created), show the teacher's own reactions to the text, model rereading of long or awkward descriptions and contradictions, and explain or model a difficult task the students must do as a follow-up to the editing.

Annotating. The teacher provides information to fill in gaps (e.g., "The author didn't tell us but. . . .").

Recapping. This strategy is used to summarize students' ideas and to signal they are ready to move on.

Setting Classroom Protocols

Beginning writers, whether 5 or 12 years old, need the basic concepts of writing taught explicitly. Just as we teach concepts of print—reading from left to right, title, author, illustrator, and so on—concepts and conventions of writing also need to be taught. Since writing is a process, ELs/SLs need to understand all the thinking behaviors related to that process.

At the prewriting stage, the understanding, teaching, and reteaching of the complex pieces of the writing process take place. The teacher simplifies instructions, develops and posts guidelines, and reteaches as needed. The language patterns or communicative functions for getting things done at each stage are also presented. The following boxes summarize guidelines, possible classroom posters, and guiding assumptions that need to be considered before assessing ELs' and SLs' writing. Teachers might also want to use these as a point of discussion in their teachers learning communities or as peer coaching topics.

The Protocols of Writing

- Understanding the writing process
- Rules and routines for process writing
- Silence during writing
- How to whisper during peer interaction
- How to do self-reflection and think aloud
- How to use forms and frames for writing
- How to get organized for each phase of the writing project
- What to do during drafting
- What to do during the revision stage and author's chair

- What to do during the editing stage
- What to do during conferencing
- How to use dictionaries, spell checkers, highlighters, different colors of ink for editing, and so on
- Creating word lists and word banks
- Keeping a notebook with thoughts, quotes, and notes for future writing
- Setting routines and timeframes
- Establishing the physical environment for writing activities

Timeframes for Writing

- How to distribute the writing activities during the daily 60-minute block for writing
- Managing time within the diverse writing activities
- What to do when finished at each phase
- Times for explicit skill instruction
- Times for peer, cooperative, and individual writing
- Times for conferencing, monitoring, practice tests, and assessment
- Additional time for students who need it

Physical Classroom Environment

- Posters with standards, rubrics, rules, and guidelines
- Posters with graphic organizers, tips on grammar, devices, and so on
- Resource center with textbooks on writing, different literature, samples of writing, frames for opening paragraphs, transitions, conclusions, and so forth
- Different types of paper, pencils, pens, markers, Post-it notes, journals, and so on
- Computer corner with directions for accessing programs, the Internet, spell checks, and so forth
- A place for conferencing
- A place for peer circles, author's chair, and discussions
- A place for student folders or work collections
- A place to display student work inside and outside the classroom

Explicit Instruction for SLLs

The goal of a recursive writing process is to get students to write often and to use their peers in the classroom as their audience. Students work with partners or in teams while planning, revising, and editing their writing, giving feedback to one another as well as learning to use feedback that has been given. Students learn a great deal about the second language just from examining each other's writing. Through this process, students get many opportunities to write, learn new words, and understand the mechanics of writing in English and Spanish. Some ideas on mini-lessons that teachers can provide on a systematic basis are offered in the following box.

Conventions for Writing in English or Spanish

Conventions of Writing

- Writing the title, author's name, date, and page numbers
- Using only one side of the paper and skipping lines
- Using words, spaces, and punctuation markers

Composition

- Using and choosing genre
- Describing characters
- Using dialogue
- Developing plot and setting
- Using a variety of an author's devices such as irony, flashback, and so on
- Using active versus passive voice

Conventions of English

- Spelling
- Capitalization, punctuation, margins, and hyphens
- Paragraphing, beginning and ending sentences, and so forth
- Subject-verb agreement
- Core words, prefixes, and suffixes

Vocabulary Development During Story-Related Writing

Beginning writers also need ways to continuously increase their vocabulary. There is strong evidence that listening comprehension leads to reading and writing competence (Biemiller, 1999; Menyuk, 1999). The instructional components of listening comprehension (Slavin, Madden, Karweit, Dolan, & Wasik, 1996) enable vocabulary and concept development. When a teacher reads texts daily that introduce new vocabulary, concepts, language structures, story elements, and the author's techniques, students build a basis for story-related writing. Story-related writing uses the patterns, words, and formats illustrated through listening comprehension.

It might be useful to create a visual such as a story map to make key elements clear. The teacher will also need to have a set of questions and prompts to help the children understand the problem in the story and literary devices such as cause and effect or irony. The teacher will also need to elicit ideas and questions from the students so that they take on as much responsibility for text interpretation as possible. In addition to this and other instructional activities, such as whole-class webbing of ideas and words during the prewriting stage, a poster in the classroom such as the one below will help guide the students toward further word refinement.

Vocabulary Study Tools During Writing

- Collect and group vocabulary in various ways (parts of speech, synonyms, antonyms).
- Incorporate new words into each draft.
- Ask partners to help incorporate new words after peer editing.
- In small groups, generate a vocabulary list of 20 or more items.
- Select 5 words and generate sentences useful for your drafts.
- Select 3 words and search for synonyms.

Assessing SLL Writing

Writing is a series of recursive processes (planning, drafting, revising, etc.), and this process allows flexibility in applying and adjusting strategies based on student background. There are several issues to consider in assessing ELs' and SLs' writing. Some of the factors that affect ELs' and SLs' writing deal with student background, while others deal mainly with the ways instruction is orchestrated. The instructional context has been summarized above; therefore, the student background factors highlighted below reinforce the need for setting the ideal classroom context. Once the student background factors have been identified and integrated into the instructional framework, a differentiated assessment process can be implemented along with all other process protocols.

Student Background Factors Affecting Writing Performance

- Level of primary-language proficiency
- Level of second-language oral proficiency (vocabulary recognition, vocabulary production, syntax, phonology, morphology, pragmatics)
- Level of primary-language literacy skills
- Level of second-language preliteracy skills (phonemic awareness, phonological awareness)
- Degree of correspondence of primary-language characteristics with the second language (same Roman alphabet)
- Age of arrival and grade level entering
- Sociocultural background factors and their interrelationship with the new culture

Differentiated Assessment for First Language (L1) and Second Language (L2)

- Differentiated growth plan
- Error correction strategies
- Differentiated grading or scoring
- Teacher and student reflection and debriefing

Differentiated Growth Plan

Where does one SLL student start in the writing process versus another student? All SLLs should tackle the same writing assignments as the other proficient students, but in a much smaller scale at the beginning and with considerably more assistance. One student might write only one paragraph and use invented spelling with creative grammatical structures during the first few weeks of school. This will give the teacher an opportunity to analyze the student's writing and work out a plan for growth with the student. The student can work on one or two skills per week. The proofreading and editing will focus on these skills. Increasingly, the student and teacher will target other skills that can be assessed in the context of the assignment for the whole class. These plans, contracts, or samples of skill mastery can be included in the student's portfolio. After a couple of months, the student's growth will be quite evident from the contents of the portfolio.

Error Correction

Error correction is a difficult and sensitive issue in writing classes (Trumbull & Sasser, 2000), especially in ELs' and SLs' writing instruction. Many students want to be corrected, but for many others, corrections can have a devastating effect. Therefore, correction is best left for the editing stage. Instead, a teacher needs to focus on teaching students how to find and correct their own mistakes as part of their editing process before the teacher corrects or grades their final work.

Grading

Assessing and grading a student's writing focuses only on those items that have been taught explicitly in class and have been announced as "grammar criteria" or other criteria for this particular writing project. Like error correction, grading is a very sensitive issue for SLLs. The grading policy needs to be made very clear so that students know in advance what they are working toward accomplishing. It is important to provide reminders of those criteria at the drafting and editing stages, particularly at the peer revision stage, where students can help one another with correction and elaboration. This is when techniques for proofreading will be appreciated by all students, especially those who want teacher correction.

A four-level rubric can be used for SLLs' writing such as the following examples for individual or team writing that are commonly used in Success for All/Éxito Para Todos (SFA/EPT) classrooms. Students' writing is scored from the perspective of their level of language proficiency.

Levels	
Level 1 – Novice	Level 3 – Competent
Level 2 – Intermediate	Level 4 – Exceptional

At each level, the following rubrics are used:

Rubric	Points
Complete	80
Almost complete	75
Still needs more detail	70
Just a skeleton	65

Rubrics Include:

Teamwork

Completion of the writing process

Teacher evaluation (contents and mechanics)

Tests of grammar, mechanics, and composition lessons

Teacher and Student Reflection

At the teacher correction or assessment phase, it is best to avoid simply crossing out and rewriting mistakes for the students. This discourages grammar/syntax awareness. Instead, a simple underlining or highlighting of errors leads students toward an adventure in self-discovery and profound dialogue as they work with their partners or teammates. They can generate questions for the teacher if they do not understand the nature of the mistakes. Students can then record these in a "mistake section" in their notebook, followed by peer or teacher conferencing on the repeated patterns of mistakes. The teacher can then review with the whole class the repeated patterns of errors and teach a specific lesson on those. The lesson can end with a mini-test on those patterns.

SUMMARY

Teachers will need continuous support and motivation to implement a complex writing process that addresses the diversity of student needs. There will also be a diversity of teachers working with SLLs—bilingual, English-language development, and mainstream teachers who are credentialed or on waivers. For these two reasons alone, it is extremely important for schools to allocate time and space for teachers to work in their own learning communities. Through teacher learning communities (TLCs), as described in Chapter 9, teachers are able to sustain an innovation and make it work. Below are some topics for discussion in TLCs. It is hoped that these questions are constantly replaced with new ones as the old questions are addressed.

Issues for Discussion in Teachers Learning Communities

- Very little research has been conducted on SLLs' writing. How can we contribute to the field?
- The teaching of writing is typically delayed for SLLs, and assessments reflect this omission. How can we prevent this happening in our school?
- Since writing is interconnected with reading and language development, how can we give equal attention to all their developmental phases?
- The diversity of student backgrounds makes assessment quite complex. How can we ensure sensitive and differentiated assessment processes?
- Agreed-on criteria and an error hierarchy have not been nationally normed. What system can we develop, pilot, and establish as our own in-house criteria?
- Frequent examination of student work is necessary to monitor student progress and inform instructional decisions. How often should we meet to do this?
- Teachers need continuous support with staff development or ongoing teachers learning communities to develop expertise in SLLs' assessment. What plan can we submit for our own professional growth?

Writing is a complementary component for language proficiency and literacy. Writing anchors knowledge of print, comprehension, grammar, and voice. When introducing writing in a second language or in two languages simultaneously, the traditional writing process has to be enriched with direct instruction on all the protocols and skills needed to be a successful writer.

Writing in TWI requires ample feedback for students and teachers. Teachers will need time during the workday to meet with colleagues to discuss stages of writing and rubrics, how to integrate skills, and how to grade their students' work.

8

Assessing Second-Language Learners

Three themes have dominated public discourse on education in the United States for the past two decades.

1. The need for public schools to demonstrate more accountability to the communities they serve and to the organizations that fund them

2. Ways in which schools should accommodate the rapid growth of English learners

3. Ways of addressing the persistent educational underachievement of many English learners

State education agencies have responded to these themes in different ways. Some states have increased the use of standardized tests once a year, while others have attempted to use authentic assessment venues on a continuous basis throughout the school year (Darling-Hammond, 2001).

An issue of inequity has been discussed in many quarters when English learners are assessed too soon in their academic English development. Research has demonstrated that it takes at least 5 years to develop the academic language skills in English (Collier & Thomas, 2001). The same would apply to other second-language learners (SLLs) if they are tested in their second language (L2) too soon with regard to the length of time it takes to develop their academic language skills. By testing SLLs in their L2 before they are ready, standardized tests are doing a disservice and underestimating the students' potential.

> A way to monitor the progress of SLLs is to make authentic assessment part of the instructional process and involve students in all phases of this process—for example, designing rubrics to assess their development.

STUDENT ASSESSMENT

Assessment or testing plays a complicated role in the education of SLLs. Some of the reasons include the following:

• It is a sensitive issue for schools and programs with underachieving SLLs.

• Schools and their programs are questioned when standards-based instruction requires certain levels of performance on state-mandated tests for all students, including SLLs. Low-performing schools are those that have standardized test scores below the norm. These schools are placed on a list developed by the state's education department and targeted for restructuring. In these circumstances, the school district is in danger of a state takeover.

• When test results are misinterpreted as a failure of the students, teachers, parents, and schools, the school's response is to protect its students and to make sure that the possible school or systemic changes do not affect them negatively and that they receive a good and equal education.

The following recommendations apply to all language programs. Two-way bilingual (TWB) programs could also benefit from these recommendations and use them to build a strong assessment system to determine the following:

- How to assess on a continuous basis the language development of SLLs and what skills to assess that include listening, speaking, reading, and writing
- How holistic the assessment should be (i.e., it sees the student as she or he performs not only in her or his L2 but also in the entire instructional context)
- What assessment measures produce results that can be channeled to effective instruction, professional development, and parental involvement

A DEFINITION OF ASSESSMENT

Assessment is the systematic measurement of educational progress over time, including the progress of individual students and groups of students, as well as the effectiveness of school instructional programs, which are usually based on various sources of evidence (O'Malley & Valdez Pierce, 1996). Assessment is also considered a key piece of the school reform movement and district systemic change. It drives the decisions that schools and school systems make about the following:

- The instructional programs they develop and implement in a TWB program, as well as the harmonious structure of the uses of two languages for instruction
- The levels of support for teachers and students in a TWB program, the ongoing professional development assistance, and the promotion of communities of learners
- The involvement of families and the community in a TWB program and the interaction and cooperation between and among all parents of SLLs
- The effective administrative strategies that make a difference in the context of schooling and the TWB program leaders' belief that the program works as a means to properly implement it

> Assessment is the systematic measurement of educational progress over time, including the progress of individual students and groups of students, as well as the effectiveness of instructional programs.

WHAT ARE THE PURPOSES OF ASSESSMENT IN TWB PROGRAMS?

For Screening and Identification. English learners are usually administered a home language survey, which is conducted when the student registers at school. The home language survey is used to identify students eligible for special language and/or content-area support programs. The survey is provided in the first language (L1) of the parents and is given in written questionnaire form, orally by parent interview, or by student interview if the student is of middle or high school age. The home language survey identifies the L1 of the student, the student's preferred language use, and family members' use of languages other than English at home (Ovando & Collier, 1998). The English speakers would also be screened to ascertain the levels of L1 and L2 development. A less elaborate screening can be offered as most of the information is already part of the admissions procedures for all English-speaking students.

For Placement. Language proficiency measures are used with SLLs to determine the language proficiency and content-area competencies of students so as to recommend an appropriate educational program for the following:

- Placement in TWB programs
- Placement in special programs
- Placement in L2 classes (beginning, intermediate, advanced)
- Language dominance assessment to determine L1 and L2 use in academics
- Ongoing assessment of linguistic and cognitive development as students move through school, monitoring their progress
- Reclassification or exit from a TWB program, as if it applies to the program model (e.g., if a SSL has acquired the language and content-area skills needed in mainstream all-English classrooms, or another SSL has acquired the expected level of achievement in his or her L2, such as Spanish, Russian, or German)
- Program evaluation of the effects of TWB instructional programs
- Accountability, to guarantee that all TWB program students attain expected educational goals or standards

For Academic Achievement. Standardized tests and/or rubrics are used with SLLs to determine student language performance and academic achievement. The results are used to recommend an appropriate educational program for

- Reading, writing, and language arts
- Ongoing assessment of academic language development as students move through school, monitoring their progress on a continuous basis
- Content-area development that combines subject matter and academic language (e.g., the language and content-area skills needed in mainstream all-English classrooms)
- Program evaluation of the effects of TWB instructional programs
- Accountability, to guarantee that students attain expected educational goals or standards

In recent years, comparisons of test scores of SLLs in TWB programs on standardized tests have yielded some results that show that Spanish learners perform better than English learners in language, reading, and mathematics over the years (Lindholm-Leary, 2001). More information, careful analysis, and dialogue are needed to explain why this happens, a goal that is beyond the scope of this how-to book. Without an extensive review and analysis of standardized tests, we could not make a fair judgment on which factors (e.g., integration, classroom delivery) can affect these results.

CHOOSING ASSESSMENT
MEASURES IN TWB SETTINGS

Over the past 15 years, we have seen a rapid expansion and interest in alternatives to traditional forms of assessment in education (Rivera, 1999). The form of assessment used for both standardized testing and classroom assessment for as long as we can remember has been the multiple-choice test (Ovando & Collier, 1998). At the same time, educators working with SLLs and the general student population have raised concerns about its usefulness as a primary source of student achievement and effective instruction, and they are seeking alternatives through multiple forms of assessment (O'Malley & Valdez Pierce, 1996). They base their concerns in terms of two issues:

1.   Current standardized assessment procedures do not assess the full range of essential student outcomes, and teachers find it difficult to use the information gained for instructional planning (Cummins, 2000). TWB programs need assessment procedures that account for the development and use of two languages for instruction when teaching SLLs.

2.   Multiple-choice tests are not adequate to assess the full range of higher order thinking skills considered important in today's curriculum (Solomon, 2002). These tests do not account for linguistic abilities present in TWB settings.

These standardized tests do not represent what and how students learn. They have emphasized the assessment of discrete skills, have been detrimental to the holistic understanding of how the student performs in a two-language setting, and do not contain authentic representations of classroom activities (Arter & McTighe, 2001; Oller, 1997).

AUTHENTIC ASSESSMENT OF SLLs

Authentic assessment is a method of finding out what a student knows or is able to do. Its purpose is to show growth and inform instruction over a period of time and is an alternative to traditional forms of standardized or one-shot deal testing such as multiple-choice testing (O'Malley & Valdez Pierce, 1996). Alternative assessment is criterion referenced and typically authentic. *Authentic* means that the assessment is based on activities that represent ongoing classroom instruction and real-life settings. It involves teachers and students developing ways to measure language and academic progress. This definition would be appropriate for TWB program instruction as authentic assessment would represent the growth and processes of L2 development and patterns of academic achievement in SLLs.

> The purpose of authentic assessment is to show growth and inform instruction over a period of time. It is based on activities that represent ongoing classroom instruction and real-life settings.

The following examples of authentic assessment relate to TWB programs.

Performance Assessment. The student constructs a response orally or in writing. The response may be elicited by the teacher in formal or informal assessment contexts or may be observed as part of a lesson during classroom instructional or noninstructional settings. SLLs may be called on to use instructional materials or perform hands-on activities in reaching solutions to problems. Beginner SLLs may also act out responses in the early stages or during their silent period of L2 acquisition and development. In performance assessments, students perform the following activities:

- Construct a response, provide an expanded response, create a product, or all of the above
- Use higher levels of thinking in constructing responses to open-ended questions, using their own linguistic output
- Perform instructional tasks that are meaningful, challenging, and engaging and that mirror effective pedagogy and teaching standards
- Integrate knowledge and skills across content areas and express themselves in L1 and/or L2
- Use step-by-step procedures and strategies for exploring multiple solutions to complex tasks
- Demonstrate depth of skills or mastery

Portfolio Assessment. This refers to the systematic collection of student work that is analyzed to show progress and academic growth over time with regards to setting instructional objectives (Taggart, Phifer, Nixon, & Wood, 1998; Valencia, 1991). A key feature is the involvement of students in selecting samples of their own work to show growth and learning over time in developing ownership and assessing their own products. SLLs would use their knowledge of two languages to have portfolios of the following:

- Writing samples in their L1 and L2
- Reading logs to account for their proficiency in two or more languages
- Drawings representing their learning and proficiencies
- Audiotapes and/or videotapes of their linguistic input in L1 and L2
- Teacher and student comments on progress made by the student related to his or her content and language learning

Portfolios have *content validity* because they represent what SLLs are producing in the classroom. We use these portfolios to assess their performance in relation to the TWB program's goals, objectives, and activities set forth by the standards-based curriculum. Furthermore, it has been shown that portfolios have the

> Sponsor a portfolio night when showcase pieces can be discussed with teachers, students, parents, and administrators.

potential to increase the quantity and quality of classroom-based activities, for example, in writing and cognitive development (Porter & Cleland, 1995; Tierney, Carter, & Desai, 1991).

Two types of portfolios that are most in use would apply to a TWB program setting and assess SLLs' academic and linguistic growth (Gottlieb, 1999):

- *Showcase Portfolios.* These are used to display students' best works in their L1 and L2 to parents, teachers, and administrators. They illustrate student achievement of instructional goals, as set by the program that meets state standards. The documentation on the process used by each student to get to the finished product is particularly important for professional development on student learning, language of instruction, teaching strategies, and effective pedagogy.

- *Collection Portfolios.* These are working folders that illustrate how SLLs deal with daily schoolwork. They contain everything (the process and the product) produced by the student in both languages.

- *Self-Assessment.* SLLs are directly involved in their own assessment and become self-regulated learners (Purdie & Hattie, 1996). They have control over their own learning and can use their knowledge of two languages and the resources available to them in and outside the classroom. Students are pleased with their own efforts and take nourishment in the new meanings and understandings because they see the connection. SLLs can do the following:

- Make choices in their own learning
- Select learning activities to enhance their knowledge
- Plan to use their time and resources to increase their language and academic development
- Have the freedom to choose challenging activities that can become learning experiences
- Take risks and gain ownership as they succeed in instructional tasks
- Advance their own learning and accomplishments and meet the standards-based curriculum
- Meet desired instructional goals and objectives set forth by the program

- Collaborate with peers and integrate with other SLLs to develop lesson products
- Exchange ideas of mutual benefit and practice discourse interaction patterns
- Construct, revise, and share meanings and explanations with peers through presentations in L1 and L2
- Help and support each other and become self-sufficient and part of the classroom community

ASSESSMENT AND TEACHING IN TWB PROGRAMS

Assessment is closely related to instruction and is indispensable in professional development. For instance, authentic assessment is possible only in the context of teaching and learning processes that are student centered. The teacher's role is to facilitate and moderate the instruction. This role is in contrast to teacher-centered instruction, in which students are passive recipients of a transmission behaviorist, cemetery-style model (Tharp, 2002). Teachers need the following:

- Ongoing professional development and support through a mentoring system
- Opportunities to collaborate with other teachers when trying out new assessments within a community of learners
- Teacher learning communities to share ways of refining the assessments for effective instruction

How Can I Integrate Portfolio Assessment in My TWB Classroom?

Set criteria and performance standards:

- Caucus or work with your SLLs to specify the standards by which their work will be judged. For example, what elements of good oral proficiency, reading comprehension, writing, problem solving, or working in groups using their languages need to be considered?
- Show, model, or demonstrate samples of exemplary benchmarks, of what good work looks like, and of work that is not exemplary so that students and their parents, teachers, and administrators have a clear idea of how their work will be evaluated (e.g., samples of student performance from previous years).
- Describe criteria charts using student input such as the following example:

Criteria Charts

To become a good writer, I can

- Plan before I write
- Write about real things
- Write stories with a beginning, middle, and end
- Write in complete sentences
- Leave spaces between words
- Put periods at the end of sentences
- Make my handwriting easy to read
- Ask my peers to read my work
- Accept my peers' suggestions about improving my work

SOURCE: Based on Clemmons et al. (1993).

Apply the criteria set as a group:

- Use criteria charts by asking students in pairs or small groups to identify the strengths and weaknesses of actual work samples, such as the following:

    Oral language samples using audiotapes and videotapes
    Reading comprehension activities with texts in L1 and L2
    Writing samples in L1 and L2 based on a hierarchy or rubric developed by the group
    Content area samples related to the program's instructional goals

- Promote *portfolio partners* to evaluate each other's work samples using the set criteria with a chart such as the one in Figure 8.1.

Set realistic improvement goals:

- Promote individual students' goals, for example,
    My goal is to read ___ books this week.
    My goal is to write in complete sentences.
    My goal is to make my handwriting easy to read.
    My goal is to improve my vocabulary in English and/or Spanish.

- Create a card such as the one in Figure 8.2.

Use assessment goals to improve instruction:

- Plan lessons or mini-lessons for areas of improvement.

Figure 8.1 Portfolio Partners

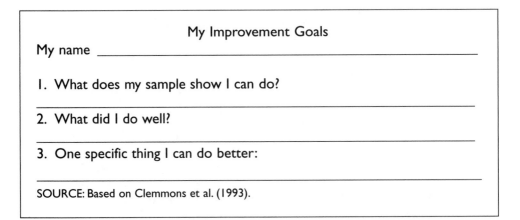

> **Portfolio Partners**
>
> My name _____ Date _____
>
> My partner's name _____
>
> 1. What do you think the sample shows your partner can do?
> _____
>
> 2. What do you think your partner can do?
> _____
>
> 3. How can your partner improve his or her sample?
> _____
>
> SOURCE: Based on Clemmons et al. (1993).

Figure 8.2 Improvement Goals

> My Improvement Goals
>
> My name _____
>
> 1. What does my sample show I can do?
> _____
>
> 2. What did I do well?
> _____
>
> 3. One specific thing I can do better:
> _____
>
> SOURCE: Based on Clemmons et al. (1993).

- Make your classroom more learner centered, and become a facilitator or catalyst of student output.
- Involve your students in the process in a cooperative way as a community of learners.
- Accept the feedback the assessment goals provide you on the effectiveness of your teaching and incorporate this in your lesson planning and delivery.

The following illustrations represent samples of rubrics to be used in the assessment of oral and written language and academic development in Spanish and English and in reading comprehension. These examples may not reflect the curriculum for all settings or be appropriate for all levels of instruction. We have skipped Levels 2 and 4 to attend to more differential characteristics in the holistic scoring rubric, with a score of 5 being the highest and 1 the lowest.

Rúbrica para la expresión oral del español como segundo idioma (Spanish as a Second Language: Oral Language Scoring Rubric)

Nivel (Level)	Descripción (Description)
5	Se comunica muy bien en contextos sociales y en el salón de clase (Communicates very well in social contexts and in the classroom)
	Habla con fluidez (Speaks with fluency)
	Domina una variedad de estructuras gramaticales (Has command of grammatical structures)
	Usa vocabulario académico (Uses academic vocabulary)
	Participa en las conversaciones en clase (Participates in classroom discussions)
3	Se comunica con cierta dificultad (Communicates with some difficulty)
	Usa la gramática adecuada en oraciones complejas pero tiene dificultad con la conjugación de los verbos (Uses adequate grammar in complex sentences but has problems with verb tenses)
	Usa un vocabulario con ciertas irregularidades (Uses vocabulary with some difficulty)
	Comprende las conversaciones en clase cuando se le repite y clarifica (Understands class conversations when they are repeated and rephrased)
	Se comunica bien en contextos sociales, su nivel de comunicación en la clase es bajo (Communicates well in social contexts, begins to communicate in the classroom)
1	Puede nombrar objetos (Can name concrete objects)
	Repite frases y palabras (Repeats words and phrases)
	Comprende poco su segundo idioma poco o nada (Understands the second language little or not at all)

English as a Second Language: Oral Scoring Rubric

Level	Description
5	Communicates very well in social and academic contexts Speaks with fluency, enunciates clearly Has command of complex grammatical structures Uses academic content-based vocabulary Participates in classroom discussions and academic exchanges
3	Communicates with some difficulty but conveys meaning Uses adequate grammar in complex sentences but has problems with verb tenses and number categories Uses content-based vocabulary with some difficulty Understands class conversations and instruction when they are repeated and rephrased Communicates well and effectively in social contexts, begins to communicate in cognitively demanding contexts in the classroom
1	Can name concrete objects displayed Repeats words and phrases Understands the L2 very little or not at all

Rúbrica para la escritura del español como segundo idioma (Spanish as a Second Language: Writing Scoring Rubric)

Nivel (Level)	Descripción (Description)
5	Se expresa en forma clara y eficiente (Expresses in a clear and effective manner) Su organización es clara, con una introducción, un desarrollo de ideas y una conclusión (Has clear organization, with introduction, development of ideas, and conclusion) Usa un vocabulario variado, preciso en todo el texto (Uses varied and precise vocabulary) Escribe con pocos errores gramaticales (Writes with few grammatical errors)
3	Se expresa en forma clara a menudo (Expresses in a clear manner frequently) Comienza a escribir párrafos (Begins to write paragraphs) Escribe con oraciones sencillas (Writes simple sentences) Usa vocabulario sencillo que se usa frecuentemente (Uses high-frequency vocabulary) Escribe con errores gramaticales que pueden impedir la comprensión (Writes with grammatical errors that may diminish communication)

1	Dibuja para poder expresarse (Draws pictures to convey meaning)
	Usa palabras y frases simples (Uses simple words and phrases)
	Escribe basado en un modelo (Copies from a model)

English as a Second Language: Writing Scoring Rubric

Level	Description
5	Expresses in a clear and effective manner
	Has clear organization in paragraphs and compositions, with introduction, development of ideas, and conclusion
	Uses varied and precise content vocabulary
	Writes with few grammatical errors but conveys meaning within a sentence
3	Expresses in a clear manner frequently
	Begins to write paragraphs with coherence
	Writes well-structured simple sentences
	Uses high-frequency and academic vocabulary
	Writes with grammatical errors that may diminish communication
1	Draws pictures to convey meaning
	Uses simple and frequent words and phrases
	Copies from a model provided

Rúbrica para la lectura del español como segundo idioma (Spanish as a Second Language: Reading Scoring Rubric)

Nivel (Level)	Descripción (Description)
5	Lee y completa una variedad de textos (Reads and completes a wide variety of texts)
	Disfruta de la lectura (Reads for enjoyment)
	Critica los textos en forma personal (Responds personally and critically to texts)
	Selecciona textos relevantes y complejos (Selects complex and relevant texts)
3	Empieza a leer en forma independiente (Begins to read independently)
	Usa una variedad de estrategias de la lectura (Uses a variety of reading strategies)
	Selecciona sus textos apropiados (Chooses appropriate texts)
	Empieza a leer independientemente (Begins to read independently)
	Reconoce fácilmente los eventos, los personajes y el tema (Recognizes easily the events, characters, and plot)

I   Repite palabras y frases (Repeats words and phrases)
Reconoce la relación entre sonido y símbolo (Recognizes sound-symbol relationships)
Empieza a contar textos conocidos y predecibles (Begins to retell familiar, predictable text)
Usa figuras para comprender mejor (Uses pictures to facilitate meaning)

English as a Second Language: Reading Scoring Rubric

Level	Description
5	Reads and completes a wide variety of texts independently Reads for enjoyment Responds in a personal manner and critically to texts Selects complex and relevant texts
3	Begins to read independently Uses a variety of reading strategies Chooses appropriate texts Begins to read independently Recognizes easily the events, characters, and plot
I	Repeats words and phrases Recognizes sound-symbol relationships Begins to retell familiar, predictable text Uses pictures to facilitate meaning

WHAT IS A PORTFOLIO CONFERENCE?

A portfolio conference is an opportunity for the teacher and student to face the student's growth together and to find ways to make the process productive and of mutual benefit. The student gets individual feedback on how to set and achieve goals, and teachers get individual feedback on how to make instruction more effective. The SLLs can prepare for the portfolio conference with answers to questions on his or her L2 literacy development. Answers to questions such as the following are needed:

- How has my English/Spanish improved since the last time we met?
- What can I do now that I could not do before?
- Can I read better in English/Spanish?
- What do I like to read? What makes it interesting?
- Do I read most in English/Spanish?
- How many books do I read per week?
- How many books do I read per month?
- What am I doing to become a better reader?

- Can I write better now in English/Spanish?
- How much do I write per week/month?
- What am I doing to become a better writer in English/Spanish?

Teachers can use the same pattern of questioning in the portfolio assessment to create a collaboration of mutual benefit:

- How has your English/Spanish improved since the last time we met?
- What can you do now in English/Spanish that you could not do before?
- How can I help you with your English/Spanish?
- Can you read better now in English/Spanish?
- What do you like to read in English/Spanish? What makes it interesting?
- What are doing to become a better reader?
- How can I help you with your reading?
- Can you write better now in English/Spanish?
- What do you like to write in English/Spanish? What makes it interesting?
- What are you doing to become a better writer in English/Spanish?
- How can I help you with your writing in English/Spanish?

STANDARDS-BASED EFFECTIVE TEACHING CONNECTED TO AUTHENTIC ASSESSMENT

The teacher is an integral partner in the assessment process and has the responsibility to continue assessing student progress and growth across the standards-based curriculum, oral language development, and reading, writing, and content areas. In a TWB program, the curricular areas taught in the L1 must be assessed in the L1, and the themes or subject areas taught through the L2 must be assessed in the L2.

If a student speaks in L1 in class during his or her L2 time slot, the teacher needs to accept the student's output but respond in the L2. In this way, the two languages will remain separate for instruction, and each language will get equal development across the curriculum. Assessment measures need to mirror this separation.

> The two languages of a TWB program must be kept separate for instruction so that each language gets equal development across the curriculum.

Standards for the teaching and assessment of rubrics for SLLs have been posed or revised by a number of organizations to implement and assess rubrics in the L1 and/or the L2. They are as follows:

- The CREDE (Center for Research in Education, Diversity and Excellence) Standards for Effective Pedagogy
- The National Science Education Standards
- The National Council of Teachers of Mathematics Standards
- The Teachers of English to Speakers of Other Languages

These standards incorporate a L2 development component and have been published and endorsed by professional organizations and research centers. These standards are based on the fact that we have moved from knowledge transmission to inquiry as a primary goal of effective pedagogy (Escamilla, Andrade, Basurto, & Ruiz, 1996; Minaya-Rowe, 2002). They point to an educational environment with students as independent thinkers and problem solvers (Slavin & Madden, 2001a).

Furthermore, these standards define the nature of language, how language is learned, and the assessment of language. Because reading and writing are very important skills to experience the whole curriculum, each content area teacher needs to assess language with every instructional activity. Table 8.1 on pages 165-166 represents a holistic comparison of these language and content area standards.

SUMMARY

We have presented why and how we assess SLLs in a TWB program, a brief overview of assessment practices and individual student assessment for placement in a program, and ongoing classroom assessment and completion of a school program. We have also examined the types of assessment tools available to us, along with their relative strengths and weaknesses in the context of the standards-based movement, which has high-stakes tests and implications for the effective teaching of SLLs. We have focused on authentic assessments and have illustrated with rubrics the ways we can incorporate assessment in daily instructional activities for oral, reading, and writing skill development. These assessments enable SLLs to construct information and learn meaningfully rather than simply choose response alternatives. These types of assessments can also be challenging for SLLs, but they can provide opportunities for them to use their L1 and L2 to demonstrate their academic knowledge across the four language skills. We have also compared existing content area and language standards and illustrated the high degree of overlap among them. With the assessments based on these standards, quality language and content instruction can be improved and benefit SLLs.

Table 8.1 Comparison of Language and Content Area Standards

Standards for Effective Pedagogy (CREDE)	National Science Education Standards	National Council of Teachers of Mathematics	Teachers of Speakers of Other Languages
• Joint productive activity Students and teacher working together Students assist one another Students develop a product	• Collaboration Groups of students analyzing and synthesizing data to defend conclusions Public communication of students' ideas and work to classmates	• Collaboration Groups of students creating and using representations to organize, record, and communicate mathematical ideas	• Collaboration Language learning through students' collaboration
• Language development Language developed in a meaningful context Oral and written language development through questioning, restating, and modeling	• Communication Communicating science explanations Understanding scientific concepts and developing abilities of inquiry	• Communication Select, apply, and translate among mathematical representations to solve problems Use representations to model and interpret physical, social, and mathematical phenomena	• Communication Language learning through meaningful and significant use The importance of developing oral, reading, and writing skills
• Contextualization Students' knowledge as a foundation for new knowledge Connecting school to students' lives	• Contextualization Process skills in context Activities that investigate and analyze scientific questions Use of multiple process skills such as manipulation and cognitive and procedural skills	• Contextualization Use various representations of objects to be able to recognize common mathematical structures across different contexts	• Contextualization The role of students' native languages in their English-language and general academic development Cultural, social, and cognitive processes in language and academic development

(Continued)

166

Standards for Effective Pedagogy (CREDE)	National Science Education Standards	National Council of Teachers of Mathematics	Teachers of Speakers of Other Languages
• Challenging activity Cognitively challenging instruction Focus on thinking and analysis of appropriate levels of tasks	• Cognitive demand Activities that investigate and analyze science questions Do more investigations to develop understanding, ability, values of inquiry, and knowledge of science content Investigation over extended periods of time	• Cognitive demand Create and interpret models of more complex phenomena, drawn from a wider range of contexts, by identifying essential features of a situation and by finding representations that capture mathematical relationships between those features	• Cognitive demand Use scaffolding to move students from challenging activities to more complex activities that require the use of more complex vocabulary
• Instructional conversation Dialogue, questioning, sharing ideas, and knowledge Assistance dialogue to develop thinking and problem solving, to express ideas orally and in writing	• Dialogic thinking Communicating science explanations and sharing ideas and work with other classmates	• Dialogic thinking Promoting dialogue and interaction among teacher-students and students-students to share ideas about mathematical problems	• Dialogic thinking The importance of language as communication Promoting active participation of students during classroom discussion and dialogue among them

SOURCE: Based on Robles-Rivas (2001).

Part III

Involving Teachers and Parents

9

Staff Development and Teacher Learning Communities

In a two-way bilingual (TWB) school, principles for effective staff development also apply and connect to bilingual and bicultural development goals (Huberman, 1992; Lieberman & Miller, 1991). These are the following:

- Staff development is culture building. Staff development activities should connect the renewal of schooling (or instituting the new TWB program) to the renewal of teachers and administrators. This should be done through collaborative cultures, where teachers assume new roles in their own development and in the development of their students.
- Staff development is teacher inquiry into practice. Staff development should provide opportunities for reflective practice; therefore, after expert workshops, there should be more time spent on teacher-led activities.
- Staff development is about human development and learning for both students and teachers. Staff development has to connect the activities it organizes and promotes for adults with learning outcomes for students.

Teachers who have access to teacher networks, enriched professional roles, and collegial work feel more positive about their profession. Teachers feel more professional when their schools provide structured time to work together on professional matters such as planning instruction, observing another's classroom, and providing feedback about their teaching (Darling-Hammond, 1996) and in constructing their own professional development activities (Calderón, 1997).

> Outstanding teachers teach the students to learn—not just pass tests.

Joyce et al. (1992) constantly emphasize in their publications how teaching can make a big difference to students and that outstanding teachers teach the students to learn—not just pass tests. Schools are now expected not only to offer education but also to ensure learning. Teachers are expected not only to cover curriculum but also to create a bridge between the needs of each learner and the attainment of challenging learning goals (Darling-Hammond, 1996). Adherence to or lack of these basic premises becomes more evident in TWB schools.

TOPICS FOR STAFF DEVELOPMENT

A strong staff development program begins at least 1 or 2 weeks before the opening of school and then schedules 5 to 8 staff development days during the year. By the following summer, the teachers will have identified additional topics they want to explore more profoundly. Therefore, ample resources and time allocation must be priority items negotiated with the district.

Topics Before School Opening

For Teachers, Administrators, Parents, and Community

- Most frequently asked questions
- The TWB design selected and why
- How the TWB program will be implemented
- Roles and responsibilities of everyone

For Teachers and Administrators

- Second-language teaching and learning (for reading and each subject matter)
- Latest research on the development of biliteracy
- Instructional strategies for biliteracy

- Observing and monitoring student progress
- Observing and monitoring our progress
- Team-teaching strategies
- Working within teachers learning communities
- Cultural understanding
- Standardized tests and alternative assessments
- Establishing linkages with families

For Parents

- What to expect from the program and school
- How to help their children at home
- What role(s) a parent can play in the program and school

Topics Throughout the Year and Summer Institutes

For Teachers, Administrators, Parents, and Community

- Updates on students' progress
- Modifications and adaptations to the program
- Additional needs

For Teachers and Administrators

- Teaching in Spanish for teachers
- Literature in Spanish and English
- Contrastive features of English and Spanish—what transfers?
- Depth of knowledge of biliteracy
- Developing an ample repertoire of instructional methods
- Supporting teachers in TWB programs
- Building on students' cultural, experiential background
- Engaging language minority parents
- Employing multiple assessment tools

The initial training consists of simulations, demonstrations, and processing of new information and methods. Teachers learn in cooperative learning teams and are always told the theories behind what they are learning, even though the emphasis is on giving them active, hands-on, pragmatic experience with strategies that will work. Throughout the year, teachers continue with training sessions on topics that they identify from their peer coaching, such as Spanish grammar for teachers, pacing, assessment, cooperative learning, classroom management, the writing process, and other topics to refine and extend topics presented earlier. At the end of the year, an evaluation session is held to determine the design of next year's professional development activities.

What Bilingual Teachers Want

In a recent national survey, TWB teachers reported their priorities for professional development (Calderón, 2002). The majority of the 100 teachers recognized the need to continue to upgrade their bilingual skills. This and other priorities were reported (see Table 9.1) and can serve as a point of departure for planning professional development activities.

More than 90 percent of the teachers checked "needs improvement in Spanish" on their survey. Some of their comments were as follows: "I'm afraid to elicit higher order discussions in Spanish because I don't know enough vocabulary." "If it's not in the manual, I'm afraid to ask questions in Spanish." "We don't have math books in Spanish, so we use key terms in English and I let the students explain to the other students."

Observations in more than one-third of the surveyed teachers' classrooms overwhelmingly revealed a gamut of spelling and grammatical errors in the teachers' and students' work that was posted, as well as in the teachers' instructional delivery. Simple phrases on the board or charts with instructions for the students contained spelling errors and lacked accents for the most part.

The implications from this study for the schools planning to implement a TWB program are that Spanish for teachers (or any other target language) will more than likely have to be included in the staff development summer institutes, binational teacher exchanges, or semester university courses. These learning activities, however, must be carefully negotiated with the trainers to ensure relevance to TWB teachers.

The national controversy about which is the "appropriate Spanish" is also a major concern for the teachers (e.g., Puerto Rican, Mexican, South American, Tex-Mex, and other regional versions have been mentioned as not being appropriate Spanish). Each region still seems quite ethnocentric about its dialect, and teachers complain about improper examples in their texts or their trainers' dialects. The implications here are that cross-cultural issues such as these also need to be addressed in TWB staff development. As classrooms become more heterogeneous in Spanish variations, teachers will need to learn, accept, and acknowledge those variations. Teachers must also learn the variations with their students. Several teachers said they would welcome glossaries of dialectical differences and regionalisms.

Time on Each Language of Instruction. Time spent on Spanish instruction varied considerably. Responses ranged from 30 to 90 percent of the day. The average was 40 percent in TWB programs. Most teachers reported that they were not certain, but they offered a percentage anyway. However, it is difficult to ascertain that these percentages reflect the actual amount, except when we visited their classrooms for systematic observations. In an earlier study, observations confirmed that bilingual teachers in TWB programs were off by at least 15 to 20 percent. In a 50-50 program, the actual total for a week averaged 65-35 (65 percent English and 35 percent

Table 9.1   Priorities for Professional Development

Response Categories	% of Teachers
1. How to improve skills in Spanish	90
2. Knowledge and teaching strategies for reading in Spanish	85
3. Knowledge and teaching strategies for reading in English	80
4. Knowledge and teaching strategies for writing in English	65
5. Proficiency in Spanish for teaching grammar and content	60
6. How to deal with the low status of the bilingual program in school	55
7. When and how to use Spanish effectively (timeframes, when to translate, etc.)	50
8. How to help students transition from Spanish to English and from English to Spanish	45
9. How to diagnose and assess students	30
10. How to teach math more effectively in Spanish and English	25

Spanish) (Calderón & Carreón, 2000). The implications here are that staff development topics need to keep this issue at the forefront. For example, when workshops are offered on math, not only should the training be offered in both languages, but the issue of how time will be allocated in each language to math has to be determined before leaving the workshop.

Strategies for Dual-Language Instruction. There was no clear tendency toward strategies for two-way immersion (TWI) or dual-language use, and findings were similar to those reported previously by other researchers and practitioners. Teachers reported using the following strategies:

- Preview-review methods for introducing a story, content lessons, and/or content texts
- Translation when introducing new concepts, when it's faster than trying to explain in English, or when a new student joins the class for the first week or so
- Kept two languages separate by team teaching, teaching in one language in the morning and the other in the afternoon, and/or teaching certain content area such as science in one language and another subject in the other language

In most programs, there was more time throughout the program devoted to reading, writing, and oral language development in English. Oral language development in Spanish was not mentioned except by the Success for All/Éxito Para Todos teachers. Some teachers mainly taught math in English and social studies in Spanish. Other teachers mainly taught math in Spanish ("because there is a lot of problem solving and reading") and science and social studies in English ("because it is more hands-on and I usually read the text to the students").

The implications here are that the school needs to first research and determine the type of strategy to use for teaching in both languages and then follow up with inservice training that models the uses selected.

In schools such as Alicia Chacón and Hueco, there is a very low turnover of teachers, but in other TWI schools, the turnover is high. Teachers reported that they were not well informed about the program's philosophy and the requirements placed on them. The implications here are that in addition to informing teachers verbally and in writing, the initial staff development inservice training needs to be very explicit about the TWI philosophy, the research base, the model selected, the amount of instruction delivered in each language, the student population, the expectations of the language capabilities of each teacher and support staff, the interests of the parents and community, and the political climate.

What Are Teachers Learning Communities (TLCs)?

> TLCs are contexts where teachers co-construct knowledge and meaning from their craft.

Teaching is art, science, and craft (Joyce et al., 1992; Lieberman & Miller, 1991). Teachers must continue to make and remake the classroom, based on updated knowledge combined with their own imagination, spirit, and inspiration. Staff development programs must maintain a fragile balance between building cultures where collaboration and collegueship are promoted and where individual integrity and artistry are allowed to flourish (Lieberman & Miller, 1991). Based on these notions, the teachers learning communities attempt to become the context for teachers' collective synergy, imagination, spirit, inspiration, and continuous learning.

TLCs are sometimes called *study groups, collegial groups,* or *communities of practice*. A TLC by any other name is basically a community of teachers working together toward success in teaching and student learning. TLCs are contexts where teachers co-construct knowledge and meaning from their craft (Calderón, 1999a, 1999b).

The goal of a TLC may be to develop new curriculum and a new assessment process; learn, apply, and evaluate an instructional practice; adopt or adapt a new program; restructure a school; or create a schooling

> TLCs are opportunities to collaboratively examine, question, study profoundly, experiment-implement, evaluate, and change.

innovation from scratch. It is an opportunity for teachers to collaboratively examine, question, do profound study, experiment-implement, evaluate, and change. Perhaps the greatest outcome from conducting these collegial activities is that teachers develop new skills, ways of working with their colleagues, and, most significantly, ways of working with their students more effectively.

Why a Community?

A *community* implies working together, as community members have done throughout the ages, for the benefit of the individual and the community as a whole. Each individual member contributes his or her talents and resources and shares in the decision making all along the way. The more each individual pitches in, the more the whole community stands to gain.

In a community, there are rainy and stormy days. Frail structures that are barely being erected might be swept away by unexpected floods, fire, or any natural event. When these catastrophes occur, a community pulls together, which makes its members' ties to one another even stronger. It also nurtures and reaches out to those most affected and most in need. A community grows together and learns together. It grows together intellectually, emotionally, and spiritually as well as physically or in resources and gains. Without growth in one area, growth in the others is stifled.

The lack of community becomes more evident in complex structures such as those required by TWB programs. A TWB teachers learning community is very much like any thriving community. It implies teachers working together for the benefit of the individual teacher and the school as a whole. Each teacher contributes his or her talents and resources and shares in the decision making in every session. The more each teacher contributes, the more the whole school stands to gain. Teachers develop nurturing relationships by moving beyond self-centeredness as they reach to others most in need. They externalize their deep moral and spiritual commitment to educating children through collaborative responsibility. They grow and stretch in multiple directions. Without simultaneous growth in the intellectual, emotional, spiritual, creative, and interpersonal realms, a teacher's or administrator's growth is stifled.

How TLCs Assist Systemic Change in the TWB School

"Schools and classes are communities of students, brought together to explore the world and learn how to navigate it productively. . . . Thus, a major role of learning communities is to create powerful learners" (Joyce et al., 1992, pp. 1-2). The learners are the teachers, students, parents, and administrators in a school. Joyce and his colleagues (1992) have found that teachers can master just about any kind of teaching strategy or implement almost any kind of sensible research-based curriculum—if the appropriate conditions are provided for teachers to learn and practice in communities of peers. Experimentation with teaching should be a normal and shared activity as teachers develop new procedures and/or develop or try out new instructional materials (p. 3). Joyce et al. also emphasized that effective teaching comes when schools set up learning communities for teachers. The concept of a community of collaborating teachers, a recognition that educational knowledge is emergent, a belief that the future science of education will be built around clinical inquiry, and a sense of an organization whose staff is truly empowered are the researchers' vision of professionalization (pp. 381-382).

Huberman (1992) cautioned that teachers still view themselves as "independent artisans" who derive their satisfaction from independent classroom "tinkering" rather than from large-scale school reforms. Hargreaves (1994) made the distinction between teacher individuality (which supports initiative and principled dissent) and individualism ("Leave me alone, I teach behind closed doors"). He reminds us that school improvement means striking a balance between teacher individuality and colleagueship and collaboration. Both need to coexist in a TWI school.

> Teaching as a craft involves planning, research, observation, and response.

Staff development and teachers learning communities need to provide teachers with what Leinhardt, Zaslavsky, and Stein (1990) called "action-based situated knowledge of teaching" (p. 23; Grimmett & McKinnon, 1992). Teaching as a craft involves planning, research, observation, and response. It is not a range of skills and proficiencies (Green & Harker, 1982). It is pedagogical procedural information useful in enhancing learner-focus teaching in a classroom full of diverse learners (Calderón, 1997). These procedural ways of dealing rigorously and supportively with learners need to be constantly upgraded, adjusted, and reconceptualized. Therefore, a teacher needs opportunities for continuous collegial construction of learning.

> The school is characterized by a profound respect for and encouragement of diversity, where important differences among children and adults are celebrated rather than seen as problems to remedy.

Communities of learners seem to be committed, above all, to discovering conditions that elicit and support human learning and to providing these conditions. Whereas many attempts to implement new programs dwell on monitoring adult behavior, controlling students, and raising test scores, the real question should be the following: "Under what conditions will principal and student and teacher become serious, committed, sustained, lifelong, cooperative learners?" (Barth, 1990, p. 45). In a learning community, students, teachers, parents, and administrators share the opportunities and responsibilities for making decisions that affect all the occupants of the schoolhouse. There is a high level of collegiality, a place teeming with frequent, helpful, personal, and professional interactions; a climate of risk taking is deliberately fostered, and a safety net protects those who may risk and stumble. The school is characterized by a profound respect for and encouragement of diversity, where important differences among children and adults are celebrated rather than seen as problems to remedy (Barth, 1990). Little (1981) found that the prevalence of collegiality in a school is closely related to four specific behaviors of the principal.

The Role of the Principal

1. States expectations explicitly for cooperation among teachers. "I expect all of us to work together, help one another, and make our knowledge available."
2. Models collegiality, that is, enacts it by joining with teachers and other principals working collaboratively to improve conditions in the school
3. Rewards collegiality by granting release time, recognition, space, materials, or funds to teachers who work as colleagues
4. Protects teachers who initially engage in collegial behavior and thereby risk the retribution of their fellows (Little, 1990)
5. Meets with team teachers on a regular basis to discuss issues regarding curriculum, instructional techniques, assessment, and student progress
6. Observes teachers and provides technical feedback
7. Becomes the strongest program advocate

Barth (1990, p. 163) concluded that in a collegial school, adults and students are constantly learning because everyone is a staff developer for everyone else.

Empirically Tested Studies of TLCs

The theoretical framework described above became the foundation for the development and continuous refinement of the TLCs, which began with a 5-year study on implementing a complex instructional model along with the TLCs (Calderón, 1994, 1998; Calderón et al., 1998). Quantitative data consisted of comparing baseline data with year-to-year results for (1) student achievement, (2) teacher professional accomplishments, and (3) the school's annual report card indicators (e.g., attendance, retentions, suspensions, and graduation rates), as well as comparative analyses of teacher, student, and administrator questionnaires. Ethnographic data, analyzed in light of the talent development perspective (Boykin, 1996; Erickson, 1996), consisted of field notes, interviews, videotapes of the TLC sessions and professional development events, and pre- and postvideo recordings of teachers applying innovations in their classrooms.

The study of TLCs in bilingual and multicultural schools was also based on the notion that learning is socially constructed. Soviet psychologist Lev Vygotsky (1978) identified the zone of proximal development (ZPD) in collaborative learning. The ZPD defines the distance between what an individual can do on his or her own and what he or she can do with peer assistance. A professional model of potential, or a talent development model, relies on interaction for the co-construction of learning. Central to the teachers' community is the direct engagement and increased participation in joint activity. For example, in communities of effective practice, students acquire linguistic and sociocultural knowledge from legitimate participation in communicative practices (Gutierrez, 1995). Along the same principles, teachers acquire pedagogical understanding and practice from legitimate participation in TLC exchanges, not from lectures, readings, or disjointed workshops.

There have been six principal studies and contexts for the TLCs: (1) the Bilingual Cooperative Integrated Reading and Composition (BCIRC) project in seven elementary bilingual schools, with equivalent control groups; (2) the cooperative learning/peer coaching project in a large high school; (3) the cooperative learning/peer coaching project in a predominately Latino student population middle school; (4) the cooperative learning/Success for All projects in Juárez, Mexico; (5) the binational researchers learning community from U.S. and Mexican universities and educational institutions; and (6) the TWB elementary schools project. Further analysis of data from these projects continues to help us build a stronger theory and implementation of TLCs (Calderón, 2000).

The results from these studies showed that TLCs could be used for various purposes, all of which have implications for TWI program implementation:

1. To improve or adjust existing instructional programs

2. To integrate complex instructional processes

3. To cope with structural barriers, isolation, and limitations imposed by schools

4. For critical pedagogy and research

5. To construct new programs

Teachers describe a TLC as:

- A talent development model—the focus is on identifying each teacher's talents and sharing those talents with peers.
- Creativity and invention—teachers are encouraged to express their creative talents and ideas.
- Significant collegial relationships—profound relationships are key in effective schools.
- An inquiry process—the concept of TWI schools is fairly new and in need of continuous inquiry.

- Personal and professional improvement—the whole staff must be willing to learn and improve its skills continuously.
- A mechanism to cope with change—as the whole staff experiences many changes, it is more comforting to have peer support.
- A sense of belonging for everyone—since TWI is new for everyone at the school, no one is the "real expert," and everyone plays an important role in building success.
- Opportunities to learn together—no matter how diverse a school staff might be, a TLC's common goal and vision give everyone an opportunity to grow professionally together.
- Shared responsibility—a TLC automatically sets a tone for shared responsibility.
- Peer coaching and friendly feedback—these are more acceptable within a safe context of a TLC.
- Mutual support—in a TLC, all teachers support each other, particularly those teachers who need more assistance.
- Teachers' voices—a place where a teacher's voice is heard and valued.

These characteristics come from extensive reviews of the literature and from pilot projects that have been conducted in a variety of bilingual/bicultural contexts throughout the United States and Mexico.

TLCs to Construct and Sustain TWB Programs or Schools

Perhaps some of the most complex and comprehensive programs today are the dual-language or two-way bilingual schools. Although most programs begin with the implementation of a few classrooms at a time, the innovation is eventually implemented schoolwide. This calls for extensive reform and rethinking. For this reason, another TLC study has been taking place in a school district that plans to eventually have a large number of two-way bilingual schools.

The TLCs in these schools have been particularly important in creating a context where bilingual and mainstream teachers learn to work together effectively, where learning in two languages becomes quality learning, and where power, language status, racism, and historical misconceptions are replaced by cultural understanding, equity, and excellence.

The ethnographic studies from these classrooms have yielded glimpses of the multiple issues of dual-language program implementation that we are sharing in this book. Most important, the studies have demonstrated the resiliency of teachers working together to create their own program: the curriculum, the orchestration of instruction in two languages, the team-teaching negotiations, and their TLC activities, which included peer coaching, action research projects, and teacher ethnographies to learn about their own performance and craft.

We recommend that conversations and activities about teaching and learning should be frequent, continuous, concrete, and precise. The following 30-minute activities have been collected from various TLCs. These also apply to a TWB. As teachers systematically meet once a week for 30 minutes, they will discover the type of activities that best meet their professional needs.

Types of Weekly 30-Minute Activities in TLCs

1. Continuous study of research on reading, writing, English as a Second Language, TWB programs, sheltered instruction, and other topics relevant to TWB. Examples: Teachers read articles from journals such as *The Reading Teacher, Review of Educational Research, Journal of Education of Students Placed at Risk, Kappan,* and so on to keep up with the field. Teachers read the articles in jigsaw fashion (teachers sit in teams of four, and each reads a portion of the article and teaches it to the other team members); afterwards, they discuss the implications and relevance to their own implementation.

2. Peer demonstrations of the teaching strategies and discourse scripts for each strategy in Spanish and English (or another primary language). Examples: A teacher can demonstrate and provide a sample script of the questions she or he uses to debrief cooperative skills, learning strategies, or the content of the learning in sheltered English. A teacher can share a script for setting up a science lesson in Spanish.

3. Analysis and discussion of student adaptation and modification of instruction to meet diverse needs. Examples: Discuss (1) how best to group students in teams, (2) how to conduct a Numbered Heads Together activity that ensures success for second-language acquirers, and (3) how to teach reading comprehension skill "x" to students who need extra support.

4. Analysis of fidelity to the model. Examples: Discuss if there are teachers who are not using the model systematically and why. Determine next steps: Is more training necessary? Are adaptations to the model necessary? Other solutions?

5. Practice peer coaching and giving technical feedback. Examples: Watch videotaped teaching segments of TWB teachers and role-play, giving them positive technical feedback. Or, two teachers can practice observing a colleague with teacher-developed observation checklists and then compare their data-gathering strategies. They can also practice giving feedback to the teacher before they actually do so.

6. Discussion of peer coaching and/or mentoring. Examples: Discuss such questions as, "What works and what needs improvement in our feedback activities?" "How can we better assist the new teachers?" "What are we learning from our peer observations?"

7. Feedback from implementation checks. Examples: Discuss such questions as, "What were the results of our implementation visits?" "How can we celebrate our successes and build on them? "How can we improve on ___ and ___?" "What's our goal for next week? What is the difference between the first visit and this one in our students' accomplishments?"

8. Joint analysis of video recordings of own teaching and student learning. Example: Teacher places a video camera in back of the room or by a team of students to record a small segment. At a TLC, the teacher selects a 5- to 10-minute segment to share with the TLC colleagues. A discussion follows, highlighting successes and areas for improvement.

9. Review of instructional essential elements. Examples: Teachers go over the schedule of reading activities for the week and ask, "Are we doing each step in an appropriate sequence and within the timeframe? What are we frequently leaving out in the process of teaching reading? Why? Where are we bogged down? Why? What do we need to do to improve?" An analysis of video recordings of the reading activities prior to this discussion is also recommended.

10. Reflection and decision-making activities to help teachers further develop their own professional development. Examples: What other workshops do we need? What about other types of professional development activities? What types of support systems do we need for this particular instructional problem?

11. Social sessions to celebrate successes. Examples: Celebrate births, birthdays, marriages, awards, and recognition such as Teacher of the Year, grant awards, terrific implementation visit reports, and so on.

12. Sessions for personal support in time of need. Examples: Attend to personal tragedies, milestones, or temporary problems (divorce, children going off to college, personal setback).

13. "Vision, Mission, Passion Sessions" for self-renewal and synergy. Example: Bring in a dynamic motivational speaker to recharge those batteries— especially around November and February-March. Create a fun activity to rekindle the passion for teaching.

14. Student product display "Galleries" or "Brag-a-Bunch & Munch" sessions. Example: Set up displays of student work in the teachers lounge and bring munchies for lunchtime. Conduct afterschool brief sessions in which teachers take turns bragging about what their students have accomplished that week. Once in a while, invite other teachers from another school to your TLC.

15. Sessions with researchers for analysis of students' performance. Example: Invite a researcher and show videos of students in cooperative teams. Discuss the following: What is the quality of the interaction? Higher order thinking and discussions? Level of cooperation? What can we learn from this instructional event?

16. Organize workshops or classroom demonstrations for other teachers. Example: Design workshops, agendas, or visuals to be delivered in teams for other teachers in your school. Rehearse with TLC members before the "big day."

17. Study student writing assessment processes, criteria, and samples. Example: Bring samples of students' writing from four categories: (1) excellent, (2) good, (3) not so good, and (4) uncertain as to how to score. Do a read-around in teams of four and score all the student samples. Discuss results and reach consensus about rubrics.

18. Analysis of student 8-week and standardized test results. Example: Bring your class's standardized scores or 8-week results. Compare with others. Analyze similarities and discrepancies. Discuss implications for instruction, and identify target strategies and projected goals.

TLCs Can Be Places to Learn Cultural Histories and Respect for Other Cultures

School personnel have the moral obligation to accommodate children's differences in cultural background, learning style, and multiple intelligences. Curriculum needs to include different kinds of families and cultural histories. All too often, the richness of the local cultural history is totally ignored or is subordinate to the "majority culture" in curriculum designs. Jeanne Oakes is critical of existing school reform literature and movements for ignoring race and being color-blind. She finds "persistent inequalities along race and social class lines as low-income students and students of color experience fewer resources and less powerful learning environments" (Oakes, Wells, Yonezawa, & Ray, 1997, p. 43). These inequalities will persist until teachers work together to liberate themselves and their students from such oppressing or restricting structures.

TLCs can become places to learn the teachers' own cultural histories. In methodologies such as "personal histories," each teacher writes his or her own and shares with the other teachers. The strategy of "writing for reflection" gives teachers an opportunity to write anonymously about a cultural concern, and then these are read and discussed in the TLCs. Eventually, teachers drop the anonymity and begin sharing profound issues from the heart. These writings help teams of teachers not only to explore their own histories but also to publish, share, and disseminate this wealth of cultural capital.

TLCs Can Be Places for Emotionally Meaningful Relationships

Andy Hargreaves (1994) argued that change efforts have been so preoccupied with skills and standardized tests that they have not gotten to the heart of change—establishing bonds and forming relationships with students. Our research community argues that it is also important for all teachers to create bonds and relationships with other teachers, administrators, and parents, particularly in bilingual/language minority schools.

> Much evidence testifies that people who are emotionally adept—who know and manage their own feelings well, and who read and deal effectively with other people's feelings—are at an advantage in any domain of life, whether romance and intimate relationships or picking up the unspoken rules that govern success in organizational politics. People with well-developed emotional skills are also more likely to be content and effective in their lives, mastering the habits of mind that foster their own productivity; people who cannot marshal some control over their emotional life fight inner battles that sabotage their ability for focused work and clear thought. (Goleman, 1995, p. 36)

Goleman (1995) defined *emotional intelligence* as self-control and empathy, zeal and persistence, and the ability to motivate oneself. Hargreaves (1994) believes that "emotional intelligence" adds value to students, classroom learning, and teachers' professional learning (p. 2). He also provides many reasons why educational change needs more depth: increased rates and changing patterns of global migration, low numbers of minority teachers, the fast pace of school reforms, and children who know more about technology and the Internet than teachers do.

Because of all these changes, teachers need a lot more collaboration to be effective today. Teachers need a community where they can share the burden, reduce duplication, provide moral support, and derive collective strength. Classroom volunteers, professional facilitators, and/or paid clerical help ought to be collectively recruited by a community of teachers rather than on an individual basis. It is this type of collective strength that can also be derived from a well-structured TLC for TWI schools.

As market competition and parental choice redefine which schools survive, TWI teachers might begin to feel the emotional burden of an uncertain future. Teachers need to find better ways to learn from their colleagues to remain "marketable" and to keep their schools "successful" in this new competitive market.

All in all, teachers must reinvent their sense of professionalism so they can cope and succeed with the changes in schools, their community, their colleagues, and most of all their student populations. Working in schools now requires emotional maturity, openness, and assertiveness.

TLCs Can Be Places to Rekindle Hope and Passion

Good teaching is not only instructional strategies and classroom management. It is also pleasure, passion, creativity, joy, and challenge (Hargreaves, 1994). It is a passionate vocation (Fried, 1995). It is also *cariño* (care), affection, and love. The passion includes enthusiasm, excitement, interest, risk taking, and hope.

However, Fullan (1997) said that the more teachers "care," the more anxious they get. Then, the more that they become emotionally detached, the poorer the decisions that they make. Understanding the intimate two-way link between emotion and hope is a powerful insight. Yet, this insight is difficult to come by when working and reflecting in isolation.

Hope can come from our profound religious beliefs or from our own optimism and moral purpose. Hope is not only a positive emotion.

> Anger, sadness, frustration, anxiety, loss of control, dissatisfaction and discomfort—all inform hopefulness for the emotionally intelligent person. The emotionally effective person knows that complexity and diversity are endemic in postmodern society. Hopeful people have a greater capacity to deal with "interpersonal discomfort." (Fullan, 1997, p. 221)

This combination of hope and spiritual and emotional intelligence is also necessary when dealing with complex change circumstances. Moments of discomfort are opportunities for reflection. But these reflections need to be tested in collegial comfort zones to be rendered valid. Therefore, TLCs can become places for rekindling hope, emotional comfort, and passion as schools begin to address the complex issues of educating all students in their schools to the highest levels possible.

WHAT HAVE WE LEARNED FROM THE STUDY OF TLCs?

We have learned that the traditional staff development practices in bilingual contexts do not work. From a survey of 100 bilingual teachers across the country, we identified characteristics of ineffective traditional staff development that are quite prevalent (Calderón, 2002).

Ineffective Traditional Staff Development

- Offers a series of one-shot workshops on the "fad of the moment" or the "guru of the day"
- Separates bilingual from mainstream teachers
- Offers no follow-up or teachers learning communities for teacher reflection after the inservice training
- Provides workshops focusing too much on skill and "fun things" to do on Monday morning
- Imparts transmission models rather than constructivist models
- Ignores an individual teacher's needs and levels of expertise
- Ignores context and diversity of classrooms
- Offers minimal support to teachers (no facilitators, coaches, researchers)

Creating TLCs is not as difficult as sustaining them. TLCs are situated models and must be constructed across contexts and schools. Just like peer coaching, they cannot be imposed. This process model is culturally sensitive and accounts for the multiple ways that participants co-construct contexts, activities, and their shared language. They are focal points for powerful transformation when continuous learning is occurring. They can also get bogged down with logistics, schedules, negative conversation, and superficial task completion.

> They can also get bogged down with logistics, schedules, negative conversation, and superficial task completion. Therefore, creating TLCs is not as difficult as sustaining them.

As Barth (1991) noted, "The term collegiality has remained conceptually amorphous and ideologically sanguine" (pp. 31-32). *Collegiality* has many meanings, some of which carry few or even negative consequences, usually because it has been mandated from above. Hargreaves and Wignall (1989) called this "contrived collegiality." Little also warned that teachers can collaborate effectively to achieve a variety of ends, including blocking reform efforts to preserve the status quo. Therefore, it is important to give considerable attention to the TLCs from the start and to continue to care for and monitor their development and progress. Studies have identified elements that need to be present for TLCs to function and persist:

Sustaining Quality TLCs

- TLC activities need to be structured by specific agendas generated by teachers—the agenda should be flexible enough to allow teachers to meet their own emergent needs (collective autonomy).
- TLC activities need to be brief—5 minutes for sharing successes, 5 minutes for problem solving, 10 minutes for instructional demos, 10 minutes for analyzing student work, and 5 minutes for celebration.
- TLC activities need to be scheduled—as part of the school's calendar—and time has to be allocated during the workday.
- Quality interaction norms are practiced—there are ground rules jointly constructed so that one person does not dominate or individuals do not participate.
- Continuous training for TLCs—teamwork, trust building, and team building are essential for initial success and to reenergize and refocus.
- Since transformation is a highly interactive process, the more teachers participate and share, the more learning that takes place.
- Teachers create their own measures of performance within TLCs and submit their accomplishments to the principal on a monthly basis.
- Administrators drop by systematically to praise teachers and to identify areas of difficulty or need.
- TLCs successes should be celebrated periodically.

TLC participants must adhere to these ground rules, schedule follow-up implementation checks, and conduct specific training when activity gets bogged down (e.g., conflict resolution strategies, communication skills, inquiry processes). It is a cycle of learning that never ends because there will always be new teachers, new things to learn, and new problems to solve.

SUMMARY

Thus, professional development designs must be carefully planned, monitored, and evaluated. The following checklist can be used to assign leadership roles and create subtasks for the staff development plan.

Staff Development Plan

- Task 1: Initiate meetings to develop design with teachers.
- Task 2: Determine how the staff development design supports, articulates, and integrates the district's as well as the school's TWB plans.

- Task 3: Map out data collection for student placement, progress, and outcomes.
- Task 4: Identify content of staff development based on research and empirical studies and determine principles, goals, and objectives for staff development and TLCs.
- Task 5: Identify teacher and staff needs and talents.
- Task 6: Map out data collection for teacher development and the overall staff development plan.
- Task 7: Identify current and future staff development sources and financial resources.
- Task 8: Implement the plan and an ongoing process for successful implementation and problem solving.
- Task 9: Evaluate and improve the plan at the end of the year.
- Task 10: Celebrate each month.

Ongoing professional development activities could also include attending TWB conferences such as the annual California Association for Bilingual Education's Dual Language summer conference. Visiting other schools with TWI programs helps refine and sustain enthusiasm, as well as form networks and partnerships within networks such as those in the Success for All regional conferences.

In essence, the philosophy of professional development is that although initial training is important, real change in teachers' practices takes place in the classroom, not the workshop. Staff development is a process that never ends. In TLCs, teachers in TWB schools are constantly refining their instructional practice, learning new strategies, discussing their accomplishments, solving everyday problems, visiting each other's classes, and using assessments of student progress to guide changes in their teaching methods. While these processes might seem time-consuming, the amount of time and resources invested in them will correlate with the success of the students and the program.

TLCs are contexts for the following:

- Profound study of a topic
- Peer coaching
- Action research
- Classroom ethnographies
- Teacher portfolios
- Teacher autobiographies
- Instructional analysis
- Analysis of student progress and outcomes
- Binational teacher exchanges to further enhance or sustain bilingual skills

10

Reaching Out to Parents

An important concern of TWB programs—as it is of schools and the school systems they represent—is the academic and language achievement of second-language learners (SLLs) and the need for parents to be involved in the school (Lindholm-Leary, 2001). Two-way bilingual (TWB) program parents have a role in their children's education. They can improve and maintain their children's achievement and can also participate as a group to have a voice in the program's and the school's decision-making process (Bermúdez & Márquez, 1996; Durán, 2000). This would particularly apply to parents of English learners who may not be familiar with the school's expectations in parent involvement outside of their homes (Minaya-Rowe, 1996; Morán & Hakuta, 1995).

Specific literature on parent involvement in TWB programs is scarce compared to what exists in transitional bilingual programs and in mainstream school programs. This chapter includes what there is in TWB parent involvement and incorporates or supplements with successful elements from the larger body of knowledge in the field. Parent involvement practices seem to be more important in the child's academic success than are race, education, and socioeconomic status (Hidalgo, Bright, Siu, Swap, & Epstein, 1995; Marvin, 1998). Clarification is needed of what schools and teachers perceive the role of parents should be in schools and what parents' expectations of their role should be. The spectrum of parental support can be described from simple parental support of school policies with home reinforcement of school skills to parents as advocates and change agents at the decision-making level (Bermúdez & Padrón, 1990).

TWB parent involvement can also be important in addressing possible tensions that may be present in the school culture between SLL parents (Cummins, 2000; Nieto, 2000).

TWB programs bring optimism in solving tensions in schools as their program design allows for student interaction and the involvement of all parents of SLLs, with an attitude of respect that places equal value on all languages and cultures. All TWB parents need to have the following:

- Access to participation in school decision making, even though some SLL parents may not yet be proficient in English
- Knowledge of political and economic resources, even though some preliterate parents may feel powerless
- Knowledge of the school instructional program design to serve the needs of all students, using the standards-based curriculum and state-mandated standards and guidelines
- Awareness that the languages for instruction are Standard English and one other standard language and that both languages are considered prestigious languages and supported by the school system
- Awareness that both languages and cultural identities are developed and maintained at school

WHO ARE THE PARENTS OF SLLs?

TWB programs have a great opportunity to involve SLL parents. For the most part, parents of English speakers are proficient and often literate in English. They belong to or are familiar with the mainstream U.S. society and the cultural values it represents, and they possess knowledge of its educational system. Parents of English learners are a diverse group with diverse backgrounds and needs (Ogbu, 1987, 1992; Ovando & Collier, 1998). The following characteristics reflect their diversity:

- They come from a working-class background, yet most have aspirations to middle-class status.
- They are immigrant minorities who have moved voluntarily to the United States for economic, social, or political reasons.
- They are indigenous minorities who have become incorporated involuntarily into U.S. society through conquest (Native Americans, Mexican Americans) or colonization (Puerto Ricans, Native Hawaiians).
- They represent diverse languages and cultures, with varied educational backgrounds, social classes, and life experiences.
- They come from rural and urban settings and from technological, industrial, or preindustrial societies.

Providing an in-depth examination of these characteristics would be beyond the scope of this chapter. However, they need to be addressed when planning any kind of agenda for parent involvement.

A DEFINITION OF PARENT INVOLVEMENT

Despite the enormous range of diversity among parents in TWB programs, we can aspire to encourage their full participation in school, as well as to link the life of the school with the life of the community in all its diversity and to celebrate it as a means of helping parents achieve a stronger sense of ownership in the education of their children (Chavkin, 1993; Delgado-Gaitan, 1993).

In this context, we define parental involvement as any of a variety of activities that allow parents to participate in the educational process at home or at school. Examples of activities are information exchange, decision sharing, volunteer services for school, home tutoring or teaching, and child advocacy (Carrasquillo & London, 1993; Durán, 2000). This definition is valid for TWB parents with the added interaction of parents from both language groups. For example,

- parents of English learners interact with parents of Spanish learners, and
- parents of Spanish learners interact with parents of English learners.

Studies on parent involvement over the past three decades have consistently demonstrated the importance of parents in the academic development of their children at all levels of instruction and as a component of effective schooling and systemic reform (Cloud et al., 2000; Hess, 1999). Children have an advantage in school when their parents encourage and support their school activities (Levine & Lezotte, 1995). The evidence is clear that students gain in personal and academic development if

- families emphasize schooling over the school years, from the early grades through high school, and
- parents let their children know on a continuous and daily basis that their schooling is important to them (Valdés, 1996).

There is some agreement on what schools should do to promote and maintain parent involvement. Two types of parent involvement have been identified in the literature and are described in terms of how each type contributes to school effectiveness. They are also described as conventional and nonconventional parent participation (Lindholm-Leary, 2001). Since these types are relevant for all school programs, they can also be important for TWB programs (i.e., the recommendations can be extrapolated to TWB programs).

CONVENTIONAL PARENT INVOLVEMENT ACTIVITIES

Schools and programs count on parents to get involved, attend parent meetings, and participate in set school activities (Gibson, 1993; Shannon & Lojero Latimer, 1996). Because parents of English learners vary in their experiences in the United States, as well as in language, academic skills, and level of adjustment to U.S. society, schools need to take active roles in helping them build positive home conditions for their children's school learning and behavior (Macroff, 1992; Moles, 1993).

In TWB programs, ideally, SLL parents are expected to act on the information they receive from school and know how to help their children succeed. At the same time, TWB program administrators and teachers are responsible for the form, frequency, and likely results of the information sent to the parents, particularly parents of English learners who may be new to the English language, the mainstream culture, and the U.S. educational system (Tinajero, 1992). TWB programs are responsible for making sure that the following occurs:

- The information can be read and understood by all SLL parents.
- They alert SLL parents to check frequently with their children for messages from the school.
- They encourage or invite SLL parents to work with the school staff to revise or improve school policies and ways of communication.
- They request SLL parents to work with the school administration and teachers if their children's attendance, grades, conduct, and course work are not satisfactory.

TWB teachers and school-community liaisons can be encouraged to phone or visit parents who cannot speak or read in the second language. An exemplary communication network is in place at Chacón School, as illustrated in Chapter 4 of this how-to book. Non-English-speaking parents and non-Spanish-speaking parents are able to communicate and help themselves and, in turn, help their children with their homework and school projects. Their participation practices include information exchange, home tutoring, volunteer service for the school, and decision sharing. Chacón School parents are pleased that their children are enrolled in the TWB program and are willing to give their time generously and collaborate with the school. Among the parent involvement assets are the following:

- Parent-teacher conferences using the languages parents feel most comfortable with or using translators
- Phone conversations with parents about their children's progress

- Detailed, frequent, and genuine communications about their children's instructional program or progress

NONCONVENTIONAL PARENT INVOLVEMENT ACTIVITIES

TWB program parents can also become involved with the school activities beyond the homework framework and traditional school attendance, such as parents' nights or parent-teacher conferences (Lindholm, 1990; Suárez-Orozco, 1993). Parents of English learners can participate more fully in their children's schooling and in a sense validate and empower their own family's social and cultural experiences and values, thus achieving a better balance of cooperation between the school and the home (Sleeter, 1991). English-speaking parents also can be involved in multicultural and bilingual experiences as an asset to their children's success and thus contribute to a better understanding of linguistically and culturally diverse students. This type of parent assistance in TWB programs includes the following:

- Assisting teachers in the classroom, on class trips, or in class parties
- Assisting administrators and teachers in the cafeteria, library, playground, computer lab, or other areas that require adult supervision
- Assisting the parent organization and school administration with fundraising, community relations, and political awareness

Of course, not many TWB parents can be active in these activities. They often work full-time or part-time, having one or two jobs to make ends meet, and cannot be in the school building during the school day. Still, the parents' presence at school can provide a two-way benefit, for parent participation and for school instructional program improvement. For example, Chacón School parents who are in charge of some afterschool program activities or who volunteer at school show teachers that they are willing to work with them to improve the school and its TWB program. At the same time, parents feel that the school is open to them. Other nonconventional opportunities include the following:

- Parents as audiences: Parents can also be involved at the school as audiences for student performances to demonstrate their bilinguality, assemblies, demonstrations, and sports events. These are infrequent events that involve minimal commitment of time from parents. These events can also be used by TWB programs as occasions to conduct other meetings or provide information to parents, as deemed necessary, on the progress of their children, their specific needs, and so forth.

- Parents as students: Parents can also come to the TWB school as students for workshops, education, and training sessions being held in the language parents feel most comfortable. For example, parents of SLLs may need to learn the second language, finish high school, and become familiar with computers, among other things.
- Parents as guests: Parents can be invited to visit the school on one of their vacation days or work holidays to observe teachers and students in the classroom, talk with their children's teachers, or help at school.

Parents and the TWB program can also work together to make necessary changes both in the home and in the program, which will benefit the overall education of the children. The joint effort on the part of the school and the parents has the potential to become an empowerment model that will enable both the families and the school to benefit (Cummins, 2000; Ogbu, 1995). Chacón School parents reported the following activities that accommodated them as process-oriented participants and helped them develop awareness of their role in the school and the conditions under which they can operate as a fundamental basis for change in the schooling process. As active participants, TWB parents have an opinion on the decision-making process and participate in governance roles and advocacy groups as follows:

- *Governance.* Their activities include participation in
      PTA/PTO or other organizations
      Formal and informal school committees
      Advisory councils or other groups at the school, district, or state levels under the leadership of school, district, or state administrators
      Advocacy for children
      School improvement plans
      Revision or reformulation of school policies
      Selection committees for new principals, teachers, or staff

- *Advocacy.* Their activities include the following:
      Speaking and working independently for TWB quality programming, presenting at educational conferences, and showcasing program components
      Providing parents and the community with information about TWB program design and standards
      Participating in making education decisions and supporting issues that affect education, such as issues of equity in bilingual education
      Ensuring school fairness and preventing discrimination in integration policies and practices regarding TWB programming

TWP PROGRAM PARENTS
IN THE GLOBAL SCENE

Recently, leaders in government, military, education, and industry have cited the United States' lack of competence in foreign languages as a national security issue (Paige, 2001, 2002; Tucker, 2001). Foreign-language competence is a major factor contributing to the country's new role in fighting terrorism and increasing its competitiveness in world economic markets.

- On the international scene, national security and international trade point to foreign-language learning as an essential prerequisite for peace and understanding (Malone, 2001).
- On the national level, many English-speaking American parents want their children to develop the skills necessary to function in a society that is becoming increasingly diverse, both culturally and linguistically.

On the basis of these national socioeconomic, political, and demographic concerns that affect local communities, English-speaking parents are showing interest in having their children develop bilingual competence through public school foreign-language instruction (González, 2000).

The expansion in the number and geographic distribution of TWB programs in public schools across the United States is an index of the increasing interest in foreign-language competence across the country (Christian, 1999; Howard & Sugarman, 2001). A major factor in the popularity and success of TWB programs has been the support of the English-speaking parents who desire foreign-language education for their children (Cazabon, 2001).

CONSIDERATIONS FOR SUCCESSFUL
PARENT INVOLVEMENT IN A TWB PROGRAM

The following considerations from research and recommendations have proven to be successful and apply to parental involvement in all programs, but they also have implications for TWB program parent participation.

- Promote and maintain parent involvement across grade levels, from pre-K through high school.

    All TWB program teachers at each grade level need to make continuous use of parent involvement activities at home. This is important because studies indicate that teachers of first-grade students make more frequent use of parent involvement in activities at home than do teachers of third- and fifth-grade students.

TWB parents need to be provided with detailed strategies of parent involvement activities at home at all grade levels, in both language and content areas. This is an important consideration because studies indicate that parents receive fewer ideas from teachers in the upper elementary grades and feel less capable of helping their older children in reading and math activities at home. The trend worsens at the middle and high school levels.

Consequently, all TWB parent activities must proceed from the fact that parents are interested in their children's schooling and success and would like information and instructions from the school about how to help their children.

- Involve and work with all types of families, regardless of the parent/family composition.

  Families have changed; more children come to school from single-parent homes than ever before. However, include single and married parents as they can be equally interested in helping their children with learning activities at home.

  TWB programs can get good results from all parents—not just those who are traditionally thought to be helpful to teachers and children. Programs need to work with parents from less or more educated backgrounds, who may be employed or unemployed, who are teenage or young parents, and who are from diverse language and cultural backgrounds.

  Regardless of their family arrangements or characteristics, almost all parents care about their children's progress in school and want to know how they can assist their children.

  Consequently, all TWB program families can be informed and productively be involved in their children's education, regardless of family structure.

- Use research findings and studies in similar settings to improve parent involvement practice in TWB programs. Use a process with at least four components:

  Identify the main goal and outline a hierarchy of goals to develop a comprehensive program for parent involvement.

  Clarify how the materials selected in learning activities at home match the goals for parent involvement.

Promote a two-way communication process so that parents can contact the teacher or other staff with questions, suggestions, or reactions.

Include follow-up and evaluation activities to determine the strengths and weaknesses of the parent involvement program.

Bilingual volunteers, school-community liaisons, other parents, paid aides, or staff can form an important communication network to translate information to parents of SLLs. As was exemplified in Chapter 4, the non-English-speaking and English-speaking parents at Chacón School become part of the group of translators as they learn their second language. Financial support from the school district is required to develop family-school contacts that support student progress.

FAMILY LITERACY WORKSHOPS

For the past three decades, a considerable amount of research—pedagogical, psycholinguistic, and sociolinguistic—has evolved in terms of first-language development, second-language acquisition, and multicultural-ism. That research has helped refine, substantiate, and restate the goals of quality education for SLLs (August & Hakuta, 1997; Hakuta, 2001):

- It has supported the positive effects of bilingualism and the use of the first and second languages to achieve true bilingualism (Lindholm-Leary, 2001).

- It has led to proposals to the society at large, the monolingual population, that bilinguals are talented and able to function in two languages (Cummins & Wong Fillmore, 2000).

Studies also indicate that all children benefit when their parents are responsive and active in their education, regardless of economic status, race, parent education, and family size, among others (Cloud et al., 2000; Hidalgo et al., 1995). Furthermore, all children benefit when the schools they attend promote home-school partnerships, with consequential bene-fits in the following areas:

- Literacy development
- Improved academic cognitive achievement
- Second-language proficiency
- Socioemotional development
- Parent-child interactions

- Home-school relations
- Improved school behavior

A Sample TWB Reading Lesson for Parents

Studies also indicate that the most common and recommended parent techniques to stress reading and books are as follows:

- Having parents read to the child or listen to the child read
- Asking parents to take their child to the library
- Loaning books and teaching materials to parents for use with children at home

Interactive reading strategies can be demonstrated to encourage parents to read and continue to read with their children. Parents can become the students and go through the lesson as their children do in the classroom. We have selected a portion of a training session for parents of SLLs who are Spanish speakers and parents of SLLs who know very little Spanish. Due to space limitations, we are not able to present the entire training session. But a sample titled *Leamos con nuestros hijos* (*Let's read with our children*) may illustrate the strategy to use to involve parents in their children's reading progress. The training session may be in Spanish. However, training needs to be prepared in both English and Spanish. The *Leamos* workshop training agenda and format are representative of the training that can be offered to parents. The training could start with a welcoming remark by the principal or TWB program coordinator.

Estrategias de la lectura interactiva: Primero, segundo y tercer grados
(Interactive reading strategies: First, second, and third grades)

1. For the first three grades, parents are exposed to the following skill development: vocabulary, classification, relation, and identification. They are asked to relate the word *cuarto* (bedroom) to things they can find in it. Parents then volunteer words such as *ventana* (window), *cama* (bed), *ropa* (clothes), and *juguetes* (toys). Subgroupings follow. For *ventana*, parents volunteer words such as *cortinas* (curtains). For *cama*, parents contribute with words such as *almohada* (pillow) and *sábana* (sheet). For *ropa*, parents say words such as *medias* (socks) and *zapatos* (shoes). Parents are reminded that these skills need to be developed by accepting all of their children's ideas and opinions. A semantic mapping can be developed, as shown in Figure 10.1.

2. Parents are presented with a big book. The trainees begin with the title and the author. They read the big book cover together: *Ada, La Desordenada* (*Ada, Messy Ada*). The trainer asks some questions: Where do we find this object? What do you think Ada is thinking about? How is she feeling? What do you think she is going to do?

Figure 10.1 A Semantic Mapping for *Cuarto/Recámara* (Bedroom)

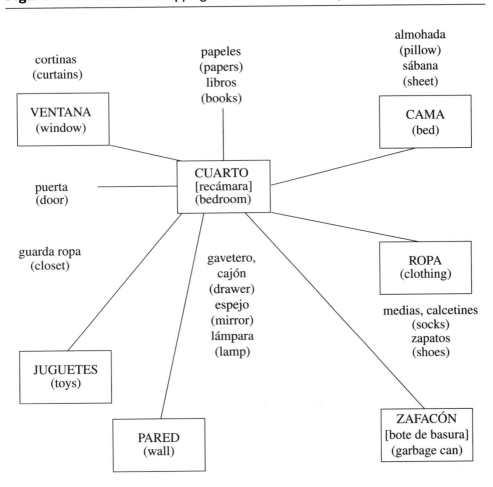

3. Parents and the trainer make a list predicting what they think is going to happen in the story. Parents are reminded that all predictions their children make must be accepted because each prediction is a personal opinion. This creates a pleasant setting. Parents are encouraged to write predictions in terms of what could happen and the final result of events. An example of a prediction/result exercise is presented in Figure 10.2.

4. Parents are encouraged to ask questions related to their children's feelings and personal experiences (e.g., "What did you think when you first saw this page? Does your daughter's or son's room look like Ada's?"). Then, they are encouraged to read together with their children.

5. The trainer gives opportunities to parents who want to read a page aloud. Nobody should be forced to participate.

Figure 10.2 *Predicciones* (Predictions)

Lo que podría suceder (What could happen)	Resultados de las predicciones (Results)
1.	1.
2.	2.
3.	3.

6.   The trainer then begins reading the first page. The teacher is the trainer who reads first. The parents are the students who repeat together. They use exclamations and questions.

7.   The trainer and parents read a page together.

8.   They talk about how Ada looks after organizing her room. The trainer asks, "Why do you think Ada is happy? Would you also be happy if you were Ada?"

9. The trainer and parents go back to the prediction/result sheet and discuss the items.

10. The trainer and parents prepare a mural to strengthen the comprehension strategy.

The trainer asks questions such as the following: "How did Ada's room look at the beginning of the story? How about at the end of the story? What did Ada use to clean her room?" The trainer gives the parents drawings of objects found in Ada's room. Parents make a mural with the figures. Later they take out each figure as Ada's room is being fixed and relate it to the final scene in the big book. If their children want to add more details to the mural, they should be allowed to do so. They should also be allowed to provide a different ending to the story and give more opinions and conclusions.

Similar interactive reading strategies could be applied to fourth, fifth, and sixth grades. Finally, a summary is presented in which all workshop components are put together to show how parents can help their children read.

What Do Parents Who Are Involved Think of Teachers?

Parents who receive frequent requests from teachers welcome the opportunity to become involved in their children's learning activities at home (Craig, 1996). Parents

- Recognize that the teacher works hard to interest them in the instructional program
- Receive most of their ideas for home involvement from the teachers
- Feel that they should help their children at home
- Understand what their children are being taught in school

- Parents who are involved welcome very good teachers with high interpersonal skills.
- Teachers rate parents who are involved higher in helpfulness and follow-through with learning activities at home, regardless of parent education, race, or socioeconomic status.

Community Engagement and School Reform

The following parental and community involvement descriptors could be used to strengthen the school district's systemic reform capacity to affect the climate and organization of the district and the overall academic performance of SLLs. The district can build strong and productive action plans that include TWB programming systemwide, which will ensure the language and academic success of SLLs when the following happens:

- The school fully engages the families and communities of its students who are SLLs.
- The school attempts to serve parents of SLLs by encouraging them to participate and involving them as equal partners in the betterment of the school.
- School leaders are knowledgeable about SLLs, are aware and sensitive to their needs and strengths, relate positively to members of all linguistic and cultural groups, and become advocates of their success in school.

- The entire school and the community share responsibility for the academic success of SLLs.
- The school environment welcomes and encourages families of SLLs and offers them training and assistance to become the primary teachers of their children and partners in the life of the school.
- The school recognizes that all SLLs are connected (cognitively, linguistically, emotionally) to the language and culture of the home.
- Teachers are encouraged to draw on and make constructive connections between the home and community experiences of SLLs and the standards-based curriculum.

AN EXAMPLE OF A PRODUCTIVE SCHOOL-PARENT PARTNERSHIP: THE ALICIA R. CHACÓN INTERNATIONAL SCHOOL

We have addressed parental involvement features at Chacón School in Chapter 4 but feel that it is necessary to list some characteristics of Chacón School's levels of parent participation. On the basis of our observations and interviews, we conclude that the parents

- Trust the educational system and believe that the TWB program is the best program for their children
- Assist their children at home and in the classroom, even though they may have little or no formal schooling
- Participate in their children's education, even though they may not be fluent in their second language (L2) or may not possess the English- or Spanish-language skills
- Are confident that their participation in school matters can affect decision making at the school and district levels
- Are supportive, are interested about, and care for their children's school success
- Spanish-speaking parents feel as important as English-speaking parents do and vice versa

At Chacón School, parents communicated a strong *integrative motivation* in placing their children in the TWB program and having them learn second and third languages to socially engage or integrate with people or other groups. They also expressed an *instrumental motivation* as they saw their children gaining intellectually and academically, allowing these children to be better off socially and economically (e.g., for career gains) by knowing two or more languages.

Chacón School parents' attitudes toward bilingualism are very favorable. Parents know about the TWB program model and the instructional design offered to their children. They understand the model and are capable of defending their decision to put their children in the program to those who do not understand the advantages of learning through two or three languages.

Chacón School parents know what to expect from their children's development at each grade level; they are aware of how their children progress through the grades. They know, for example, that children begin formal English reading by the end of second grade or in third grade.

PARENT TRAINING RECOMMENDATIONS

- Teach parents about the TWB program model.
- Provide training about what to expect at each of the grade levels.
- Provide training on what to expect from children's development at each of the grade levels.
- Train parents to promote language proficiency.
- Provide language training for parents.

Chacón School expects parents to participate in their children's schooling. They communicate with the school and help the children in the home. Parents also actively participate in the school. They are informed about the school system, the TWB program, and how it functions. Chacón School staff, for their part, maintain continual dialogue with families through structures and support parents in their efforts to become involved. The school provides various formal avenues through which teachers and parents may communicate and participate such as annual open-house events and biannual teacher-parent conferences.

In addition, Chacón School parents have represented the school at national and regional conferences, where they have presented the program and its characteristics, stages in language development, literacy development, and so forth.

The Chacón School parent involvement process is one of shared power between families and the school that has led to empowerment of the Mexican American community. This process is made evident as follows:

- They possess equal status as parents of SLLs.
- All parents have strengths and needs.
- In the school's democratic setting, parents have choices, goals, and opportunities to exercise that power.

- The history of the Mexican American community is valued, including its language, traditions, and so forth, as essential elements to reduce inequalities.
- Parents are exposed to new roles with access to resources, and the learning of those roles occurs through participation in those settings.
- Parents have opportunities for collective critical reflection, which is an integral process of participation and empowerment.

Furthermore, parents are empowered in an ongoing process in the Chacón School community, involving the following:

- Mutual respect
- Group participation
- Critical reflection

Chacón School teachers and administrators have unanimously agreed on the importance of parent participation for student achievement and expect parents to attend the parent meetings and activities. Most of the teachers report that they have a high rate of parent involvement. Parents participate in the school and know how to help their children succeed.

Chacón School parents seem to participate more fully due to a number of things. Chacón School validates the families' social and cultural experience, which allows them to feel part of their children's schooling and thus achieve a better balance of power and cooperation between the school and home. Parents and the school work together as a group and agree to make necessary changes both in the home and the school that will benefit the overall education of their children.

The joint effort on the part of the school and the parents makes it an empowerment model that enables both the families and the school to benefit. These activities accommodate parents as a process, not a conclusion.

SUMMARY

TWB programs are effective because parents of SLLs have equal status. Programs use two languages for instruction for the effective integration of SLLs and parents with common goals. Students learn each other's language and experience the other's culture through a bilingual curriculum, and parents learn to function in a bicultural context in the school. Parent training also has the potential to help SLLs.

Parental involvement activities in the TWB program mirror those for *all* parents, with the added linguistic and cultural dimension. Involvement includes learning and helping children with homework; planning school-related activities with teachers and school administrators; making presentations on the benefits of the TWB program with other parents or school personnel; having a voice in school meetings to make decisions regarding program design, curriculum, and school personnel; assisting teachers in the classroom; assisting administrators in the school; training other parents in course content and second-language development; participating in school governance and management decisions; assisting their children in family-school projects, such as library projects; and supporting and defending the benefits of the TWB program.

For the most part, TWB program parents tend to have higher levels of involvement. In fact, the Chacón School parent model allows parents to support collectively the concepts of the program and to assume responsibilities within the school and program, in addition to the activities of support they offer their children at home with their school projects, homework, and so forth. As stated earlier, this involvement functions very well regardless of parents' background factors such as economic background, ethnicity, language background, status as immigrant or native born, or educational background.

11

Evaluation, Research, and Conclusions

This last chapter stresses the need to evaluate two-way bilingual (TWB) programs on a continuous basis. Although some of the suggestions relate to general program designs, a connection and description to TWB programs will be made. In addition, it will examine action research activities that can be conducted in TWB programs.

TWB PROGRAM EVALUATION

The TWB program needs to have an evaluation design at the core of its implementation. Its purpose is to provide the means for determining whether it is meeting its goals and objectives (i.e., how on target it is by comparing achieved outcomes with intended ones) (Holcomb, 1999; Worthen, Sanders, & Fitzpatrick, 1997). When the evaluation is conducted on an ongoing basis, evaluation results allow the school to state with a degree of confidence what program components are working (Ramírez, 1995; Willig, 1985).

Types of Program Evaluation

A TWB program benefits from an evaluation design that is formative, summative, and

> TWB programs require continuous evaluation for program implementation and improvement.

ethnographic or that has an action research component. TWB program evaluation is quantitative when based on the collection of numerical data. It is also qualitative when based on the collection of ethnographic or other types of qualitative data. Consider the following, for example:

- A formative evaluation can be part of a TWB program design. It determines the extent to which measured results on the objective match intended results. Results are then fed back into the TWB program to improve its function, components, and quality. The purpose is not to judge but to improve program operation. It is based on comparing program outcomes with program goals and objectives.

- A summative evaluation can also be part of a TWB program. It determines the extent to which measured results on the objective match intended results from alternative systems for purposes of demonstration and documentation. Alternative ways to achieve program goals are compared on a systematic basis across a variety of outcomes in an effort to use the most effective ones.

- Ethnographic or case study descriptions can also be part of the TWB evaluation. They are based on observational data and interviews. Case study research reflected in the latest trends has the potential of covering all areas of the TWB program. The accumulation of such data can render a rich and robust picture of the program that can benefit practice and influence policy (Barone, 2001; Cummins, 1999).

- Action research can also be part of the TWB evaluation design. It is a concurrent and cooperative process that facilitates reflection and action. TWB programs can become action research mini-centers. Immediate results can be obtained and implemented in the curriculum, in the classroom, in teaching strategies, during professional development, and in parent involvement and student progress. Action research allows practitioners (usually teachers, curriculum specialists, and staff developers) and theoreticians (usually university professors, researchers, and specialists) to become co-researchers. For example, first-language (L1) and second-language (L2) teachers can conduct action research in the classroom, where they can try out innovative instructional strategies. Their strategies may or may not work, but teachers have the opportunity and empirically tested insights to either continue or seek alternatives (Slavin, 2002).

STUDENT ASSESSMENT IN EVALUATION

In TWB program evaluations, emphasis is placed on quantitative data. Therefore, the evaluation design focuses on student achievement goals and objectives (Ovando & Collier, 1998). Two major types of assessments are used to obtain student academic achievement outcomes: norm-referenced testing and criterion-referenced testing.

- Norm-referenced tests (NRTs) compare a student performance to the performance of other students in a "norm" group of students from school districts all over the country. These tests often emphasize multiple-choice items. Commercial tests such as the *Iowa Tests of Basic Skills* (1993) and the *California Achievement Tests* (1992) are norm referenced.

- Criterion-referenced tests (CRTs) compare students' performance to a performance criterion or standard set prior to the assessment. Although CRTs rely on multiple-choice items, some current tests provide for authentic assessment features, so that student abilities to construct are assessed. CRTs are tests preferred by educators because they focus on curricular objectives that are easy to teach.

TWB program evaluation designs should consider that second-language learners (SLLs) need experience and exposure to these kinds of assessments for their own benefit, and educators need to look at the totality of student outcomes (including those from qualitative data), follow the progress of their students on all measures across time, and relate student progress, if possible, to the same data on the achievement of former students.

A TWB PROGRAM EVALUATION DESIGN

A TWB program needs to build a framework for its evaluation design based all the factors mentioned so far. The first step is to design the program's goals and objectives. This can be achieved through (1) a needs assessment, (2) existing lists of operational objectives, or (3) program participants (administrators, teachers, parents, etc.), who develop goals and objectives for instruction, professional development, uses of languages for instruction, effective teaching, and program effectiveness, among others. The development of objectives and their evaluation is shown in Figure 11.1.

Data that address each of the goals and objectives need to be collected and analyzed. Teachers, administrators, students, and their parents play an important role in all areas of program evaluation. Everyone's involvement strengthens the program components and instills a sense of ownership of the program and its evaluation.

Figure 11.1 Preparing for the TWB Program Evaluation

1. Needs Assessment
(Process)

2. TWB Program Goals and Objectives
(Product)

3. TWB Program Design and Development
(Process)

4. TWB Program Evaluation
(Product)

5. TWB Program Refinement and Implementation
(Product)

The TWB program evaluation is an important means of improving the quality of instruction, the program implementation, and the evaluation design.

FIVE PRINCIPLES OF EFFECTIVE EVALUATION DESIGN

The Office of English Language Acquisition (OELA, 2001) recommends five principles for effective evaluation design to its grantees, as a guidance to improve evaluation practices in its many funding programs. These principles apply to TWB program design, implementation, and evaluation:

1. Link TWB program components. A cohesive relationship between program components helps to ensure meaningful and applicable results.
   (a) Base the program goals and objectives on yearly assessment of needs at the TWB program to improve student language and academic achievement.
   (b) Design program activities to support program goals and objectives.
   (c) Outline the relationship between needs, goals, program objectives, program activities, and evaluation.
   (d) Develop evaluation questions to guide program and evaluation planning. For example:

   > How do SLLs compare in academic progress to non-SLLs in state performance goals?
   > How do SLLs compare among themselves in academic progress?
   > How effective are professional development plans in improving student reading achievement?
   > How can parents of SLLs work together to help their children in L1 and L2 development and academic achievement?

2. Include indicators of expected TWB program performance in the goals and objectives. Specify expected outcomes for the following:
   (a) Student learning and achievement. These include student progress in each academic area as students develop curricula and obtain or achieve levels of mastery in L1 and L2 proficiency.
   (b) Improvement of TWB program components in the school and district—these include new curricula, new professional development practices, improved support services for program participants, and stronger parent/family participation.

3. Use quantitative and qualitative measures to produce data on TWB program effectiveness. Include multiple measures for each performance objective. For example:
   (a) Attrition and completion and transfer rates of students
   (b) Performance on achievement tests
   (c) Degree to which the program reflects TWB content-based instructional standards and teaching effectiveness
   (d) Portfolio assessments incorporated into classroom activities
   (e) Parent, teacher, and student surveys during facets of program implementation
   (f) Student achievement data for instruction

4. Use evaluation data to improve TWB program components on a continuous basis.
   (a) Incorporate formative evaluation tools.
   (b) Collect data throughout the year to provide continuous feedback to determine areas of needed improvement or to indicate effective features.
   (c) Specify in an evaluation plan how and when data will be reviewed and how they will be used to make ongoing improvements in the program.

5. Manage the evaluation with a team.
   (a) Coordinate evaluation activities with partners (e.g., administrator, teachers, and parents).
   (b) Specify responsibilities of partners: timeframes for assessment, data collection, data analysis, feedback, and reporting.

6. Funding agency evaluation requirements. The U.S. Department of Education (OELA, 2001) specified the following criteria in its fundable projects, and the secretary of education considered the following factors in determining the quality of the evaluation to be conducted of the funded project:
   (a) The methods of evaluation need to provide for examining the effectiveness of project implementation strategies.
   (b) The methods of evaluation need to include the use of objective performance measures that are clearly related to the intended outcomes of the project and will produce quantitative and qualitative data to the extent possible.
   (c) The methods of evaluation need to provide performance feedback and permit periodic assessments of progress toward achieving intended outcomes.
   (d) The instructional outcomes of the program should allow the students to participate.

EVALUATION-RELATED QUESTIONS

The U.S. Department of Education also posits a number of questions for its fundable projects that are relevant to the evaluation design and the entire project. We have revised them to be considered in the TWB program evaluation:

- What are the specific responsibilities of the TWB program/school, districts, and/or other partnership organizations in planning, implementing, and evaluating the program?

- How does the program support instruction for SLLs that reflects content standards for learning and proficiency in two languages?
- How does the program assist in systemically reforming policies and practices in the TWB program and school district?
- What professional development is provided to new and experienced TWB teachers on an ongoing basis?
- What evidence of effectiveness supports the TWB model?
- What are the expected outcomes for student learning, effectiveness in the instructional setting, reform, and improvement in the school?
- What measures does the TWB program use to collect data on the effectiveness of the program in meeting its objectives, such as national or state benchmark tests and surveys of students and their families?
- How are needs, objectives, activities, and measures linked?
- How will the program evaluation incorporate strategies for assessing progress and performance of SLLs, providing effective communication between teachers and parents, improving the quality of the staff development, identifying exemplary program features, and reporting on specific data related to the number of SLLs completing the program?

EVALUATION STEPS

The following four evaluation steps have been adapted for TWB program evaluation, as proposed by Airisian (1997):

1. Specify the TWB outcomes and their measurement. Decide what you are trying to achieve in the TWB program and how to determine whether you have achieved it.

2. Specify and evaluate inputs and process. Identify the elements of your TWB program that you plan to implement and evaluate.

3. Construct a design. Set the standards and identify the principles behind a design that will yield valid and generalizable conclusions for the TWB program.

4. Carry out the evaluation. The program evaluator develops or obtains existing evaluation measures to administer, analyze, interpret, and report on the TWB program.

We would add the following:

5. Use the evaluation results to improve the TWB program implementation. For TWI programs to continue offering quality standards-based curricula in L1 and L2 and effective teaching, a process of ongoing feedback must be set in place.

For federally funded TWB programs, a program evaluator is usually hired to conduct the evaluation. The following TWB program evaluation checklist would include the following components:

Evaluation Checklist for TWB Programs

- All stated goals and objectives are measured.
- Measures provide longitudinal, qualitative, and quantitative data on program effectiveness.
- All data gathered are interpreted and analyzed.
- Data analysis provides meaningful and useful information and highlights strengths and weaknesses to implement the program.
- Program improvement and capacity building are assessed so that the TWB program will continue after federal funding ceases.
- Effective program features are described and examined.
- The evaluation report is clearly written, concise, and suitable for a variety of audiences that include parents, administrators, teachers, and policymakers.
- Program implementation revisions and anticipated changes are described in detail.

SOURCE: Based on OELA (2001).

ACTION RESEARCH FOR TWB PROGRAMS

A number of research activities can be conducted in TWB programs in areas such as effective instruction, standards-based curriculum, professional development, and SLL parent involvement, among others. The results from these can be implemented in instructional activities, teacher training, and overall TWB program improvement.

The TWB program's teachers and administrators have an important role in action research because they are the closest to what is going on in the schooling process and in the L1 and L2 classrooms. They can provide the most critical information about what is going on in L1 and L2 development, biculturalism, and curriculum such as the following:

- Articulate the instructional, linguistic, and sociocultural principles on which the program is operating
- Determine the research needs of the program
- Design research with some degree of confidence

ACTION RESEARCH CRITERIA

A review of the literature on TWB programs points to the following principles that can be followed to delineate action research activities:

- Conduct long-range or longitudinal research. For example, to collect information about SLLs' emerging bilingualism, we need to follow their progress, or lack of progress, from the time they enter the TWB program, across the program duration, and beyond it. We can then look at the cumulative effects of educational and social experiences of students becoming bilingual across grades, as they are involved in different types of interaction in the classroom while they are learning the standards-based curriculum (Laturnau, 2001).

- Bring together quantitative research and qualitative methodological approaches. For example, the observation of general patterns and minute detail of L1 and L2 uses by SLLs in the classroom can explain "why" certain students continue to perform poorly ("what") on certain tests.

- Look at the context of the classroom, the home, and the community. For example, we need to understand and improve our explanation of the so-called academic failure of English learners in the U.S. school system: Why does an English learner, who is the English translator to his or her monolingual parents, goes to the store, and makes transactions, fail in math? The classroom instruction and schoolwork need to be considered in the context of effective teaching, the culture, and the cognitive processes associated with day-to-day interactions.

First, *effective* needs to be satisfactorily defined. If one is interested in studying "effective teaching," then some of the questions to pose for the study might be as follows:

1. What are the characteristics of effective TWB teachers?

2. What are teachers' beliefs about teaching and learning?

3. What is the nature of their decision making? For using each language? For assessing student progress in a second language?

4. What characterizes their professional lives?

Broader questions need to be researched, even at a national level. Your school could contribute to any of these domains, which in themselves generate many questions yet unanswered:

1. What is the relationship between L2 oral language proficiency and L2 literacy? At what level of L2 oral language proficiency should second-language learners begin formal L2 reading instruction?

2. What are the best instructional practices for developing literacy in L1? In L2?

3. What instructional practices facilitate transfer from L1 to L2?

4. How can we best assess student linguistic and academic progress in TWB?

5. How can we organize TWB instructional components to meet the diversity of student needs?

6. What must a TWB teacher know to be able to teach effectively in TWB programs?

7. What type of staff development program is most effective with TWB teachers and instructional assistants?

Concerning biliteracy, many micro-level questions still need answers. Longitudinal scientific studies on biliteracy could easily focus on just one of these reading components:

1. Word recognition—differences between L1 and L2

2. Vocabulary knowledge—building L1 and L2 simultaneously

3. Reading fluency—automaticity in L1 and L2

4. Comprehension—ways of assessing

5. Orthography—spelling across two languages

Qualitative studies on these issues will help to understand the mechanism behind the "effectiveness" or ineffectiveness of the factors in the different categories. Qualitative studies will inform the quantitative evidence of effectiveness or ineffectiveness. Both types of research methods are complementary and lend themselves to collaborative teams of researchers and practitioners.

ACTION RESEARCH AND EVALUATION

Action research and evaluation often overlap. The same themes can be studied for either purpose. Table 11.1 presents some overlapping themes.

Table 11.1 Research and Evaluation Activities

Areas of Evaluation	*Sample of Evaluation Activities*
1. Student selection criteria	• Language dominance and language proficiency testing • Academic and affective indicators for exit criteria
2. Student proportions for each class	• Linguistic indicators • Program goals and objectives • Community characteristics and parent wishes
3. Type of program	• Effects of instruction in a 50-50 language model • Effects of instruction in an 80-20 model • Effects of instruction in a 90-10 model
4. Implementation strategy	• Grade levels per program year • Language and academic goals for each level
5. Whole school or school within a school	• Advantages of whole-school implementation • Ways to improve TWB program within the school • Characteristics of Success for All schools
6. Governance	• Effectiveness of school improvement plans • Roles of political action committees • School-community relations • Infrastructure for success
7. Funding	• Needs assessment for proposal development • Commitments to state and federal government
8. Facilities	• Needs of the program and its participants • Organizational and physical structures
9. Curriculum for all subjects	• Effectiveness of curriculum by levels of instruction • Curriculum tied to state and national standards
10. Literacy programs	• First-language literacy • Transfer of reading skills from L1 to L2 • Development of writing skills in L1 and L2

(Continued)

Table 11.1 Continued

Areas of Evaluation	Sample of Evaluation Activities
11. Student assessments	• State- or district-mandated testing • Assessment of comprehension (receptive) and communicative (productive) competence • Relation to achievement testing
12. Teacher selection criteria	• Teacher recruitment strategies • Teacher incentives
13. Team-teaching configurations	• Teacher strengths and professional development needs • Content and language pair teaching
14. Family support services	• Conventional and nonconventional family involvement
15. Early intervention programs	• Characteristics of early interventions • Patterns that fit specific English learners and Spanish learners
16. High goals and expectations for everyone	• Factors for full proficiency development in L1 and L2 • Profiles of high achievers
17. Contract for parents	• Parent involvement contract • Parents as teachers • Parents as advocates
18. Contract for teachers	• Profiles of effective teachers • Profiles of bilingual and bicultural teachers
19. Professional development plan for Year 1	• Surveying the faculty strengths and needs • Research-based training
20. TLC plan for Year 1	• Training for high-quality teachers • Support systems
21. Program evaluation plan	• Integrating designs • Reporting frameworks
22. Dissemination plan	• Presenting strengths of the program • Defending the principles underlying TWB instruction

SUMMARY

The TWB program evaluation can provide information on and interpretation of the context in which the TWB program operates. This context includes the resources to implement the program—educators, parents, students, policymakers, and/or researchers. As pointed out in Chapters 1 and 4, they can promote a more equitable school climate for school improvement and systemic reform and accept the challenge to become part of the TWB educational transformation. For example, Chacón School's TWB program affirms the equal worth of ethnic backgrounds and the inseparability of language and culture.

The evaluation also identifies the degree to which the program operates as planned. Chapter 2 provides a path for planning and designing TWB programs at least a year before implementation. The evaluation design then considers gathering information on program development and implementation, how it was shared with all stakeholders—teachers, administrators, parents, and the community—and how all stakeholders were involved in the information and decision-making processes that are used.

The TWB evaluation also examines the implementation of the instructional methods and strategies that the program employs. Chapter 5, 6, and 7 focus on some of the best ways to teach SLLs that make any L2 comprehensible using the four language skills. The quality of the teacher's delivery of instruction to teach any content material—math, science, social studies, or language arts, reading, and writing—is also evaluated. The comprehensive reading program also needs to be part of the evaluation so that the model becomes effective and replicable.

The TWB evaluation also examines assessment practices for SLLs. Chapter 8 provides an evaluative sequence for placement in a program, ongoing classroom assessment, and completion of a school program. The types of assessment tools for oral, reading, and writing skill development need to be reviewed in the context of high-stakes testing.

The TWB evaluation should include the kinds of professional development to support program implementation. As stated in Chapter 9, teachers are constantly refining their instructional practices, learning new ones, using peer mentoring, and assessing student progress to guide changes in their methods. The evaluation design needs to examine the correlation between the time and resources invested and the success of the students in the TWB program.

The evaluation design should consider how parental involvement activities benefit the TWB program. Chapter 10 describes a number of parent participation activities that could be observed and documented—for example, the amount of time parents help their children with homework; the kinds of school-related activities involving parents, teachers, and school administrators; and parents' input at school meetings in making decisions regarding program design, curriculum, and school personnel.

Furthermore, the TWB program evaluation needs to be part of a planning process that includes components, such as a set of outcomes of project objectives, a set of standards or criteria to attain when implementing the objectives, and a set of measuring devices (e.g., rubrics, tests, surveys, interviews, observations) that reveal what was accomplished when implementing the objectives. Evaluation incorporates input from all TWB program participants and guides the improvement of the program.

Finally, this chapter concludes that TWB program evaluation needs to be continuous to affect the program's implementation. It should also be part of a long-term process, with qualitative and quantitative outcomes of project objectives, standards, or criteria to attain when implementing the objectives and measuring devices (e.g., rubrics, tests, surveys, interviews, observations) that reveal what was accomplished.

Resource A:
Resources for Two-Way Bilingual Programs

Organizations

National Clearinghouse for English Language Acquistion and Instruction Educational Programs
www.ncela.gwu.edu

Center for Applied Linguistics
www.cal.org/db/2way

National Association for Bilingual Education
www.nabe.org

(Also contact the California Association for Bilingual Education, Texas Association for Bilingual Education)

Center for Research on Education, Diversity and Excellence
www.crede.ucs.edu

Center for the Education of Students Placed at Risk, Johns Hopkins University
www.csos.jhu.edu/crespar

Success for All Foundation
www.successforall.net

Alicia Chacón Elementary School
www.aliciachacon

Videotapes

Learning Together, Center for Applied Linguistics, www.cal.org

Juntos! Into the Future: Two-Way Bilingual Immersion at River Glen Elementary School, San Jose Unified School District, www.sjusd.k12.ca.us

The Korean/English Dual Language Program, Los Angeles Unified School District, Asian Pacific and Other Languages Office, www.lausd.k12.ca.us/lausd/offices/bilingual/apolo.html

Osborne School, Turlock School District, www.turlock.k12.ca.us

Books, Chapters, Articles, and Other Sources

2001

Effective Programs for Latino Students. Robert E. Slavin and Margarita Calderón (Eds.). Mahwah, NJ: Lawrence Erlbaum, 2001. Pp. ix-394.

Two-Way Immersion Programs: Features and Statistics. Elizabeth R. Howard and Julie Sugarman. Washington, DC: ERIC Clearinghouse on Languages and Linguistics, 2001. Pp. 1-5 [Online]. Available: www.cal.org/ericcll/digest/0101twi.html

Dual-Language Education: Who Benefits? Alexa Lee. Cable News Network, 2001. Pp. 1-2 [Online]. Available: http://fyi.cnn.com/2001/fyi/news/0604/bilingual.education/index.html

Development and Maintenance of Two-Way Immersion Programs: Advice From Practitioners. Julie Sugarman and Elizabeth R. Howard. Santa Cruz, CA: Center for Research on Education, Diversity and Excellence, 2001. Pp. 1-2.

Dual Language Education. Kathryn J. Lindholm-Leary. Clevedon, England: Multilingual Matters.

2000

Dual Language Instruction: A Handbook for Enriched Education. Nancy Cloud, Fred Genesee, and Else Hamayan. Boston: Heinle & Heinle, 2000. Pp. xii-227.

Biliteracy for a Global Society: An Idea Book on Dual Language Education. Kathryn Lindholm-Leary. Washington, DC: National Clearinghouse for Bilingual Education, 2000. Pp. 1-38.

A Two-Way Bilingual Program. Promise, Practice, and Precautions. Margarita Calderón and Argelia Carreón. Baltimore, MD: Center for Research on the Education of Students Placed at Risk, 2000. Pp. 1-57.

The Foundations of Dual Language Instruction. Judith Lessow-Hurley. New York: Addison Wesley Longman, 2000. 3rd ed. Pp. xvii-186.

Two-Way 101: Designing and Implementing a TWI Program. Elizabeth R. Howard and Julie Sugarman. Washington, DC: Center for Applied Linguistics, 2000. Pp. 1-10.

Implementing Two-Way Immersion Programs in Secondary Schools. Chistopher L. Montone and Michael I. Loeb. Santa Cruz, CA: Center for Research on Education, Diversity and Excellence, 2000. Pp. 1-19 [Online]. Available: www.cal.org/crede/pubs/edpractice/EPR5.htm

Asymmetry in Dual Language Practice: Assessing Imbalance in a Program Promoting Equality. Audrey Amrein and Robert A. Peña, 2000. *Educational Policy Analysis Archives*, 8(8), 1-9 [Online]. Available: http://epaa.asu.edu/epaa/v8n8.html

1999

Program Alternatives for Linguistically Diverse Students. Fred Genesee. Santa Cruz, CA: Center for Research on Education, Diversity and Excellence, 1999. Pp. vi-43.

Teachers Learning Communities for Cooperation in Diverse Settings. Margarita Calderón, 1999. *Theory Into Practice*, 38(2), 94-99.

1998

Becoming Bilingual in the Amigos Two-Way Immersion Program. Mary T. Cazabon, Elena Nicoladis, and Wallace E. Lambert. Santa Cruz, CA: Center for Research on Education, Diversity and Excellence, 1998. Pp. 1-17 [Online]. Available: www.cal.org/crede/pubs/research/rr3.htm

Bilingual Education: From Compensatory to Quality Schooling. María Estela Brisk. Mahwah, NJ: Lawrence Erlbaum, 1998. Pp. xx-206.

In Their Own Words: Two-Way Immersion Teachers Talk About Their Professional Experiences. Elizabeth R. Howard and Michael I. Loeb. Washington, DC: ERIC Clearinghouse on Languages and Linguistics, 1998. Pp. 1-5 [Online]. Available: www.cal.org/ericcll/digest/intheirownwords.html

Encyclopedia of Bilingualism and Bilingual Education. Colin Baker and Sylvia Prys Jones. Clevedon, England: Multilingual Matters, 1998. Pp. x-758.

Bilingual and ESL Classrooms: Teaching in Multicultural Contexts. Carlos J. Ovando and Virginia P. Collier. Boston: McGraw-Hill, 1998. Pp. xix-388.

1997

Effects of Two Way Immersion on the Ethnic Identification of Third Language Students: An Exploratory Study. Kellie Rolstad, 1997. *Bilingual Research Journal*, 21(1), 43-63.

Critical Components for Dual Language Programs. Nicole S. Montague, 1997. *Bilingual Research Journal*, 21(4), 1-9 [Online]. Available: http://brj.asu.edu/articles/ar5.html

1996

Dual-Language Planning at Oyster Bilingual School: "It's Much More Than Language." Rebecca D. Freeman, 1996. *TESOL Quarterly, 30*(3), 557-582.

Parental Attitudes Toward Bilingualism in a Local Two-Way Immersion Program. Barbara A. Craig, 1996. *Bilingual Research Journal, 20*(3-4), 383-410.

The Effects of Acculturation on Second Language Proficiency in a Community With a Two-Way Bilingual Program. C. Ray Graham and Cheryl Brown, 1996. *Bilingual Research Journal, 20*(2), 235-260.

1995

Bilingual Proficiency as a Bridge to Academic Achievement: Results From Bilingual/Immersion Programs. Kathryn J. Lindholm and Zierlein Aclan, 1995. In *Compendium of Research in Bilingual Education*, G. González & L. Maez (Eds.). Washington, DC: National Clearinghouse for Bilingual Education. Pp. 71-80.

The ESL Component of Bilingual Education in Practice. 1996. *Bilingual Research Journal, 19*(3-4), 353-684.

1994

Two-Way Bilingual Education: Students Learning Through Two Languages. Donna Christian. Santa Cruz, CA: National Center for Research on Cultural Diversity and Second Language Learning, 1994. Pp. 1-5 [Online]. Available: www.cal.org/ericcll/digest/ed379915.html

Two-Way Bilingual Education Programs in Practice: A National and Local Perspective. Donna Christian. Santa Cruz, CA: National Center for Research on Cultural Diversity and Second Language Learning, 1994. Pp. 1-19 [Online]. Available: http://ncbe.gwu.edu/miscpubs/ncrcdsll/epr12/

1993

Emerging Literacy in a Two-Way Bilingual First Grade Classroom. Natalie A. Kuhlman, Mary Bastian, Lilia Bartolomé, and Michele Barrios, 1993. *Annual Conference Journal.* Washington, DC: National Association for Bilingual Education. Pp. 45-59.

Two-Way Bilingual Education: A Progress Report on the Amigos Program. Mary T. Cazabon, Wallace E. Lambert, and Geoff Hall. Santa Cruz, CA: National Center for Research on Cultural Diversity and Second Language Learning, 1993. Pp. 1-31.

1990

Bilingual Education: Issues and Strategies. Amado M. Padilla, Halford H. Fairchild, and Concepción Valadez (Eds.). Newbury Park, CA: Sage, 1990. Pp. 1-261.

A Spanish-English Dual-Language Program in New York City. Sydney H. Morison, 1990. *The ANNALS of the American Academy of Political and Social Science, 508,* 160-169.

Foreign Language Education: Issues and Strategies. Amado M. Padilla, Halford H. Fairchild, and Concepción M. Valadez (Eds.). Newbury Park, CA: Sage, 1990. Pp. 1-256.

1989

Bilingual Education: History, Politics, Theory, and Practice. James Crawford. Trenton, NJ: Crane, 1989. Pp. 1-204.

1987

Learning Through Two Languages: Studies of Immersion and Bilingual Education. Fred Genesee. Cambridge, MA: Newbury House, 1987. Pp. x-213.

1984

Studies on Immersion Education: A Collection for United States Educators. Office of Bilingual Bicultural Education. Sacramento: California State Department of Education, 1984. Pp. viii-184.

Resource B:
List of Acronyms

BCIRC: Bilingual Cooperative Integrated Reading and Composition

CAL: Center for Applied Linguistics

CREDE: Center for Research in Education, Diversity and Excellence

CRT: Criterion-referenced tests

CSRD: Comprehensive school reform demonstration models

DLTA: Directed listening thinking activity

DSS: Dominant-speaking student

EL: English learner

ELD: English-language development

EPISD: El Paso Independent School District

ERIC: Educational Resource Information Center

ESL: English as a Second Language

GED: General educational development

L1: Primary language

L2: Secondary language

LC: Listening comprehension

NABE: National Association for Bilingual Education

NCELA: National Clearinghouse for English Acquisition and Language Instruction Education Programs, formerly called the National Clearinghouse for Bilingual Education (NCBE)

NCES: National Center for Education Statistics

NCLR: National Council of La Raza

NRC: National Research Council

NRT: Norm-referenced tests

OELA: Office of English Language Acquisition, formally called the Office of Bilingual Education and Minority Languages Affairs (OBEMLA)

QAR: Question-answer relationship

RRI: Rapid retrieval of information

SL: Spanish learners

SLL: Second-language learners

SSL: Spanish as a Second Language

TABE: Texas Association for Bilingual Education

TBE: Transitional bilingual education

TLC: Teachers learning communities

TPR: Total physical response

TWB: Two-way bilingual

TWI: Two-way immersion

YISD: Ysleta Independent School District

ZPD: Zone of proximal development

References

Adult Bilingual Curriculum Institute. (2002). *Adult bilingual workplace curriculum units*. El Paso, TX: CRESPAR/ Johns Hopkins University.

Airisian, P. (1997). *Classroom assessment* (2nd ed.). New York: McGraw-Hill.

Allington, R. (1990). The legacy of "slow it down and make it more concrete." In J. Zuten & S. McCormick (Eds.), *Learner factors/teachers factors: Issues in literacy research and instruction* (40th Yearbook of the National Reading Conference, pp. 19-30). Chicago: National Reading Conference.

Allington, R. (2001). Research on reading/learning disability interventions. In S. J. Samuels & A. Farstrup (Eds.), *What research says about reading instruction*. Newark, DE: International Reading Association.

Amrein, A., & Peña, R. A. (2000). Asymmetry in dual language practice: Assessing imbalance in a program promoting quality. *Educational Policy Analysis Archives, 8*(8), 1-9 [Online]. Available: http://epaa.asu.edu/epaa/v8n8.html

Anderson, R.C., Reynolds, R. E., Schallert, D. L., & Goetz, E. T. (1977). Frameworks for comprehending discourse. *American Educational Research Journal, 14*(4), 367-381.

Arter, J., & McTighe, J. (2001). *Scoring rubrics in the classroom. Using performance criteria for assessing and improving student performance*. Thousand Oaks, CA: Corwin Press.

Au, K. H. P. (1993). Participation structures in a reading lesson with Hawaiian children: Analysis of a culturally appropriate instructional event. *Anthropology and Education Quarterly, 11*(2), 91-115.

August, D., Carlo, M., & Calderón, M. (2002). *Transfer of reading skills from Spanish to English: A study of young learners*. Report ED-98-CO-OO71 to the Office of Bilingual Education and Minority Languages Affairs, U.S. Department of Education, Washington, DC.

August, D., & Hakuta, K. (Eds.). (1997). *Improving schooling for language-minority children: A research agenda*. Washington, DC: National Academy Press.

August, D., & McArthur, E. (1996). *Proceedings of the conference on inclusion guidelines and accommodations for limited English proficient students in the National Assessment of Educational Progress, December 5-6, 1994*. Washington, DC: U.S. Department of Education, Office of Educational Research and Improvement.

Baker, C., & Prys Jones, S. (1998). *Encyclopedia of bilingualism and bilingual education*. Clevedon, England: Multilingual Matters.

Barone, T. (2001). Science, art, and the predisposition of educational research. *Educational Researcher, 30*(7), 24-28.

Barth, R. (Ed.). (1991). *Improving schools from within: Teachers, parents, and principals can make the difference.* San Francisco: Jossey-Bass.

Bear, D. R., Invernizzi, M., Templeton, S., & Johnson, F. (1996). *Words their way.* Upper Saddle River, NJ: Merrill.

Beck, I. L, McKeown, M. G., Worthy, J., Sandora, C. A., & Kucan, L. (1999). *A year long implementation to engage students with text.* Chicago: The Elementary School Journal Press.

Bermúdez, A. B., & Márquez, J. A. (1996). An examination of a four-way collaborative to increase parental involvement in the schools. *Journal of Educational Issues of Language Minority Students, 16,* 1-16.

Bermúdez, A. B., & Padrón, Y. N. (1990). Improving language skills for Hispanic students through home-school partnerships. *Journal of Educational Issues of Language Minority Students, 6,* 33-43.

Bialystok, E., & Hakuta, K. (1994). *In other words: The science and psychology of second-language acquisition.* New York: Basic Books.

Bickart, T. (1998). *Summary report of preventing reading difficulties in young children.* Report prepared for U.S. Department of Education Reading Summit, Washington, D.C.

Biemiller, A. (1999). *Language and reading success.* Cambridge, MA: Brookline.

Boykin, A. W. (1996, April). *A talent development approach to school reform: An introduction to CRESPAR.* Paper presented at the annual meeting of the American Education Research Association, New York.

Brisk, M. E. (1998). *Bilingual education: From compensatory to quality schooling.* Mahwah, NJ: Lawrence Erlbaum.

Calderón, M. (1991). The benefits of cooperative learning for Hispanic students. *Texas Researcher Journal, 2,* 39-57.

Calderón, M. (1994). Mentoring, peer support, and support systems for first-year minority/bilingual teachers. In R. A. DeVillar, C. J. Flatis, and J. P. Cummins (Eds.), *Cultural diversity in schools: From rhetoric to practice,* pp. 117-141. Albany, NY: University of New York Press.

Calderón, M. (1997). Preparing teachers and administrators to better serve the needs of Latino students. In *Proceedings from the 1996 ETS Invitational Conference.* Princeton, NJ: ETS.

Calderón, M. (1998). *Staff development in multilingual multicultural schools.* New York: ERIC Clearinghouse on Urban Education.

Calderón, M. (1999a). *Including culturally and linguistically diverse students in standards-based reform: A report on McRel's Diversity Roundtable I.* Aurora, CO: Mid-continent Regional Educational Laboratory.

Calderón, M. (1999b). Teacher learning communities for cooperation in diverse settings. *Theory Into Practice Journal, 38*(2), 94-99.

Calderón, M. (2000). *Teachers learning communities (TLCs): Training manual.* El Paso, TX: CRESPAR.

Calderón, M. (2001a). Curricula and methodologies used to teach Spanish-speaking limited English proficient students to read English. In R. E. Slavin & M. Calderón (Eds.), *Effective programs for Latino children* (pp. 251-306). Mahwah, NJ: Lawrence Erlbaum.

Calderón, M. (2001b). Success for All in a two-way immersion school. In D. Christian & F. Genesee (Eds.), *Case studies in bilingual education* (pp. 27-40). Alexandria, VA: TESOL.

Calderón, M. (2002). Trends in staff development for bilingual teachers. In L. Minaya-Rowe (Ed.), *Teacher training and effective pedagogy in the context of student diversity* (pp. 121-146). Greenwich, CT: Information Age.

Calderón, M., & Carreón, A. (2000). *A two-way bilingual program: Promise, practice, and precautions.* Baltimore, MD: Center for Research on the Education of Students Placed at Risk.

Calderón, M., Hertz-Lazarowitz, R., & Slavin, R. E. (1998). Effects of Bilingual Cooperative Integrated Reading and Composition on students making the transition from Spanish to English reading. *The Elementary School Journal, 99*(2), 153-165.

California achievement tests (5th ed.). (1992). Monterey, CA: McGraw-Hill.

Carnevale, A. P. (1999). *Education-success: Empowering Hispanic youth and adults.* Princeton, NJ: Educational Testing Service.

Carrasquillo, A. L., & London, C. B. G. (1993). *Parents and schools: A source book.* New York: Garland.

Cazabon, M. T. (2001). *Coming together in the planning team: Considering seven vital focal points in the planning and development of two-way programs.* The New England Equity Assistance Center [Online]. Available: www.alliance.brown.edu/eac/coming_together.shtml

Cazabon, M. T., Lambert, W. E., & Hall, G. (1993). *Two-way bilingual education: A progress report on the Amigos Program.* Santa Cruz, CA: National Center for Research on Cultural Diversity and Second Language Learning.

Cazabon, M. T., Nicoladis, E., & Lambert, W. E. (1998). *Becoming bilingual in the Amigos two-way immersion program.* Santa Cruz, CA: Center for Research on Education, Diversity and Excellence [Online]. Available: www.cal.org/crede/pubs/research/rr3.htm

Center for Applied Linguistics (CAL). (2002). *Directory of two-way bilingual immersion programs in the U.S.* Washington, DC: Author [Online]. Available: www.cal.org/twi/directory/

Chall, J. S. (1996). *Learning to read: The great debate.* New York: McGraw-Hill.

Chavkin, N. F. (Ed.). (1993). *Families and schools in a pluralistic society.* Albany: SUNY Press.

Christian, D. (1996). *Two-way bilingual education: Students learning through two languages.* Santa Cruz, CA: National Center for Research on Cultural Diversity and Second Language Learning.

Christian, D. (1999). Looking at federal education legislation from a language policy/planning perspective. In T. Huebner & K. A. Davis (Eds.), *Sociopolitical perspectives on language policy and planning in the USA* (pp. 117-130). Amsterdam: John Benjamins.

Christian, D., Montone, C., Lindholm, K., & Carranza, I. (1997). *Profiles in two-way bilingual education.* McHenry, IL: Delta Systems.

Clemmons, J., Areglado, L., & Dill, M. (1993). *Portfolios in the classroom.* New York: Scholastic.

Cloud, N., Genesee, F., & Hamayan, E. (2000). *Dual language instruction: A handbook for enriched education.* Boston: Heinle & Heinle.

Collier, V. (1998). *Promoting academic success for ESL students: Understanding second language acquisition for school.* Elizabeth: New Jersey Teachers of English to Speakers of Other Languages–Bilingual Education.

Collier, V., & Thomas, W. (2001, February 22). *California dreamin': The real effect of Proposition 227 on test scores.* Feature speech presented at the National Association for Bilingual Education conference, Phoenix, AZ.

Cortes, C. (1986). The education of language minority students: A contextual interaction model. In California State Department of Education (Ed.), *Beyond language: Social and cultural factors in schooling language minority students* (pp. 3-33). Los Angeles: Evaluation, Dissemination and Assessment Center, California State University.

Craig, B. A. (1996). Parental attitudes toward bilingualism in a local two-way immersion program. *Bilingual Research Journal, 20*(2), 235-260.

Crandall, M., & Loeb, M. (2000). The next step: Implementing two-way immersion programs in secondary schools. *NABE News, 24*(1), 17, 35.

Crawford, J. (1989). *Bilingual education: History, politics, theory and practice.* Trenton, NJ: Crane.

Crawford, J. (1992). *Hold your tongue: Bilingualism and the politics of "English only."* New York: Addison-Wesley.

Crawford, J. (1997). *Best evidence: Research foundations of the Bilingual Education Act.* Washington, DC: National Clearinghouse for Bilingual Education.

Crawford, J. (2000). Language politics in the United States: The paradox of bilingual education. In C. J. Ovando & P. McLaren (Eds.), *The politics of multiculturalism and bilingual education: Students and teachers caught in the cross fire* (pp. 106-125). Boston: McGraw-Hill.

Cummins, J. (1979). Linguistic interdependence and the educational development of bilingual children. *Review of Educational Research, 49,* 222-251.

Cummins, J. (1981). Age on arrival and immigrant second language learning in Canada: A reassessment. *Applied Linguistics, 2,* 132-149.

Cummins, J. (1984). *Bilingualism and special education: Issues in assessment and pedagogy.* Clevedon, England: Multilingual Matters.

Cummins, J. (1986). Empowering minority students: A framework for intervention. *Harvard Educational Review, 56,* 18-36.

Cummins, J. (1991). Interdependence of first- and second-language proficiency in bilingual children. In E. Bialystok (Ed.), *Language processing in bilingual children* (pp. 70-89). Cambridge, UK: Cambridge University Press.

Cummins, J. (1996). *Negotiating identities: Education for empowerment in a diverse society.* Ontario, CA: California Association for Bilingual Education.

Cummins, J. (1999). Alternative paradigms in bilingual education research: Does theory have a place? *Educational Researcher, 28* (7), 26-32.

Cummins, J. (2000). *Language, power and pedagogy: Bilingual children in the crossfire.* Clevedon, England: Multilingual Matters.

Cummins, J., & Wong Fillmore, L. (2000). *Language and education: What every teacher (and administrator) needs to know* (Cassette Recording No. NABE 00-FS10A). Dallas, TX: CopyCats.

Curtis, M. E., & Longo, A. M. (1999). Development of components of reading skill. *Journal of Educational Psychology, 72,* 565-669.

Darling-Hammond, L. (1996). The quiet revolution rethinking teacher development. *Educational Leadership, 53*(6), 4-10.

Darling-Hammond, L. (2001, April 11). *Educational research and educational reform: Drawing the connections between research, policy, and practice.* Invited address presented at the annual meeting of the American Educational Research Association, Seattle, WA.

Delgado-Gaitan, C. (1993). Research and policy in reconceptualizing family-school relationships. In P. Phelan & A. L. Davidson (Eds.), *Renegotiating cultural diversity in American schools* (pp. 139-158). New York: Teachers College Press.

Delpit, L. D. (1988). The silenced dialogue: Power and pedagogy in educating other people's children. *Harvard Educational Review, 58,* 280-298.

Denzin, N. K., & Lincoln, Y. S. (Eds.). (2000). *Handbook of qualitative research* (2nd ed.). Thousand Oaks, CA: Sage.

Department of Labor. (2001). *Working in the 21st century.* Washington, DC: Bureau of Labor Statistics.

Donato, R. (1997). *The other struggle for equal schools: Mexican Americans during the civil rights era.* Albany: SUNY Press.

Durán, R. (2000, June 28). *Parents' and children collaborative learning supported by electronic technology.* Paper presented at the CREDE Teaching English Language Learners Summer Institute, Storrs, CT.

Echevarria, J., Vogt, M., & Short, D. J. (2000). *Making content comprehensible for English language learners.* Boston: Allyn & Bacon.

Elmore, R. F., Peterson, P. L., & McCarthy, S. J. (1996). *Restructuring in the classroom: Teaching, learning and school organization.* San Francisco: Jossey-Bass.

Erickson, F. (1996). Ethnographic microanalysis. In S. L. McKay & N. H. Hornberger (Eds.), *Sociolinguistics and language teaching* (pp. 283-306). Cambridge, UK: Cambridge University Press.

Escamilla, K., Andrade, A. M., Basurto, A., & Ruiz, O. A. (1996). *Instrumento de observación de los logros de la lecto-escritura inicial* (Observation instrument of initial reading and writing achievement). Portsmouth, NH: Heinemann.

Fashola, O. S., & Slavin, R. E. (2000). Effective dropout prevention and college attendance programs for Latino students. In R. E. Slavin & M. Calderón (Eds.), *Effective programs for Latino students* (pp. 67-100). Mahwah, NJ: Lawrence Erlbaum.

Fashola, O. S., Slavin, R. E., Calderón, M., & Durán, R. (2000). Effective programs for Latino students in elementary and middle schools. In R. E. Slavin & M. Calderón (Eds.), *Effective programs for Latino students* (pp. 1-66). Mahwah, NJ: Lawrence Erlbaum.

Foorman, B. R., Francis, S. E., Fletcher, C. S., & Mehta, P. (1998). The role of instruction in learning to read: Preventing reading failure in at-risk children. *Journal of Education Psychology, 90,* 37-55.

Fried, R. L. (1995). *The passionate teacher.* Boston: Beacon.

Fullan, M. (1997). Emotion and hope: Constructive concepts for complex times. In A. Hargreave (Ed.), *Rethinking educational change with hearth and mind: 1997 ASCD yearbook* (pp. 216-233). Alexandria, VA: ASCD.

Garcia, E. (1999). *Student cultural diversity: Understanding and meeting the challenge* (2nd ed.). Boston: Houghton Mifflin.

Garcia, E. (2001). *The education of Hispanics in the United States: Raíces y Alas.* Boulder, CO: Rowan & Littlefield.

Garcia, O. (1999). Educating Latino high school students with little formal schooling. In C. J. Faltis & P. Wolfe (Eds.), *So much to say: Adolescents, bilingualism & ESL in the secondary school* (pp. 61-82). New York: Teachers College Press.

Genesee, F. (1987). *Learning through two languages. Studies of immersion and bilingual education.* Cambridge, MA: Newbury House.

Genesee, F. (1999). *Program alternatives for linguistically diverse students.* Santa Cruz, CA: Center for Research on Education, Diversity and Excellence.

Gibson, M. A. (1993). The school performance of immigrant minorities: A comparative view. In E. Jacob & C. Jordan (Eds.), *Minority education: Anthropological perspectives* (pp. 113-128). Norwood, NJ: Ablex.

Goldenberg, C. (1993). Instructional conversations: Promoting comprehension through discussion. *Reading Teacher, 46*(4), 316-326.

Goleman, D. (1995). *Emotional intelligence.* New York: Bantam.

González, J. (2000). *A history of Latinos in America: Harvest of empire.* New York: Viking.

González, J. M., & Darling-Hammond, L. (1997). *New concepts for new challenges: Professional development for teachers of immigrant youth.* Washington, DC: Center for Applied Linguistics.

Gottlieb, M. (1999). Assessing ESOL adolescents: Balancing accessibility to learn with accountability for learning. In C. J. Faltis & P. Wolfe (Eds.), *So much to say: Adolescents, bilingualism and ESL in the secondary school* (pp. 176-201). New York: Teachers College Press.

Graves, N., & Graves, T. (1983). Creating a cooperative learning environment. In R. Slavin, S. Sharan, S. Kagan, R. Hertz-Lazarowitz, C. Webb, & R. Schmuck (Eds.), *Learning to cooperate, cooperating to learn* (pp. 403-436). New York: Plenum.

Graves, N., & Graves, T. (1994). *Scaffolding reading experiences: Designs for student success.* Norwood, MA: Christopher-Gordon.

Green, J., & Harker, J. (1982). Gaining access to learning: Conversational, social, and cognitive demands of group participation. In L. C. Wilkinson (Ed.), *Communicating in the classroom* (pp. 183-219). New York: Academic Press.

Greenfield, W. D. (1995). Toward a theory of school administration: The centrality of leadership. *Educational Administration Quarterly, 31,* 61-85.

Grimmett, P. P., & McKinnon, A. M. (1992). Craft knowledge and the education of teachers. In G. Grant (Ed.), *Review of Research in Education #18.* Washington, DC: American Educational Research Association.

Gutierrez, K. (1995). Unpacking academic discourse. *Discourse Processes, 19*(1), 21-37.

Hakuta, K. (1986). *Mirror of language: The debate on bilingualism.* New York: Basic Books.

Hakuta, K. (2001, February 24). *What can we learn about the impact of Proposition 227 from SAT-9 scores?* Keynote address presented at the annual conference of the National Association for Bilingual Education conference, Phoenix, AZ.

Hargreaves, A. (1994). *Changing teachers, changing times: Teacher's work and culture in the postmodern age.* New York: Teachers College Press.

Hargreaves, A., & Wignall, R. (1989). *Time for the teacher: A study of collegial relations and preparation time use.* Toronto: Ontario Institute for Studies in Education.

Hernández-Chávez, E. (1984). The inadequacy of English immersion education as an educational approach for language minority students in the United States. In J. Lundin & D. P. Dolson (Eds.), *Studies on immersion education: A collection for United States educators* (pp. 144-183). Sacramento: California State Department of Education.

Hess, F. M. (1999). *Spinning wheels: The politics of urban school reform.* Washington, DC: Brookings Institution.

Hidalgo, N. M., Bright, J. A., Siu, S., Swap, S. M., & Epstein, J. L. (1995). Research on families, schools, and communities: A multicultural perspective. In

J. A. Banks & C. A. McGee Banks (Eds.), *Handbook of research on multicultural education* (pp. 114-132). New York: Macmillan.

Hill, P. T. (1997). Contracting in public education. In D. Ravitch & J. P. Viteritti (Eds.), *The redesign of urban education* (pp. 61-85). New Haven, CT: Yale University Press.

Hoffman, D. M. (1998). A therapeutic moment? Identity, self, and culture in the anthropology of education. *Anthropology & Education Quarterly, 29,* 324-346.

Holcomb, E. L. (1999). *Getting excited about data: How to combine people, passion, and proof.* Thousand Oaks, CA: Sage.

Howard, E. R., & Sugarman, J. (2001). *Two-way immersion programs: Features and statistics.* Washington, DC: ERIC Clearinghouse on Languages and Linguistics [Online]. Available: www.cal.org/ericcll/digest/0101twi.html

Huberman, A. M. (1992). *Successful school improvement: Critical introduction to M. Fullan.* London: Open University Press.

Iowa tests of basic skills. (1993). Chicago: Riverside.

Johnson, S. M. (1996). *Leading to change: The challenge of the new superintendency.* San Francisco: Jossey-Bass.

Johnston, P., & Allington, P. (1991). Remediation. In P. D. Pearson (Ed.), *Handbook of reading research* (Vol. 2, pp. 984-1012). New York: Longman.

Joyce, B., Weil, M., & Showers, B. (1992). *Models of teaching.* Boston: Allyn & Bacon.

Lambert, W. E. (1984). An overview of issues in immersion education. In D. P. Dolson (Ed.), *Studies in immersion education* (pp. 8-30). Sacramento: California State Department of Education.

Laturnau, J. (2001). *Standards-based instruction for English language learners.* Honolulu, HI: Pacific Resources for Education and Learning.

Lau v. Nichols, 414 U.S. 563 (1974).

Leinhardt, F., Zaslavsky, O., & Stein, M. K. (1990). Functions, graphs, and graphing: Tasks, learning, and teaching. *Review of Educational Research, 60*(1), 1-64.

Lessow-Hurley, J. (2000). *The foundations of dual language instruction* (3rd ed.). New York: Addison Wesley.

Levine, D. U., & Lezotte, L. W. (1995). Effective schools research. In J. A. Banks & C. A. McGee Banks (Eds.), *Handbook of research on multicultural education* (pp. 525-547). New York: Macmillan.

Lieberman, A., & Miller, L. (1991). *Staff development for education in the '90s: New demands, new realities, new perspectives.* New York: Teachers College Press.

Lindholm, K. (1990). Bilingual immersion education: Criteria for program development. In A. M. Padilla, H. H. Fairchild, & C. Valadez (Eds.), *Bilingual education: Issues and strategies* (pp. 91-105). Newbury Park, CA: Sage.

Lindholm-Leary, K. J. (2000). *Biliteracy for a global society: An idea book on dual language education.* Washington, DC: National Clearinghouse for Bilingual Education.

Lindholm-Leary, K. J. (2001). *Dual language education.* Clevedon, England: Multilingual Matters.

Little, J. W. (1981). *School success and staff development in urban desegregated schools: A summary of recently complete research.* Boulder, CO: Center for Action Research.

Little, J. W. (1990). *School success and staff development in urban desegregated schools: A summary of recently completed research.* Boulder, CO: Center for Action Research.

Macedo, D., & Bartolomé, L. I. (1999). *Dancing with bigotry: Beyond the politics of tolerance.* New York: St. Martin's.

Macroff, G. I. (1992). Reform comes home: Policies to encourage parental involvement in children's education. In C. E. Finn & T. Rebarber (Eds.), *Education reform in the '90s* (pp. 157-171). New York: Macmillan.

Malone, S. E. (2001, April). *When "Education for All" includes everyone: Providing relevant education for minority languages communities.* Paper presented at the World Bank Seminar on Language and Instruction, Summer Institute of Linguistics, Dakar, Senegal.

Marcos, K. (1998). *The benefits of early language learning.* ERIC Clearinghouse on Language and Linguistics [Online]. Available: www.cal.org/ericell/fafs/rgos/benes.html

Marvin, I. J. (1998). *Puerto Rican home involvement practices and their effect on achievement.* Unpublished doctoral dissertation, University of Connecticut, Storrs.

Menyuk, P. (1999). *Reading and linguistic development.* Cambridge, MA: Brookline.

Meyer, J. W., & Rowan, B. (1991). *Institutionalized organizations: Formal structure as myth and ceremony.* Columbus, OH: Merrill.

Minaya-Rowe, L. (1988). A comparison of bilingual education policies and practices in Perú and the United States. In H. S. García & R. Chávez Chávez (Eds.), *Ethnolinguistic issues in education* (pp. 100-116). Lubbock: Texas Tech University.

Minaya-Rowe, L. (1996). Bilingual teachers involving parents in the teaching-learning process: A practicum experience. *Journal of Educational Issues of Language Minority Students, 16,* 57-76.

Minaya-Rowe, L. (Ed.). (2002). *Teacher training and effective pedagogy in the context of student diversity.* Greenwich, CT: Information Age.

Moles, O. (1993). Collaboration between schools and disadvantaged parents: Obstacles and openings. In N. F. Chavkin (Ed.), *Families and schools in a pluralistic society* (pp. 21-49). Albany: SUNY Press.

Moll, L. C. (1992). Bilingual classroom studies and community analysis: Some recent trends. *Educational Researcher, 21*(2), 20-24.

Montague, N. S. (1997). Critical components for dual language programs. *Bilingual Research Journal, 21*(4), 1-9 [Online]. Available: http://brj.asu.edu/articles/ar5.html

Morán, C., & Hakuta, K. (1995). Bilingual education: Broadening research perspectives. In J. A. Banks & C. A. McGee Banks (Eds.), *Handbook of research on multicultural education* (pp. 97-113). New York: Macmillan.

Nadeau, A. (1996). *The role of leadership in sustaining school reform: Voices from the field* [Online]. Available: www.ed.gov/pubs/Leadership/covpg. html

National Alliance of Business. (1998). *Workforce diversity: A business imperative in the global economy.* Washington, DC: Author.

National Center for Education Statistics (NCES). (1997). *1993-94 schools and staffing survey: A profile of policies and practices for limited English proficient students: Screening methods, program support, and teacher training.* Washington, DC: U.S. Department of Education.

National Center for Education Statistics (NCES). (1999). *Schools and staffing survey.* Washington, DC: U.S. Department of Education.

National Center of Education Statistics (NCES). (2001). *The condition of education 2001.* Washington, DC: U.S. Department of Education.

National Clearinghouse for Bilingual Education (NCBE). (1999). *The growing numbers of limited English proficient students.* Washington, DC: Author.

Newmann, F. M., King, M. B., & Rigdon, M. (1997). Accountability and school performance: Implications for restructuring schools. *Harvard Educational Review, 67,* 41-74.

Nieto, S. (1998). Fact and fiction: Stories of Puerto Ricans in U.S. schools. *Harvard Educational Review, 68,* 133-163.

Nieto, S. (2000). *Affirming diversity: The sociopolitical context of multicultural education* (3rd ed.). New York: Longman.

Oakes, J., Wells, A. S., Yonezawa, S., & Ray, K. (1997). Equity lessons from detracking schools. In A. Hargreaves (Ed.), *Rethinking educational change with hearth and mind* (pp. 43-72). Alexandria, VA: Association for Supervision and Curriculum Development.

Office of English Language Acquisition (OELA). (2001, December 17). *The do's and don'ts of administering ED grants.* Presentation made by OELA staff at the Improving America's Schools Conference, San Antonio, TX.

Ogbu, J. U. (1987). Variability in minority school performance. *Anthropology and Education Quarterly, 18*(4), 312-334.

Ogbu, J. U. (1992). Understanding cultural diversity and learning. *Educational Researcher, 21*(8), 5-14.

Ogbu, J. U. (1995). Understanding cultural diversity and learning. In J. A. Banks & C. A. McGee Banks (Eds.), *Handbook of research on multicultural education* (pp. 582-596). New York: Macmillan.

Oller, J. W. (1997). Monoglottosis: What's wrong with the idea of the IQ meritocracy and its racy cousins? *Applied Linguistics, 18*(4), 467-507.

O'Malley, J. M., & Valdez Pierce, L. (1996). *Authentic assessment for English language learners: Practical approaches for teachers.* New York: Addison-Wesley.

Osterling, J. P. (1998, April 16). *Moving beyond invisibility: The sociocultural strengths of the Latino community: The case of Arlington's Salvadoran families.* Paper presented at the annual meeting of the American Educational Research Association, San Diego, CA.

Ovando, C. J., & Collier, V. P. (1998). *Bilingual and ESL classrooms: Teaching in multicultural context.* Boston: McGraw-Hill.

Ovando, C. J., & McLaren, P. (2000). Multiculturalism: Beyond a zero-sum game. In C. J. Ovando & P. McLaren (Eds.), *The politics of multiculturalism and bilingual education: Students and teachers caught in the cross fire* (pp. 225-227). Boston: McGraw-Hill.

Ovando, C. J., & Pérez, R. (2000). The politics of bilingual immersion programs. In C. J. Ovando & P. McLaren (Eds.), *The politics of multiculturalism and bilingual education* (pp. 148-165). Boston: McGraw-Hill.

Paige, R. (2001, December 19). Luncheon address at the Improving America's Schools Conference, San Antonio, TX.

Paige, R. (2002, September 9). Remarks at the National Press Club, Washington, DC [Online]. Available: www.ed.gov/speeches/09-2002/09092002. html

Palincsar, A. S., & Brown, A. L. (1984). Reciprocal teaching of comprehension-fostering and comprehension-monitoring activities. *Cognition and Instruction, 1*(2), 117-175.

Pearson, P. D., & Fielding, L. (1997). Comprehension instruction. In M. Kamil, R. Barr, P. Mosenthal, & P. D. Pearson (Eds.), *Handbook of reading research* (Vol. 2, pp. 815-860). New York: Longman.

Pearson, P. D., Hansen, J., & Gordon, C. (1979). The effect of background knowledge on young children's comprehension of explicit and implicit information. *Journal of Reading Behavior, 11*(3), 201-209.

Porter, C., & Cleland, J. (1995). *The portfolio as a learning strategy.* Portsmouth, NH: Heinemann.

Pressley, M., Johnson, C. J., Symons, S., McGoldrick, J., & Kurita, J. (1990). Strategies that improve memory and comprehension of what is read. *Elementary School Journal, 90,* 3-32.

Pressley, M., Rankin, J., & Yokoi, L. (2000). A survey of instructional practices of outstanding primary-level literacy teachers. *Elementary School Journal, 96,* 363-384.

Purdie, N., & Hattie, J. (1996). Cultural differences in the use of strategies for self-regulated learning. *American Educational Research Journal, 33*(4), 845-871.

Ramírez, J. D. (1995). Executive summary to the final report: Longitudinal study of structural English immersion strategy, early exit and late-exit transitional bilingual education programs for language minority children. In G. González & L. Maez (Eds.), *Compendium of research in bilingual education* (pp. 195-230). Washington, DC: National Clearinghouse for Bilingual Education.

Rigg, P., & Allen, V. G. (1989). *When they don't all speak English.* Urbana, IL: National Council of Teachers of English.

Riley, R. W. (2000, March). *Excelencia para todos—excellence for all: The progress of Hispanic education and the challenges of a new century.* Remarks as prepared for delivery by U.S. Secretary of Education Richard W. Riley at Bell Multicultural School, Washington, DC [Online]. Available: www.ed.gov/Speeches/03-2000/200315.html

Rivera, C. (1999, April). *Policies and practices relating to inclusion and accommodation of limited English proficient students in state and district assessment systems.* Paper presented at the annual meeting of the American Educational Research Association, Montreal.

Rong, X. L., & Preissle, J. (1998). *Educating immigrant students: What we need to know to meet the challenges.* Thousand Oaks, CA: Corwin Press.

Rossi, R. J., & Stringfield, S. C. (1996). *Education reform and students at risk: Findings and recommendations* [Online]. Available: www.ed.gov/pubs/SER/AtRisk/title/html

Sarason, S. (1996). *Revisiting the culture of school and the problem of change.* New York: Teachers College Press.

Secada, W. (1990). Research, politics, and bilingual education. In C. B. Cazden & C. E. Snow (Eds.), *English plus: Issues in bilingual education* (pp. 81-106). Newbury Park, CA: Sage.

Shannon, S. M., & Lojero Latimer, S. (1996). Latino parent involvement in schools: A story of struggle and resistance. *Journal of Educational Issues of Language Minority Students, 16,* 301-319.

Sharan, Y., & Sharan, S. (1994). Group investigation in the cooperative classroom. In S. Sharan (Ed.), *Handbook of cooperative learning methods* (pp. 97-114). Westport, CT: Greenwood.

Sharan, S., & Sharan, Y. (1997). Cooperative learning in small groups: Recent methods and effects on achievement, attitudes, and ethnic relations. *Review of Educational Research, 50*(2), 241-271.

Sizer, T. (1996). Hard-won lessons from the school reform battle: A conversation with Ted Sizer. *The Harvard Educational Letter, 12,* 3-6.

Slavin, R. E. (1997). Team assisted individualization: Cooperative learning and individualized instruction in the mainstreamed classroom. *Remedial and Special Education, 5*(6), 33-42.

Slavin, R. E. (2002). Evidence-based education policies: Transforming educational practice and research. *Educational Researcher, 31*(7), 15-21.

Slavin, R. E., & Calderón, M. (2001). *Effective programs for Latino children.* Mahwah, NJ: Lawrence Erlbaum.

Slavin, R. E., & Fashola, O. S. (1998). *Show me the evidence! Proven and promising programs for American schools.* Thousand Oaks, CA: Corwin Press.

Slavin, R. E., & Madden, N. (2001a). Effects of bilingual and English-as-a-second-language adaptations of Success for All on the reading achievement of students acquiring English. In R. E. Slavin & M. Calderón (Eds.), *Effective programs for Latino students* (pp. 207-230). Mahwah, NJ: Lawrence Erlbaum.

Slavin, R. E., & Madden, N. A. (2001b). *Success for all.* Thousand Oaks, CA: Corwin Press.

Slavin, R. E., & Madden, N. A. (2001c). Roots & wings: Effects of whole-school reform on student achievement. *Journal of Education for Students Placed at Risk, 5*(1-2), 109-136.

Slavin, R. E., Madden, N. A., Dolan, L., Wasik, B. A., Ross, S. M., Smith, L. J., & Dianda, M. (1996). Success for All: A summary of research. *Journal of Education for Students Placed at Risk, 1,* 41-76.

Slavin, R. E., Madden, N., Karweit, N., Dolan, L., & Wasik, B. (1996). *Success for All: A relentless approach to prevention and early intervention in elementary schools.* Arlington, VA: Educational Research Service.

Sleeter, C. E. (Ed.). (1991). *Empowerment through multicultural education.* Albany: SUNY Press.

Snow, C. E., Burns, S. M., & Griffin, P. (1998). *Preventing reading difficulties in young children.* Washington, DC: National Academy Press.

Solomon, P. G. (2002). *The assessment bridge: Positive ways to link tests to learning, standards, and curriculum development.* Thousand Oaks, CA: Corwin Press.

Spener, D. (1988). Transitional bilingual education and the socialization of immigrants. *Harvard Educational Review, 52,* 301-314.

Suárez-Orozco, M. M. (1993). "Becoming somebody": Central American immigrants in U.S. inner-city schools. In E. Jacob & C. Jordan (Eds.), *Minority education: Anthropological perspectives* (pp. 129-143). Norwood, NJ: Ablex.

Taggart, G. L., Phifer, S. J., Nixon, J. A., & Wood, M. (Eds.). (1998). *Rubrics: A handbook for construction and use.* Lancaster, PA: Technomic.

Tharp, R. (1999). *Effective teaching: How the standards came to be.* Santa Cruz, CA: Center for Research in Education, Diversity and Excellence.

Tharp, R. (2002, July 16). *The CREDE standards for effective pedagogy.* Keynote address presented at the Administrators' Summer LEADership Institute, Hartford, CT.

Thomas, W., & Collier, V. (1997). *School effectiveness for language minority students.* Washington, DC: NCBE Resource Collection Series [Online]. Available: www.ncbe.gwu.edu/ncbepubs/resource/effectiveness/index.htm

Thomas, W. P., & Collier, V. P. (2002). *A national study of school effectiveness for language minority students' long-term academic achievement.* Santa Cruz, CA:

Center for Research in Education, Diversity and Excellence [Online]. Available: www.crede.ucsc.edu/research/llaa/1.1_final.html

Tierney, R. J., Carter, M. A., & Desai, L. E. (1991). *Portfolio assessment in the reading-writing classroom*. Norwood, MA: Christopher-Gordon.

Tinajero, J. V. (1992). Raising educational and career aspirations of Hispanic girls and their mothers. *Journal of Educational Issues of Language Minority Students, 2*, 27-43.

Trumbull, E., & Sasser L. (2000). Making standards-based assessment work for English language learners. In Southern California Comprehensive Assistance Center (Ed.), *Writing assessment for English language learners (Grades 6-8)* (pp. 5-12). Long Beach: Southern California Comprehensive Assistance Center.

Tse, L. (2001). *"Why don't they learn English?" Separating fact from fallacy in the U.S. language debate*. New York: Teachers College Press.

Tucker, G. R. (2001). A global perspective on bilingualism and bilingual education. In J. E. Alatis & A. Tan (Eds.), *Proceedings of the Georgetown University Round Table on Languages and Linguistics, 1999*. Washington, DC: Georgetown University Press.

Turner, J., & Paris, S. G. (1995). The influence of classroom contexts on young children's motivation for literacy. *Reading Research Quarterly, 30*(3), 410-441.

Tyack, D. B., & Cuban, L. (1995). *Tinkering toward Utopia: A century of public school reform*. Cambridge, MA: Harvard University Press.

U.S. Bureau of the Census. (2000). *Census 2000 briefs* [Online]. Available: www. census.gov/population/www/cen2000/briefs/html

Valdés, G. (1996). *Con respeto: Bridging the distances between culturally diverse families and schools*. New York: Teachers College Press.

Valdés, G. (1997). Dual-language immersion programs: A cautionary note concerning the education of language-minority students. *Harvard Educational Review, 67*(3), 391-429.

Valdés, G. (1998). The world outside and inside schools: Language and immigrant children. *Educational Researcher, 27*(6), 4-18.

Valencia, R. R. (Ed.). (1991). *Chicano school failure and success: Research and policy agendas for the 1990s*. New York: Falmer.

Valencia, R. R. (1997, Winter). Latino demographic and educational conditions. *ETS Policy Notes, 8*(1), 1-4, 11.

Valenzuela, A. (1999). *Subtractive schooling: U.S. Mexican youth and the politics of caring*. Albany: SUNY Press.

Vygotsky, L. S. (1978). *Mind in society: The development of higher psychological processes*. Cambridge, MA: Harvard University Press.

Waggoner, D. (1999). Who are secondary new comers and linguistically different youth? In C. J. Faltis & P. Wolfe (Eds.), *So much to say: Adolescents, bilingualism & ESL in the secondary school* (pp. 13-41). New York: Teachers College Press.

Willig, A. (1985). A meta-analysis of selected studies on the effectiveness of bilingual education. *Review of Educational Research, 55*, 269-317.

Wong Fillmore, L. (1991). When learning a second language means losing the first. *Early Childhood Research Quarterly, 6*, 323-346.

Worthen, B. R., Sanders, J. R., & Fitzpatrick, J. L. (1997). *Program evaluation: Alternative approaches and practical guidelines* (2nd ed.). New York: Longman.

Index

Acronyms, 227–28
Action research, 208, 214–18
Advocacy, 194
Alicia R. Chacón International
    School, 53–82
    background, 54–55
    evaluation, 64–78
    fieldwork, 56–57
    instructional program, 57–78
    model programs, 30, 40–41
    parent involvement, 68–78, 192–94,
        202–4
    program design, 60–61
    site selection, 56
    student evaluations, 78–81
    teacher involvement, 66–70
Amato, Anthony, 24
Assessment
    authentic assessment, 153–56, 163–64
    criteria, 156–62
    definition, 150–51
    performance assessment, 154
    planning bilingual programs, 32–33
    portfolio assessment, 154–55, 156–63
    purposes, 151–52
    reading comprehension, 159–62
    reading strategies, 112
    self-assessment, 155–56
    standardized testing, 149–50, 152–53
    standards, 163–66
    students, 150
    writing strategies, 143–46

Basals, 108–9
Benefits of bilingual programs, 5–6, 15,
    20–21, 27–28
Bilingual Cooperative Integrated Reading
    and Composition (BCIRC) project, 178
Bloom-type questions, 127–28

California English-language development
    (ELD) standards, 97–101
Center for Applied Linguistics
    (CAL), 4, 24
Center for Research in Education,
    Diversity, and Excellence (CREDE), 4
Chacón, Alicia R., 55
Chacón School. *See* Alicia R. Chacón
    International School
Characteristics of bilingual programs,
    4–5, 6–7, 28–31
Choral reading, 124–25
Cognates, 93–94
Cognitive effects of bilingualism, 18, 19–21
Collegiality, 185–86
Community. *See* Teachers Learning
    Communities (TLCs)
Comprehensive School Reform Model
    (CSRD), 42–48
Conceptual issues
    educational reform, 10, 14–17
    equitable educational programs,
        10, 12–14
    instructional program, 11, 17–20
Content instruction, 33
Contextual communication, 19–21
Contextual interaction model, 13–14
Cooperative learning strategies, 33,
    98–105, 178
Costs, 35
CREDE. *See* Center for Research in
    Education, Diversity, and Excellence
    (CREDE)
CREDE Standards for Effective Pedagogy,
    165–66
Criterion-referenced tests
    (CRTs), 209
Culturally responsive instruction,
    5–9, 63–64, 136, 182–83

Curriculum
    components, 32, 49–51
    Comprehensive School Reform Model
        (CSRD), 42–48
    culturally responsive instruction,
        182–83
    elementary grades, 46–51, 60–63,
        114–16
    50-50 model, 41–42
    high school, 115–16
    kindergarten, 43–45, 49–51, 60, 62–63,
        113–14
    models, 32–33, 39–51
    obstacles, 39–40
    thematic units, 41–42, 44
    time allocation, 59, 172–73

Del Valle High School (Texas), 56
Dimensions of language proficiency, 19–21
Directed Listening Thinking Activity
    (DLTA), 122–23
Dual-language schools, 179–82

Echo reading, 125
Educational reform, 6, 10, 14–17, 201–2,
    80-20 model, 29–31, 40–41
ELD. *See* California English-language
    development (ELD) standards
Elementary school curriculum, 46–51,
    60–63, 114–16
El Paso Independent School District
    (Texas), 41–42
El Paso, Texas, 54–55
Emotional intelligence, 183–84
Equitable educational programs, 10, 12–14
ERIC Clearinghouse, 4
Ethnographic case studies, 208
Evaluation, 207–20
    action research, 208, 214–18
    evaluation design, 209–12
    guidelines, 212–14
    program design, 35
    student assessment, 208–9
    types of evaluations, 207–8
    See also Planning bilingual programs
        50-50 model, 29–31, 41–42

Foreign language competency, 195
Formative evaluations, 208
Funding sources, 35

Governance, 35, 194
Grouping/Classifying, 90, 93

High school curriculum, 115–16
Hueco Elementary School (Texas), 42–48

Imagery, 121
Implementation of bilingual programs,
    26, 28–31
Independent reading, 130–31
Instructional models, 107–31
    comprehensive reading model
        components, 111–12
    effectiveness, 110–11
    instruction sequencing, 112–16
    IRE (initiate, respond, evaluate)
        model, 109
    reading strategies, 108–17
    traditional models, 108–9
    types of models, 108
Instructional techniques, 85–106
    Comprehensive School Reform Model
        (CSRD), 42–48
    cooperative learning strategies,
        98–105, 178
    Directed Listening Thinking Activity
        (DLTA), 122–23
    guided discussion, 112, 138–46
    imagery, 121
    independent reading, 130–31
    instructional delivery strategies, 86–89
    interactive reading strategies, 96–97,
        124–30, 198–201
    language acquisition strategies, 97–101,
        173–74
    listening comprehension, 96, 118–24
    separation of languages, 60, 66–67
    sheltered instruction, 86
    Teachers Learning Communities
        (TLCs), 179–82
    think-aloud process, 95, 96, 119–21
    typographical signals, 123
    vocabulary building, 89–96, 105–6,
        111–12, 116–18
Interactive reading strategies, 96–97,
    124–30, 198–201
IRE (initiate, respond, evaluate)
    model, 109

Kindergarten curriculum, 43–45, 49–51,
    60, 62–63, 113–14

Language acquisition strategies,
    97–101, 173–74
Language distribution, 29–31
Latino students, 7–10

Lau vs. Nichols (1974), 55
Listening comprehension, 44, 47, 96, 112, 118–24
Literacy instruction, 33, 42–48, 66, 107–31, 197–201
    See also Instructional models; Reading strategies; Writing strategies
Literature circles, 130

Metacognition, 95
Model programs, 29–31, 36, 40–51, 53–82
Models. *See* Instructional models
Monolingual programs, 9–10

National Clearinghouse for Bilingual Education (NCBE). *See* National Clearinghouse for English Language Acquisition and Language Instruction Educational Programs (NCELA)
National Clearinghouse for English Language Acquisition and Language Instruction Educational Programs (NCELA), 4
National Council of Teachers of Mathematics Standards, 165–66
National Research Council (NRC), 111–13
National Science Education Standards, 165–66, 90-10 model, 29–31, 49–51
Norm-referenced tests (NRTs), 209

Oakes, Jeanne, 182
Office of English Language Acquisition (OELA), 210

Parent involvement, 189–205
    advocacy, 194
    Alicia R. Chacón International School, 68–78, 192–94, 202–4
    conventional involvement, 192–93
    curriculum models, 48
    definition, 191
    governance, 194
    guidelines for success, 195–97
    literacy instruction, 197–201
    nonconventional involvement, 193–94
    parental diversity, 190–91
    program design, 34–35
    school involvement, 201–2
    teacher involvement, 69–70, 74, 192–93, 201
    training recommendations, 203

Partner reading, 125–26
Phonemic awareness, 45, 126
Planning bilingual programs
    assessments, 32–33
    content instruction, 33
    curriculum, 32–33
    frequently asked questions (FAQs), 27–36
    guidelines, 25, 37–38
    implementation, 26, 28–31
    information gathering, 24, 38
    information sharing, 24–25
    language distribution, 29–31
    literacy instruction, 33
    staffing issues, 34
    stakeholders, 23–26, 36–37
    student selection, 31
    teaching methods, 31–32
    See also Evaluation
Popcorn reading, 126
Portfolio assessment, 154–55, 156–63
Predictions, 122, 199–200
Principals, 60, 75, 177
Program development
    importance, 7–10
    support, 10–20

Rapid Retrieval of Information (RRI), 129
Reading strategies, 45, 96–97, 108–17, 124–31, 198–201
    See also Instructional models
Resources, 221–25

Scaffolding, 138
Schulte, Robert, 57, 75
Semantic mapping, 90, 92, 103–4, 199, 70-30 model, 29–31, 42–51
Sheltered instruction, 29, 86
Socorro Independent School District (Texas), 42–48
Staff development
    Alicia R. Chacón International School, 67–68
    collegiality, 185–86
    Comprehensive School Reform Model (CSRD), 42–43
    curriculum models, 48
    emotional intelligence, 183–84
    guidelines, 186–87
    ineffective development, 184–85
    obstacles, 40
    principles, 169–70
    program design, 34

Teachers Learning Communities
(TLCs), 48, 67–68, 146, 174–87
teaching priorities, 172–74
30-minute activities, 180–82
topics, 170–71
Staffing issues, 34
Stakeholders, 23–26, 36–37
Standards, 97–101, 134–35, 137, 163–66
Student assessment, 150, 208–9
Students at risk, 7
Student selection, 31, 58
Success for All/Éxito Para Todos, 32,
42–48, 49–51
Success for All (SFA) Foundation, 24
Summative evaluations, 208

Teachers Learning Communities (TLCs),
48, 67–68, 146, 174–87
Teachers of Speakers of Other Languages
Standards, 165–66
Teaching methods, 31–32, 85–106
See also Instructional techniques;
Reading strategies; Writing
strategies
Team teaching, 34, 41, 63
Tea party, 104
Think-aloud process, 95, 96, 119–21
Threshold hypothesis, 17–19
Transitional bilingual education, 8–10
Trilingual development, 63, 79–80
Types of bilingualism, 18
Typographical signals, 123

U.S. Department of Education, 212

Vocabulary building techniques
Comprehensive School Reform Model
(CSRD), 44
instructional process, 89–96, 105–6,
111–12, 116–18
writing strategies, 135, 142–43

Word banks, 93, 94
Writing strategies, 133–47
assessments, 143–46
community of writers,
135, 137–38
cooperative learning strategies, 103
culturally responsive instruction, 136
curriculum models, 45, 47
grading policy, 145
guided discussion, 138–46
instructional process, 136–38
protocols, 140–41
reading strategies, 112
sociocultural context, 137–38
standards, 134–35, 137
vocabulary building, 94–95,
135, 142–43
writing conventions, 142

Ysleta Independent School District
(Texas), 54–57

Zone of proximal development, 177–78

**CORWIN
PRESS**

The Corwin Press logo—a raven striding across an open book—represents the happy union of courage and learning. We are a professional-level publisher of books and journals for K-12 educators, and we are committed to creating and providing resources that embody these qualities. Corwin's motto is "Success for All Learners."